ARNIM AND BISMARCK

ARNIM AND BISMARCK

BY

GEORGE O. KENT

OXFORD
AT THE CLARENDON PRESS
1968

Oxford University Press, Ely House, London W. 1

GLASGOW NEW YORK TORONTO MELBOURNE WELLINGTON
CAPE TOWN SALISBURY IBADAN NAIROBI LUSAKA ADDIS ABABA
BOMBAY CALCUTTA MADRAS KARACHI LAHORE DACCA
KUALA LUMPUR HONG KONG TOKYO

PRINTED IN GREAT BRITAIN

PREFACE

HARRY VON ARNIM has been a controversial figure in modern German history ever since his conflict with Bismarck became public in the Arnim affair of 1874. Member of a prominent Prussian family, of good appearance, with a keen mind, he rose rapidly in the Prussian diplomatic service. During the latter part of his career—with which this study is mainly concerned—he was Minister to the Holy See, representative at the peace conference at Brussels and Frankfurt, Minister and later Ambassador to France. His contemporaries variously described him as brilliant, incompetent, an irresponsible intriguer, and a gifted statesman. Some even thought of him as a rival to Bismarck and a leader of a conservative opposition. The trial, the attendant publicity, and Arnim's conviction dramatized his conflict with Bismarck, made the matter a partisan affair, and did much to perpetuate a lopsided picture.

Stripped of its partisan overtones, the conflict between Arnim and Bismarck raises two questions: the cause of the conflict, and Arnim's competence as a diplomat. These are the main issues with which this study is concerned. In dealing with these problems, an account of Arnim's activities and his relationship with Bismarck from the time of the Vatican Council (1869) to his second trial (1875) will also be presented.

The conflict between the two men developed from their different personalities and positions. Bismarck, the autocratic Chancellor and Foreign Minister, was seldom inclined to receive advice (especially when it ran counter to his own views) and demanded absolute loyalty and prompt execution of his orders from his subordinates. Arnim loved to be the centre of attraction, to give advice to anybody on anything, to plot, to discuss, to be busy. Outwardly pliable and accommodating, he had definite convictions on many subjects—not least his own abilities—and could be very stubborn in their pursuance.

The position of these two men was that of superior and subordinate, but this was by no means as clear-cut as a corresponding relationship in modern times. Bismarck was responsible to the King only. His position depended on the personal confidence his royal master placed in him and his abilities. Until Bismarck's day, the position of the Prussian Minister President was neither particularly strong nor greatly exalted. He ranked first among the King's many advisers, without any special distinction. It was Bismarck who, during his long tenure of office, managed to enhance its status by virtue of his personality and achievements. The official relationship remained, however, the same. The Minister President had to possess the confidence of the King at all times. Arnim, though nominally under Bismarck, considered himself the personal representative of his sovereign abroad and used the ancient (and by now somewhat outmoded) right of immediate access to the King.

Assessment of Arnim's diplomatic achievements is difficult. It must be based primarily on official documents: his reports and memoranda, and the directives and instructions sent to him from Berlin, and these obviously cannot tell the whole story. But they tell a great deal; and with the documents now made available a better picture emerges than we have had so far.

Arnim's activities as a diplomat, as discussed in this study, covered an important period of transition in the history of Europe: the final unification of Italy, the loss of the temporal power of the Pope, the decline of France, and the rise and unification of Germany. Against the background of these events, a deficient David fought a brilliant Goliath—and lost.

ACKNOWLEDGEMENTS

I AM indebted to the following persons for assistance and advice: Mr. M. H. Fisher, Mr. J. Joll, Professor W. N. Medlicott, Dr. G. B. Noble, the late Mr. E. J. Passant, Professor N. Rich, Mrs. A. Scheips, Mr. A. J. P. Taylor, my former colleagues on the German War Documents Project, and my wife. Without her distractions and interruptions I might have managed to complete this study sooner.

GEORGE O. KENT

Washington, D.C.

CONTENTS

I

INTRODUCTION

HARRY CARL CURT EDUART VON ARNIM was born at
Moitzelfitz in Pomerania on 3 October 1824. His
family, on his father's side, was of the lesser Prussian
nobility. It owned estates in Pomerania and West Prussia and
its members had, at various times, attained high office in the
service of the state. Harry studied law and later took a degree
of doctor of law, then a most unusual step for a young man
of his background and upbringing. In 1847, before entering
government service, he married Elizabeth Louise von Prillwitz,
illegitimate daughter of August, Prince of Prussia. Three years
later he entered the diplomatic service, passed his examination
in 1851, and served as secretary of legation between 1851 and
1862 in Munich, Rome, Cassel, and Vienna. His wife died
in 1854, and in April 1857 he married Sophie Adelheid,
daughter of Adolf Heinrich, Count von Arnim-Boitzenburg,
a distant relative and a prominent member of the senior
branch of the family.[1] On 20 October 1864 he was sent to
Rome as diplomatic representative of Prussia at the Holy See.
During those years he was close to Bismarck, who considered
him an able and intelligent young man.[2]

In 1864 France and Italy were greatly concerned with Rome
and the Holy See, because the aspirations of Italian nationalism
clashed there with the rights of the temporal sovereignty of the
Pope. The September Convention, concluded in Paris on
15 September 1864, temporarily solved their dispute over
possession of the city. France, which had protected the Pope

---

[1] Adolf Heinrich Graf von Arnim-Boitzenburg (1803–68) had been Prussian
Minister of Interior 1842–68, and Minister-President of Prussia for ten days
during the Revolution of 1848. Harry was also distantly related to Bismarck,
through the Chancellor's sister, Malvine, being married to Friedrich Ernst Karl
Albrecht Oskar Heinrich von Arnim-Kroechelndorff.

[2] Otto, Fuerst von Bismarck, *Die Gesammelten Werke* (Friedrichsruher Ausgabe),
15 vols. (Berlin, 1923–35), ii. 224; iii. 68, 253, 256, 259; xiv/i. 206, 448, 450, 451,
454, 462, 463, 492, 497, 554, 565, henceforth cited *GW*.

with troops, agreed to withdraw them gradually from Rome, and Italy bound herself not to attack papal territory and to move her capital from Turin to Florence.[1] Three months later, on 8 December 1864, the Pope issued the Encyclical *Quanta Cura* and the *Syllabus of Errors*, and disclosed to the cardinals his intention to call an Ecumenical Council to Rome.[2] Thus the Vatican's problems attained global significance, not only because they touched upon territorial matters and questions of sovereignty, but because they involved matters of faith and morals for all who belonged to the Roman Catholic Church.

With the news of the approaching Council, governments of countries with Roman Catholic subjects became concerned lest official declarations at the Council, particularly those dealing with papal infallibility, interfered with the established laws and customs of the land. Their concern was summed up by Ollivier, the French Prime Minister: 'Rome wishes to be separated from the state, but she does not wish the state to be separated from her.'[3] This was the situation when Arnim arrived in Rome.

He believed neither that the Pope would be able to continue to wield his temporal sovereignty over the Papal States, nor that a joint intervention by the Powers would make it possible for the Pope to uphold his reign as he had in the past. Still, he was convinced that it was essential for temporal power to continue in one form or another. The main problem was to accommodate the conflicting interests of the Roman Church and the new Italian state. He rejected the proposal of Napoleon III to recognize the existence of two sovereign bodies in Italy because this would have distorted the true relationship of power between the two states. Moreover, a clear understanding between Rome and Florence was impossible for lack

[1] The French withdrew their troops from Rome in December 1866. They returned the following year after the defeat of Garibaldi and his forces at the battle of Mentana, 3 Nov. 1867. The French troops finally withdrew from Rome on 19 Aug. 1870.

[2] J. Friedrich, *Geschichte des Vatikanischen Konzils*, 3 vols. (Bonn, 1877–87), i. 651 ff., henceforth cited Friedrich, *Geschichte*. Dom Cuthbert Butler, *The Vatican Council*, 2 vols. (London, 1930), i. 81 ff., henceforth cited Butler.

[3] Émile Ollivier, *L'Église et l'État au Concil du Vatican*, 2 vols. (Paris, 1879), i. 397, as quoted by Lillian Parker Wallace, *The Papacy and European Diplomacy 1869–1878* (Chapel Hill, 1948), p. 56, henceforth cited Wallace. See also Friedrich, *Geschichte*, i. 760.

of common ground between the two. Only through mediation of a third party could a solution be found. This third party, Arnim believed, could be composed of those states which combined the necessary interests for the endangered institutions with a recognition and understanding of the requirements of the times: Prussia and France. After these two powers had agreed on a common basis for negotiations, the other powers should be invited by the Pope to a general conference.

Arnim's plan for an accommodation between the Papal States and Italy contained these features: the continuation of the Papal States as then constituted; the transfer of their entire school system to the jurisdiction of the Italian Church; the amalgamation of the Roman with the Italian Bank; a customs union between Italy and the Papal States, with a guarantee of a lump sum of two million *scudi* for the Pope; the unrestricted choice and rights of Italian citizenship to the subjects of the Pope; the recognition of the Italian Kingdom by the Vatican and the continuation of the rights of the Church in the annexed provinces; the separation of the administration from the Church in the Papal States; the limitation of the Papal Army to police duties; the obligation of the Italian Government to come to the assistance of the Pope in case of revolts; the creation of a Diet to be consulted about the budget and general legislation; the neutrality of the Papal States and a guarantee of its possessions by the Powers participating in the general conference.[1] It seems that, in addition to this plan, Arnim contemplated a still greater scheme: the possibility of a Franco-Prussian alliance.[2] This idea as well as his plan for an Italian-Papal accord was far-fetched. It considered the interests of the Pope to a great extent, but lacked sympathy for the national aspirations of the Italian people.[3]

Bismarck was cautious and hesitant. Prussia did not want to alienate its Catholics by appearing unsympathetic to the Pope, but neither did it care to offend its Protestants, nor, indeed,

---

[1] Arnim to Bismarck, 7 Nov. 1866, in *Die Auswaertige Politik Preussens, 1858–1871*, 10 vols. (Munich, 1932–45), viii. 123, fn. 3, henceforth cited *APP*. Erich Schmidt, *Bismarcks Kampf mit dem politischen Katholicizmus* (Hamburg, 1942), pp. 232–3, henceforth cited E. Schmidt.

[2] Ibid., p. 249.

[3] Arnim thought very little of the stability of the Italian monarchy or the vitality of the Italian State. Arnim to Bismarck, 7 Feb. 1868.

most other Germans, who wanted the Italians to succeed in their struggle for unity. Support of the Pope would, furthermore, have embittered Italy, Prussia's ally of 1866. This in turn might have led to a triple alliance of Italy, France, and Austria against Prussia, a possibility to which Bismarck had referred many times.[1]

[1] See p. 121 below, and F. Engel-Janosi, 'The Roman Question in the Diplomatic Negotiations of 1869–70', *Review of Politics*, iii. 3 (July 1941), pp. 332 ff.

II

PREPARATIONS FOR THE COUNCIL

ON 29 June 1868 the Holy See issued invitations to the princes and dignitaries of the Church to attend the Vatican Council. No invitations were sent to the temporal rulers.[1] This calculated slight to the heads of state was explained by Antonelli, the Cardinal State Secretary: modern states did not adhere to one religion; as for those with constitutional governments, the members of parliament would also have to be invited.

Most Catholic rulers either ignored or were indifferent to this arrangement; only Napoleon III, the Eldest Son of the Church, made an attempt to have the ancient rights of France recognized by the Holy See on this occasion.[2] As time went on, however, and as the proposed resolutions of the preparatory commissions became known, concern about the decisions of the Council increased. Still, none of the great powers made a move. Then on 9 April 1869 Hohenlohe, the Prime Minister of Bavaria, sent a circular note to the Powers suggesting that a common policy regarding the Council be agreed upon.[3]

It is not to be expected [Hohenlohe wrote] that the Council will occupy itself solely with matters of faith and questions of theology; for problems of that sort, which demand conciliar attention, are, at present, non-existent. The only dogmatic question which, as I have learned from a reliable source, is being considered in Rome, and for which the Jesuits are agitating a great deal in Italy, in Germany,

[1] Friedrich, *Geschichte*, i. 716 ff., 759 ff.
[2] E. Schmidt, p. 274.
[3] The Note had been drafted by Doellinger, who had sent the draft to Hohenlohe on 23 Mar. 1869. For Doellinger's part in this, see Ignaz von Doellinger, *Briefwechsel 1820–1890*, bearbeitet von Victor Conzemius, 2 vols. (Munich, 1965), ii. 127, fn. 1, 134, fn. 6, henceforth cited Doellinger, *Briefwechsel*. For the text of the Note, see Chlodwig zu Hohenlohe-Schillingsfuerst, *Denkwuerdigkeiten*, 2 vols. (Stuttgart, 1906–7), i. 351–3, henceforth cited Hohenlohe, *Denkwuerdigkeiten*. For Hohenlohe's motives in circulating the Note, see his directive to Perglas of 12 July 1869, ibid. 383.

and elsewhere, and which they would like to have decided by the Council, is the question of the infallibility of the Pope.

This question extends, however, far beyond the scope of pure religion and is of a highly political nature; for with it the secular power of the popes over all princes and people, even the schismatic ones, would have been decided and would have been elevated to a dogma.[1]

Other indications that the Council intended to deal with secular, or secular and ecclesiastical matters, were revealed by a programme of one of the preparatory commissions, which called for a discussion of political-ecclesiastical (*staatskirchliche*) questions only. And an article in the *Civilita Cattolica* considered one task of the Council to be the transformation of the papal syllabus of 8 December 1864 into positive resolutions and conciliar decrees. Since the articles of the syllabus were directed primarily against several important doctrines of the modern state, the question arose of how to call the attention of the ecclesiastical authorities to the dangerous consequences which any change in the existing relationship between Church and State might have.[2]

On the whole, Bismarck's reaction to the Hohenlohe circular was favourable; but he advised Werthern, the Prussian Minister at Munich, to be careful in his support of the Prime Minister's policy, lest the suspicion of Bavarian ultramontane and particularist circles be aroused.[3]

Arnim's views on the proposed Council and the Hohenlohe circular, which was communicated to him by the Foreign Ministry on 2 May 1869, are contained in a long report of 14 May.[4] He correctly assumed that Doellinger had drafted the Bavarian Note but, contrary to his subsequent views, blamed Doellinger's animosity toward Rome for his exaggerated opinions about the dangers that the decrees of the Council would hold for the modern state. On the other hand, Arnim conceded that future developments at Rome should be observed carefully.

The dogma of papal infallibility as such was of no concern

[1] Hohenlohe, *Denkwuerdigkeiten*, i. 351.
[2] Ibid. 351–2.
[3] Bismarck to Werthern, 5 May 1869, *GW* vi b. 70–1.
[4] Printed in the *Norddeutsche Allgemeine Zeitung*, 18 Apr. 1874; see p. 131 below; Friedrich, *Geschichte*, i. 778 ff.; E. Schmidt, p. 283.

to the secular governments; whether ecclesiastical decrees were pronounced by an infallible Pope or by a constitutional church assembly made little difference. What was important were the decrees prepared by the political-ecclesiastical commission which might unbalance the existing agreements between Church and State. It could be argued that there would be time for the governments to wait until these decrees, certain to cause conflicts with the secular authorities, had been promulgated by the Church. But to wait until that moment had arrived would put the governments at a serious disadvantage. For, though it was true that the resolutions of the councils were of no greater importance to the governments than the published theses of learned societies, a decree, once proclaimed by the Church, bound the conscience of millions of people. Should the governments then oppose these decrees, they would fail to convince their subjects of the necessity of their own policy, and, should the governments persist in their opposition to the Church, they would find themselves in a most awkward position.[1] How could the governments avoid being put into this position? Arnim asked. Hohenlohe's attempt to find agreement among the European Powers in their attitude toward the Vatican Council seemed too complicated. It would be more practicable for the German governments to decide on a common policy toward Rome. But the time for lodging a protest, as suggested by the Bavarian Note, had not arrived. The outcome of the deliberations of the commissions was unknown and there was no basis for a *démarche*. The only action by the Vatican to which the governments could take exception was that the relationship between the Church and the State was being discussed without participation of the governments as equal partners. Against this, the governments could protest, Arnim asserted. The German governments ought to ensure the influence which they had always exercised at councils of the Church. Protests alone, however, would not be sufficient. A demand should be made for the admission of one or several *oratores* to take part in the deliberation of the Council to ensure that the governments would be adequately informed of the course of the negotiations. This would make it possible for them, at the appropriate moment, to gain influence, lodge

[1] Friedrich, *Geschichte*, i. 793–4.

protests, bolster timid elements, and prevent political machinations which might otherwise be tried to their own detriment.
Therefore an agreement between the North German Confederation, Bavaria, and the other German states should be concluded and the Holy See should be requested to admit one or
more representatives of the united German governments to
the deliberations of the Council.[1]

In his next report Arnim elaborated his plan. As a possible
objection, the Holy See could raise the question of religious
preference and point out that Wilhelm I, head of the North
German Confederation, was not a Roman Catholic. But this
argument was invalid, Arnim asserted, because representatives
of princes belonging to the Augsburg confession had been
invited to the Council of Trent.

The appointment of a representative should be made in close
consultation with the Bavarian Government; otherwise the
possibility of having two German representatives would only
please those at the Council who would like to exploit this situation and render his plan ineffective. If it were confronted with
the choice of accepting one representative or none at all, the
Holy See would then have to choose between recognizing
the right of the German Governments to be represented at the
Council and facing the opposition of both Germany and Italy.

As to the position and task of this German representative,
Arnim believed that his foremost duty would be that of an
observer. It was not his vote which would count—'What
would two or three votes do against five hundred?'—but rather
his presence at discussions, his knowledge of intrigues, his
ability to raise protests and to make difficulties, and his
capacity to strengthen the opposition and to provide leadership for those men who, like Doellinger, had purposely been
pushed into the background. Nobody could foresee what
influence these men might be able to exercise, especially if the
situation should suddenly change or the present Pope should
die. To dispel any doubts that he might be considering himself
for this position, Arnim added that he took it for granted that

    [1] Arnim to Bismarck, 14 May 1869, E. Friedberg, *Aktenstuecke die altkatholische
Bewegung betreffend* (Tuebingen, 1876), pp. 516–20. According to Bucher, Arnim
got the idea of the *oratores* from the book *Istoria del Concilio Tridentino*, by Fra Paolo.
Moritz Busch, *Tagebuchblaetter*, 3 vols. (Leipzig, 1902), iii. 168, henceforth cited
Busch.

anybody chosen as representative would have to be a Roman Catholic.[1]

(1) It would be desirable if all European Powers would, by tacit agreement, stay away from the Council, for the responsibility for a conflict between the governments and their Roman Catholic subjects would then be slight.

(2) If, however, other governments, particularly the French, should be represented at the Council, prudence as well as dignity would demand that the Prussian Government should also be represented.

(3) Should this be the case, it would be important for Prussia to act in common with Bavaria and the rest of Germany. Arrangements should be made that the Vatican, in dealing with these questions, should not differentiate between Protestant and Catholic Germans, and that in Rome no conflicts based on religious differences between German representatives should take place.[2]

Arnim's proposal had many constructive and plausible features and some of these were adopted by Bismarck. The idea of sending *oratores* to the Council was neither nonsensical nor the solution of a very complicated situation, as has variously been claimed since. It probably was true that the Holy See would not have admitted any such representatives of the governments and that it would have been difficult to define their status and their task.[3] Later on, the minority bishops at the Council found themselves without a leader and in a predicament where a man in the position suggested by Arnim could have performed a valuable service. That the presence of such a man would not have changed the outcome of the Council can reasonably be assumed.

Bismarck transmitted Arnim's report, together with his own recommendations, to the King.[4] The Chancellor agreed with Arnim about close co-operation with Bavaria and other South German states and obtained the King's approval for this policy. Arnim's other proposal, the sending of *oratores*, Bismarck dismissed as impracticable. He did not believe that an appropriate position at the Council could be found for them—even if the Holy See did not reject this proposition forthwith—

[1] Arnim to Bismarck, no. 11, 15 May 1869.
[2] Arnim to Bismarck, 17 May 1869.
[3] Friedrich, *Geschichte*, i. 782 ff.
[4] Bismarck to the King, 25 May 1869, *GW* vib. 84–6.

particularly in the case of Prussia, because its Government was being looked upon by the Vatican as a Protestant, that is, a heretical, one.[1] Any statement by the Prussian Minister would be regarded with suspicion and disfavour and the dignity of his sovereign would suffer. He would not be accorded veto powers and his protests would be ignored.[2] Thus, should the Council pass resolutions that Prussia could not accept, his presence would put his Government in a more difficult position than if the Council were left to itself and considered as an ecclesiastical convention only. Against any transgressions by the Council in secular affairs the existing laws of the state would be applied. In any case, the decision to send a representative to Rome should not be made dependent on Napoleon's action.[3]

The King's understanding of this matter seems to have been vague. While he agreed with Bismarck and Arnim regarding co-operation with other German states, his agreement was so qualified that it is difficult to ascertain what he really meant. It would seem that he was, in part at least, more impressed with Arnim's arguments than with Bismarck's.[4]

By the end of May no further details of Hohenlohe's policy regarding the Council had reached Berlin. Bismarck then, in accordance with the decision of the King, suggested to Hohenlohe a *démarche* at the Vatican in the name of all German governments. This *démarche*, Bismarck wrote, should be confidential and undertaken in such a way that, according to its reception, it could, if the need arose, be repeated in stronger

---

[1] According to a memorandum by Thile of 11 June 1869, Cardinal Antonelli had told Odo Russell that the Pope would not agree to have non-Catholic Powers represented at the Council.

[2] This was, on the one hand, a clever approach to the King by playing on his dignity and rights. On the other hand, it was—intentionally or not—a misrepresentation of Arnim's proposals. Arnim had foreseen these facts and had made the point that the value of such an ambassador would not be in taking part in the deliberations, but rather as a steadying influence and rallying-point for the minority bishops.

[3] Bismarck to the King, 25 May 1869, *GW* vi*b*. 84–6.

[4] The King's decision, according to his marginal notes on Bismarck's report, was as follows: 'To 1: Agreed. To 2: Agreed in principle that no ambassador should be sent to the Council unless a French decision should cause a change [in this policy]. But should an ambassador be accredited to Rome, outside and for the duration of the Council, to raise those objections which have been recognized as necessary if the dreaded decisions [mentioned] in par. 1 should be passed, he would have to await [special] instructions, because those issued normally for such a case would hardly be appropriate . . . W 25. 5. 69.' Ibid. 86.

terms later on. It should not be in the form of a fruitless protest but should be presented in the spirit of a friendly but serious warning. It should also stress that under no circumstances could the governments agree to a unilateral declaration of policy by the Vatican regarding their interest in and their relationship to the Holy See. The *démarche* should also state that the governments would not attempt to interfere in any affairs concerning problems of dogma and they would therefore touch upon the question of infallibility only to the extent that its implications concerned matters of state. The steps leading to the *démarche* should be co-ordinated and agreed upon by all governments so that the Holy See would be convinced that it was confronted by a united Germany regardless of the differences of the religious faiths of its sovereigns.[1]

In his reply to Arnim, Bismarck went into great detail to convey his views. In the past, secular Powers had participated at a Council because there had been only one universal Church. Even at the Council of Trent, Protestant governments participated because it was believed that they had not left the Church irrevocably. The Church had at that time been in an intimate, closely circumscribed relationship with the State, and canon law had significant meaning to secular governments.

For these reasons it had been possible for the governments, under certain judicial provisions, to intervene in the deliberations and regulations of ecclesiastical affairs. This they had done through their *oratores* at the Council. Then, too, a number of European governments had explicitly accepted and published the decisions of the Council of Trent. Prussia had not done so then, and there could be no question that it would do so now. If, on the other hand, the Prussian Government, through its representative, should take part in the deliberations of the forthcoming Council, it would have to accept or reject its decisions as part of its secular or ecclesiastic law. This made it impossible for Prussia to send *oratores* to Rome. Instead, while the Government recognized the complete freedom of the Church in ecclesiastical affairs, it firmly rejected any transgressions by the Church into the secular sphere. Napoleon's plan to send a representative to Rome could not have any

---

[1] Bismarck to Werthern, 28 May 1869, *GW* vi*b*. 90–1. Hohenlohe, *Denkwuerdigkeiten*, i. 374–6.

influence on the decisions of the Prussian Government. In general, Prussia and the North German Federation were to seek close co-operation with Bavaria and the other South German governments to pursue a common policy toward the Holy See.[1]

But Arnim was not easily persuaded. In his next report he reiterated many of his previous arguments in favour of the *oratores*, comparing their status at the Council to that of government representatives in parliament or police officials at public meetings.[2] He must have realized though that his proposals were falling on barren ground, because in another report he offered this suggestion: to send an official memorandum to the German bishops in Rome in which the policy of the governments was clearly stated and in which the bishops were made aware of the responsibilities they would assume if they contributed to any decisions which would upset the religious peace in Germany.[3] Contrary to the views expressed in his previous report, Arnim now opposed a joint protest by the German governments. He had had several conversations with Cardinal Antonelli, he wrote, that made it clear that the Holy See would give only evasive answers to the proposed *démarche*.[4]

All these plans and counterplans came to naught, however, because Hohenlohe's circular note failed to produce any tangible results. Both Austria and France declined to participate in a common policy as suggested by the Bavarian Prime Minister and their refusal led to the collapse of the entire plan.[5] This may have been the reason Arnim's suggestion that a memorandum be presented to the German bishops was

[1] Bismarck to Arnim, 26 May 1869, *GW* vib. 86–8. Friedrich, *Geschichte*, i. 783 ff. T. Granderath, *Geschichte des vatikanischen Konzils*, 3 vols. (Freiburg, 1903), i. 369 ff., henceforth cited Granderath.

[2] Arnim to Bismarck, no. 19, 3 June 1869.

[3] Arnim to Bismarck, 29 May 1869.

[4] Arnim to Bismarck, 31 May 1869.

[5] On Austria's policy toward the Holy See and the Vatican Council, see F. Engel-Janosi, *Oesterreich und der Vatican*, 2 vols. (Graz, 1958), i. 150 ff. On Austria's refusal to follow the suggestions contained in Hohenlohe's circular, see Friedrich Ferdinand Graf von Beust, *Aus Drei Vierteljahrhunderten*, 2 vols. (Stuttgart, 1887), ii. 278–81, henceforth cited Beust. Regarding French policy, see H. Oncken, *Die Rheinpolitik Kaiser Napoleons III von 1863 bis 1870 und der Ursprung des Krieges von 1870–1*, 3 vols. (Stuttgart, 1926), iii. 208, henceforth cited Oncken. Friedrich, *Geschichte*, i. 786.

accepted in Berlin for Abeken, the State Secretary in the Foreign Ministry, referred to it in a conversation with Hohenlohe as part of the proposed Prussian policy in regard to the Council.[1]

On 17 June, before going on leave, Arnim had an audience with the Pope. Their discussion centred mainly on the forthcoming Council. Arnim told the Pope of the serious apprehensions which many countries, including Prussia, had about the preparations and the foreseeable decisions. Pius IX received these remarks sympathetically. He dismissed the forebodings of the governments by saying that he was a powerless old man, without army or navy, whose only concern was to speak the truth and do his duty. He hoped that the Council would take place and that much good would come of it. Arnim observed that, even without the help of armed forces, Pius dominated the souls of people and these would be agitated by the papal pronouncements to the great embarrassment of all Christendom. The Pope did not reply to this but remarked that it was impossible for the Church to co-operate with governments which were inimical to the Church and which made common cause with atheism and materialism.[2] Arnim's rejoinder was that this could not be applied to either Prussia or the other German governments. He then mentioned the activities of the Jesuits, who, in many instances, had made it difficult for the governments to co-operate with the Holy See. In his reply Pius as much as disavowed the Jesuits. He liked them very much, he said, because they had done a great deal of good; but they had not a decisive influence at the papal Court. For the rest, no decision had as yet been taken as to what the attitude of the Council would be on these problems, nor what position Rome would be able to offer to the governments. He was considering further communications to the governments in September. The Pope's remarks were rather vague at that point, Arnim

---

[1] Abeken memorandum of 14 June 1869 in Hohenlohe, *Denkwuerdigkeiten*, i. 375–6. *GW* vib. 96–7, 128–30. On 10 Oct. 1869 the Prussian Minister for Cultural Affairs sent a letter to the Archbishop of Cologne and to other Prussian bishops, warning them that by participating in the Council they took advantage of a privilege granted to them by the Constitution and that all other constitutional principles concerning religious freedom applied only to the then existing situation. A similar letter was sent to the Bavarian bishops by the Bavarian Minister on 1 Nov. 1869. Friedrich, *Geschichte*, i. 795–7.

[2] Ibid. 801.

reported, and he did not think it appropriate to ask for further details. Opinion on this subject seemed to be divided, because Cardinal Antonelli had told Odo Russell, the British representative, that the Holy See could neither desire representatives from Catholic countries, nor admit those from non-Catholic ones. But this was only a private opinion of the Cardinal and the question of admitting representatives of non-Catholic governments to the Council was still open.[1]

During his leave, Arnim went to Berlin for consultations. There he talked to Abeken, suggesting that, instead of sending *oratores*, a special representative to the Pope be commissioned for the duration of the Council. As a Catholic such a representative would be in a better position to gather information and influence the German bishops.[2] Bismarck did not think much of this idea. He felt it would accord undue significance to the Council and make it appear that Prussia was paying the Council extraordinary attention.[3] And, while he outwardly supported the mission of a special Bavarian envoy to Rome to represent the German governments, privately he did not really believe that it would materialize and doubted if a suitable person could be found in Munich.

Arnim followed the affairs at Rome while on leave, and, when the *Correspondance de Rome* attacked Hohenlohe and his anti-Roman policy in an article of 7 August 1869, he suggested that this attack be made an occasion to deal a telling blow to the reigning clique in Rome. This would also, he observed, awaken Antonelli to his duties and responsibilities regarding the Roman press.[4] Before leaving Berlin he sent a report to the Foreign Ministry outlining the problems and difficulties he faced at the Vatican: he was really not the most suitable man to represent Prussia during the Council, but as the King had expressed a personal interest in his attendance he would do his best to discharge his duties satisfactorily. Since both France and Austria had decided to send no special representative, Prussia could hardly do otherwise. His own purpose would be to exert his influence on the Papal Government and on the

[1] Arnim to Bismarck, 24 June 1869.
[2] Abeken memorandum, 29 July 1869.
[3] Bucher memorandum, 31 July 1869.
[4] Arnim (to Balan), 26 Aug. 1869. A directive, as suggested by Arnim, was sent to Limburg-Stirum on 4 Sept. 1869, *GW* vi*b*. 141–2.

German bishops and gather reliable information. Compared with his Austrian, French, and even Bavarian colleagues he was, however, at a disadvantage. He was a Protestant.[1] No matter how much confidence he enjoyed with a few Roman prelates and German bishops, the deep antipathy between the two religions could not be erased. This went so deep that those bishops who had tried to become better acquainted with him found themselves suspect to their own colleagues and superiors. Of almost equal disadvantage was the difference in rank which existed between himself and the French and Austrian representatives, who were ambassadors while he was only a minister, inasmuch as it was customary in Rome for each bishop to present himself personally to the foreign ambassadors on his arrival.[2] Because of his lower rank he could not ask for this courtesy; consequently his personal relationship was restricted to two or three bishops. The Austrian Embassy was the gathering-place of all German bishops where anti-Prussian tendencies were freely expressed. The French Ambassador too had no trouble, because his rank and his ample financial resources assured his influence on the French and perhaps even some German bishops. He mentioned these points, Arnim wrote, not for the sake of his own advancement or to have the Prussian Legation elevated to an Embassy,[3] but only to point out how little his abilities were being supplemented by adequate official status. He also wanted to apologize beforehand if his performance during the Council did not quite measure up to the demands which might perhaps be made of him.[4]

Bismarck's marginalia and Arnim's subsequent conversation with Bucher show no great alarm. The Chancellor even thought at one point of closing the Legation in Rome and

---

[1] Arnim to Thile, 22 Oct. 1869, and Bismarck's marginalia: 'A Cath[olic] just *ad hoc*? Better permanently.'

[2] 'Involuntary decision valueless', ibid.

[3] 'Would not be useful politically either', ibid.

[4] Bismarck underlined 'demands' and put a '?' on the margin, ibid. One historian characterized the position of the representatives of the Powers in Rome as follows: in the centre, the representatives of France and Austria; slightly to the right, the official representative of England; 'at the left, Count Arnim disturbs the atmosphere with conferences, memoranda, and plans'. F. Engel-Janosi, 'Die oesterreichische Berichterstattung ueber das Vatikanische Konzil, 1869–70' in *Mitteilungen des Instituts fuer oesterreichische Geschichtsforschung*, vol. 62 (1954), p. 599; henceforth cited Engel-Janosi, *Berichterstattung*.

taking the same position as Britain and Russia, which had only unofficial representatives at the Vatican. But he reconsidered and suggested instead that Arnim should disregard minor obstacles and carry on as usual.[1] But Arnim's report, in spite of its apologies, petty detail, and exaggerated fears, made sufficient impression on Bismarck for him to state once more his views and those of the Government regarding Prussian policy toward Rome and the Council.

The difficulties and problems that confronted him in Rome, Bismarck wrote to Arnim, were appreciated in Berlin, and the King and he himself would make all the necessary allowances in their demands upon him and his staff. These difficulties did not amount to so very much, if one considered how little cause the Government had to emphasize the significance of the Council. This did not mean, Bismarck wrote, that the religious aspects were being underestimated or that the Council's influence on the conscience of Catholics in matters of faith and doctrine and internal Church discipline were overlooked. Neither the demands, hopes, and fears which this assembly might raise among the people, nor the connections which it might establish with religious communities outside the Roman Catholic Church, were of any concern to the Government.

These were all spiritual matters which could be safely left to the various religious organizations. Attempts to disturb the religious peace in other, non-ecclesiastical, areas, however, would have to be dealt with decisively by the Government. It would be futile, Bismarck went on, to go into details and attempt to foresee how the Council would act in these matters. The mere fact that it might consider these subjects, as shown by the works of the various commissions, caused no apprehension, and the Government, calm and undisturbed, was awaiting the deliberations of the Council. It was important, Bismarck advised Arnim, that he too should remain calm and that through him this attitude be conveyed to the Council. Fear had been expressed that the Council might come under the influence of extremist elements and that this would disturb the relationship between Church and State. It was partly for that reason that Prussia had co-operated with Bavaria. But it was quite wrong to attribute this co-operation to any grave apprehensions. Quite

[1] Bucher memorandum, 25 Oct. 1869.

the contrary. It was firmly believed in Berlin as well as in Munich that any dangers that might arise from the Council would only accrue to the Catholic Church. It would, of course, be highly regrettable, Bismarck continued, should the decisions of the Council lead to difficulties between the Church and the Government; and if Rome wanted to heed advice Berlin would counsel moderation and would do so more for the sake and the interest of the Holy See than for its own.

The Prussian Government was convinced that it had all the means at its disposal to meet any transgression on the part of the Church, and it would safeguard its rights in all respects. The Government was certain that the political as well as the patriotic awareness of the German people, including the Catholics, was strong enough to give the support necessary to overcome any real or imaginary dangers in this respect. It was to be hoped that the traditional common sense and reasonableness of the Holy See would save it from these dangers. It was fortunate that the other German governments were in accord with these views and it was desirable that the unity of German policy be openly and frequently expressed in Rome. As to the Prussian and German bishops, they should, without making it too obvious, be influenced toward a moderate and reasonable policy; but most of all, Bismarck concluded, they should be impressed with the absolute firmness and trustworthiness of their governments.[1]

Arnim found an opportunity to carry out Bismarck's instructions shortly after his return to Rome. On the occasion of an audience with the Pope, Pius recalled their conversation of the previous June and reaffirmed the absence of any intention to disturb the peace. Arnim assured him that the Prussian Government was not in the least disturbed.[2] But his calm confidence appeared not to have penetrated very deeply as far as Arnim himself was concerned, for in his very next report he once more raised his voice of doom and gloom.

There had been rumours, he wrote, that the German and French bishops had a moderating effect on the Holy See. These rumours were unfounded. In spite of assurances to the contrary,

---

[1] Bismarck to Arnim, 12 Nov. 1869, *Acta et Decreta Sacrorum Conciliorum Recentiorum. Collectio Lacensis*, vii/ii. 1209–11, henceforth cited *Col. Lac.*
[2] Arnim to the King, 20 Nov. 1869.

it was unlikely that the bishops had complete freedom of discussion. Those who opposed the majority at the Council would presumably not try to enforce decrees by majority resolutions, and, as a result, these conflicts of opinion could lead to latent schisms in the Church.[1]

Discussing the main subject of the Council, the dogma of papal infallibility, Arnim made some shrewd observations.[2] Prince Hohenlohe in his famous circular note, and many Catholics on other occasions, had expressed apprehension that, once the dogma of papal infallibility had been pronounced, no government would be assured of the obedience of its Catholic subjects. These fears were without foundation, Arnim asserted. Should Catholics ever give their allegiance in political affairs to the Pope rather than to the temporal powers, the great mass of people would not ask if the Pope was, or was not, infallible in 1870. The whole question was much rather a theological problem and an internal affair of the Church. Its solution gave only an indication to what degree the Bishop of Rome had infringed upon the jurisdiction of his colleagues. This was brought about by the bishops themselves and they were to be blamed for it, because the majority of them had for years preached and recognized the supremacy of the Bishop of Rome based on supernatural origins. The Holy See was only drawing the logical conclusions from these adulations which the bishops had offered up to the last minute.

Indeed, one would have to recognize the fact [Arnim wrote] that the Pope had a certain right [to assume] the most extreme consequencies. For, if his God-given supremacy is being wrecked on this most important point, the whole structure on which the Pope's Holy See is erected will collapse. After that, Rome would no more be the Holy Ark as provided for before the beginning of time, but it [will become] a suburb, created for utilitarian purposes for the administration of the Church, [a fact] with which even the Protestants could go along. . . .

From the point of view of the secular governments, Arnim continued, and especially that of Prussia and Germany, it

[1] Arnim to Thile, no. 44, 22 Nov. 1869.

[2] Arnim to Thile, 26 Nov. 1869, and the King's marginalia: 'Dies Dogma in der 2ten Haelfte des 19. Jahrhunderts von neuem proklamiert muss aber bei der Verfuehrungskunst unseres politischen Jahrhunderts zum Religionskrieg fuehren. Dem ist also *nicht entgegen* zu treten sondern dasselbe zu staerken. W 14/12/69.'

would be difficult to forecast which decision would, in the end, be most desirable. 'Even if one would not be guided by the wicked principle that one should never begrudge a man the rope on which he wants to hang himself, it would still be permissible to think that the turn of events which is most objectionable to our instincts might, in the last analysis, have the most favourable results.'[1] Most of all, it should not be thought that every champion of infallibility was Prussia's enemy, and every bishop in opposition Prussia's good friend. Yet the result of this crisis showed that those bishops who were about to loose their support from Rome demonstrated a definite desire for support from the secular powers.

[1] Ibid.

III

THE VATICAN COUNCIL

SOON after the sessions of the Council had begun, Arnim reported on the restrictions imposed by Pope Pius IX on discussion and initiation of propositions. A number of bishops—German, Hungarian, and Croatian, some French and some American—resented these restrictions. This group was vocally strong but numerically weak. Arnim estimated that it numbered about 100, against 500 adherents of the Pope. Furthermore, the opposition was divided along national lines and without a leader or a programme. It had made no protest against the standing rules nor did it seem to have any plan to express its views. Should this group develop into a formal opposition to the papal party, Arnim thought that he should give its German bishops the necessary support. Such support should, however, be limited to repelling encroachment of the Italians on the rights of the German bishops.[1]

Bismarck seems to have been unduly agitated over Arnim's rather vague and innocuous suggestions. He may have felt that a plot was brewing, for he directed Thile, who temporarily replaced Abeken, to send a sharply worded instruction to Rome. Because Arnim's scheme to support the bishops was an undertaking of great importance, Thile asked him to furnish more details. 'I may expect from Your Excellency's proved tact', Thile wrote, 'that you will observe all necessary precautions . . . and that you will especially avoid any initiative for which you have not received specific authorization from here.'[2]

When Arnim received this instruction he was justifiably annoyed. It can be assumed that he had had no specific plan in mind when he wrote about the conditions in Rome and that even if he had there was no harm in looking ahead. The situation in Rome had changed completely since he had sent his suggestion, he replied, and there was no occasion whatever to

[1] Arnim to Thile, 16 Dec. 1869.   [2] Thile to Arnim, 27 Dec. 1869.

give support to the bishops. There was therefore no danger that he would take any initiative not previously authorized. For this, he wrote acidly, there was no need to have any 'proved tact' (*bewaehrten Takt*)—just ordinary tact, of the sort that any government could expect of its agents, was quite enough.[1]

In the meantime, too, Arnim had become disillusioned with the abilities of the German bishops and their behaviour at the Council. 'We Germans should be properly ashamed of the deplorable role which the German bishops here play', he told Friedrich, the prominent German theologian. 'If it were not for the Hungarian bishops, who are being considered here as half Germans, they [the German bishops] would wander about like lost sheep. The German clerics, or rather the episcopate, have no feelings at all for their nation.'[2]

It was his dissatisfaction with the behaviour and activities of those bishops who opposed the papal party that caused Arnim once more to advocate governmental intervention at the Council. He took the occasion of a proposed address of the German and Austro-Hungarian bishops to the Council to assert that a grave crisis was at hand. There were many factors to be considered in this situation which could not be dismissed simply by referring to one's own legislative means, Arnim wrote, with a clear stab at Bismarck's favourite argument. Aside from several other possibilities, one alone gave the governments sufficient cause to interfere in the current proceedings. This was that the assembly gathered in the Vatican was not a council in which all the parts of the Church, the bishops, and the laity, had sufficient opportunity and liberty to be inspired by the Holy Ghost. It was rather an assembly which for the greater part was composed of servants of the Pope and only to a much lesser part of independent men and bishops. Supported by his majority, the Pope was absolute ruler of the Church and the Council and in that way dominated its order of business as well as its discussions and decisions. It was this vastly increased power of the Pope, now being elevated to a constitutional principle in the government of the Church, which was so

[1] Arnim to Bismarck, no. 2, 8 Jan. 1870. That Arnim had given up his idea of intervention before Thile's directive had arrived is clear from Arnim's report of 23 Dec. 1869.

[2] Quoted by J. Friedrich, *Tagebuch* (Noerdlingen, 1873), p. 55, henceforth cited Friedrich, *Tagebuch*.

dangerous and, Arnim warned, infinitely more important than the promulgation of the dogma of papal infallibility. The Ministers of Bavaria and Portugal and Strossmayer, Bishop of Bosnia, had come to him to discuss the situation and suggest common action. At the end of his report Arnim proposed the organization of an anti-Council composed of the diplomatic representatives of the Powers in Rome.[1]

But these reports did not change Bismarck's attitude and opinion. Arnim's description of the Council gave the Chancellor the impression of chaotic conditions in Rome. It was difficult, he thought, to foresee what course the Council would take. Too hasty action might cause more harm than good, and too much activity might easily lead to undesirable results. It was not Arnim's task, Bismarck advised, to initiate measures against the Council or to prod the bishops into action against the papal party. He should instead express the conviction and propagate the idea that the Prussian Government was fully capable of handling the situation at home with the means it had at its disposal. Public opinion and the strong national feelings of all segments of the population, including the Catholics, gave firm support to the Government in all its actions. Special assurances by the Pope that the decisions of the Council would not change the established relationship between the Holy See and the governments were therefore quite unnecessary. Apart from that, Bismarck continued, it was not the Government's intention to bring about a conflict with the Holy See. The Government was anxious, in the interest of its Catholic subjects and the continuance of peaceful internal developments of the country, that the relationship between Church and State should remain undisturbed. It was the Government's aim that the religious life and the intellectual freedom, characteristic of German Catholics, be maintained, and not destroyed by foreign elements through majority decisions in Rome. But for these very reasons the Government's concern could not be translated into governmental action on behalf of the German bishops at the Council. They would have to stand on their own feet. The

---

[1] Arnim to Bismarck, 23 Dec. 1869. To Arnim's proposal of an anti-Council, Bismarck put on the margin, 'with Trauttmansdorff?' In a postscript Arnim qualified his proposal as not being opportune at the moment. Friedrich, *Geschichte*, iii. 264–5, 267.

Government could only express its sympathies and, if need be and if so requested, could assure the bishops of its support. To make demands on the Holy See on behalf of the German bishops, however, was not the duty of the Prussian Government. Nor should it be Arnim's task. The reason for this passive policy was obvious, Bismarck explained. Should the Government intervene in Rome, and should its intervention be rejected, it could neither conceal its defeat nor retaliate. Should its intervention be accepted, on the other hand, its independent position toward the Council would be sacrificed, its decisions could not be tested impartially before the courts, and, as a result, the Government would be bound by the decrees of the Council. This too was one of the reasons why a conference of the representatives of the Powers in Rome could not be considered feasible. Another more practical consideration was that few diplomatic representatives would actually get together for a meeting of this kind. The bishops could be encouraged verbally, they could be given moral support, and, if worse came to worse, they could be assured that their rights would be safeguarded in their own country. It could also be pointed out to them that any radical changes in the organization of the Church, as the autocratic displays of the papal party seemed to foreshadow, would, of necessity, affect the relationship between Church and State and, through it, the bishops' own position toward the Government. Should this occur, repressive legal and administrative measures might be taken against them.[1]

Bismarck's admonitions and expositions had little effect on Arnim. The situation in Rome was too serious, events happened too fast and were too important for him to just sit and watch. Measures of great significance and incalculable consequence were being discussed and prepared at the Council and it was practically impossible for anyone present not to take an active part and not to join the quarrelling factions. To preserve a calm disposition, a clear head, and a moderating and steady voice in this turmoil, as Bismarck demanded, was asking a great deal. It was too much to expect of Arnim.

Possessing a quick-witted, sometimes brilliant, somewhat vain, and easily excitable nature, Arnim was a man of action

---

[1] Bismarck to Arnim, 5 Jan. 1870, *GW* vi*b*. 197–200. The Chancellor's views had the approval of the King and the Cabinet.

and movement. He loved discussion and dispute, especially as a leading participant. His position, his personal charm, and his entertaining conversation had gained for him a conspicuous position among the diplomats in Rome[1]—a situation which he undoubtedly enjoyed and was not slow to exploit. Not satisfied with being a mere observer, reporter, and occasional counsellor, Arnim wanted to initiate policy; rather than listening to advice, he wanted to dispense it. That his attitude would eventually get him into opposition to Bismarck could easily be anticipated.[2] While Arnim was in Rome, however, no serious disagreement arose between the two. Bismarck continued to advise non-intervention, patience, and moderation. Arnim kept insisting on an active policy against the Holy See. That his opinion and his judgement of events in Rome were shared by others is well attested.[3] He subsequently advocated a joint *démarche* with the Austrian Government,[4] joint intervention by the Powers,[5] and Prussian support for the French Note.[6] Nor did he cease to forecast dire consequences if his advice were not followed. For greater effectiveness, or perhaps because of

[1] For sympathetic views of Arnim in Rome, see K. Schloezer, *Roemische Briefe 1864-9* (Berlin, 1926), pp. 171, 175, 182. Friedrich called him one of the most outstanding diplomats in Rome, *Tagebuch*, p. 55. Radowitz considered him one of the most intelligent (*geistvollsten*) diplomats with the most pleasant manners, H. Holborn, *Aufzeichnungen und Erinnerungen aus dem Leben des Botschafters Joseph Maria von Radowitz*, 2 vols. (Berlin, 1925), i. 289. Morier thought that 'his [Arnim's] fault is an excessive vanity which disturbs his judgement the moment his own person comes into play', R. Wemyss, *Memoirs and Letters of Sir Robert Morier*, 2 vols. (London, 1911), ii. 303.

[2] At that time, too, Bismarck admonished Arnim to distinguish in his reports facts from opinion, '. . . I shall be relieved if Your Excellency would, in your reports, keep the presentation of facts and conditions as objective as possible and separated from your judgements; the latter, however, which I value no less, should be included in separate reports.' Bismarck to Arnim, 18 Jan. 1870, *GW* vib. 219.

[3] Thile memorandum, 22 Feb. 1870, in which the State Secretary noted that Oubril, the Russian Ambassador, had shown him reports from Rome which, on the whole, agreed with those of Arnim. A similar note is in a directive from Bismarck to Werthern, of 10 June 1869, about the reports of the Bavarian Ambassador in Rome. *GW* vib. 99–100. See also Lord Acton, 'The Vatican Council', *North British Review*, liii. 204 ff.; Hohenlohe, *Denkwuerdigkeiten*, i. 365–6.

[4] Arnim to Bismarck, 12 Feb. 1870.

[5] Arnim to Bismarck, no. 33, 4 Mar. 1870.

[6] Arnim to Bismarck, 15 Mar. 1870. It would seem that at least part of Arnim's militant position regarding the Council can be attributed to the influence of Lord Acton, whom he saw frequently in these days and with whom he was on friendly terms. Doellinger, *Briefwechsel*, ii. 305–6.

new information, he changed the details in his reports, but his main theme was constant: governmental intervention in support of the minority bishops and against the papal party. The idea of applying national laws to the decrees of the Council would be erroneous, he asserted, clearly aiming at Bismarck's much-used argument. There just would not be any decrees to which national legislation could be applied. For if the Council fulfilled the far-reaching expectations of the Pope, there would be no changes in the organization of the Church or in its relationship with the governments. The danger would lie rather in the extreme power which the radical party within the Church would be using throughout Christendom. It would use this power in the education of the clergy and the youth, and would terrorize the conscience of all Catholics without in any way coming into conflict with secular laws. Once the decrees of the Council were promulgated, the great majority of bishops would, at first silently, later openly, submit to them, and within ten years all bishoprics in Germany would belong to the ultramontane party because there would no longer be any independent priests in the land. Theology would sink irresistibly into the morass of Jesuit formulation and there would be nothing left to oppose the pernicious influence which Rome wanted to exercise over the nations.[1]

As consistently as Arnim advised intervention, Bismarck counselled abstention.[2] Only if another, Catholic, Power would take the lead in Rome, would Prussia and the North German Confederation join in a *démarche*.[3] The opportunity to do so came late in February 1870, when it became known that France had sent a Note to the Holy See. In it the French Foreign Minister, Daru, requested admission of a French representative to the Council because, according to his information, other than purely ecclesiastical matters were being discussed and decided upon in Rome.[4]

[1] Arnim to Bismarck, no. 33, 4 Mar. 1870.

[2] Bismarck to Arnim, 19 Feb. 1870, *GW* vib. 251; (Foreign Ministry) Circular Directive, 21 Feb. 1870, ibid. 255–6; Bismarck to Arnim, 13 Mar. 1870, ibid. 283–4; Bismarck to Arnim, 15 Mar. 1870, ibid. 292.

[3] Bismarck to the Prussian representatives in Munich, Dresden, Brussels, 15 Mar. 1870, *GW* vib. 289–91; Bismarck to the Prussian representatives in Paris and London, 16 Mar. 1870, ibid. 292–6.

[4] Friedrich, *Geschichte*, iii. 673 ff.; Doellinger, *Briefwechsel*, ii. 169, fn. 9; *Col. Lac.* vii/ii. 1546–69.

Arnim, instead of welcoming the *démarche* by the French Government, showed little enthusiasm. He thought little of its contents or the way it was being carried out. And in this he was quite right, for this much-advertised step proved a great disappointment to the anti-papal faction.[1] The French Government demonstrated with its Note a lack of planning and a confusion of policy which had characterized its entire attitude toward the Council, Arnim reported to Berlin. According to his information, the time might not be far off when the French Government might feel it desirable to get together with other European governments to find support for its policy. Should this occur, it might then be desirable for Prussia to consider supporting this policy, if only in a restricted way.[2]

In advocating this policy, Arnim used many of the old arguments he had employed on previous similar occasions. He also looked into the past and recalled the Reformation and the support the Protestant reformers had received from their princes. 'Without Henry VIII England would even today be a province of the Pope and without the German princes Brandenburg and Magdeburg would still be seats of Roman legates.' To this Bismarck noted on the margin: 'Henry VIII took, as we do, successfully, the road of legislation and not that of exchanging [diplomatic] notes.'[3]

Continuing his report, Arnim outlined what practical steps might be taken by Prussia to support France. In doing so, he assumed that the Austrian Government too would take an active part. In this he was mistaken. Bismarck, who knew better, realized almost immediately that the French step in Rome was but a perfunctory manœuvre and that it would be dangerous to accept it at face value.[4] The Chancellor was further strengthened in his view by two conversations with Benedetti, the French Ambassador in Berlin. In them, Bismarck, apparently to test French intentions, mentioned the possibility of consultations among the Powers in regard to papal policy at the Council. Benedetti, who may have misunder-

[1] Friedrich, *Geschichte*, iii. 676.
[2] Arnim to Bismarck, no. 43, 15 Mar. 1870, and Bismarck's marginal note: 'already done'.
[3] Ibid.
[4] Bismarck to Werther, 12 Mar. 1870, *GW* vib. 280.

stood Bismarck at that point, reported to Paris that the Chancellor had suggested a conference of the Powers.[1] This Daru
rejected. In turn he asked for the support of the Powers for the
French Note. Bismarck's impression from these conversations
with the French Ambassador was that France did not care to
take any firm steps in Rome, or to join with the other Powers
in a common policy. This impression was furthermore also
prevalent in Munich and Vienna.[2]

Informing Arnim of these developments, Bismarck stressed
once more his belief that the initiative for a policy against the
Council could be taken only by a Catholic power. As to the
German bishops, they could not be protected against voluntary
submission, only against oppression—and this neither by forc-
ing Prussia's assistance on them nor by taking over their
problems.[3]

Meantime, and before this directive reached him, Arnim
had been busy gathering support for his view. The representatives of Austria and Bavaria had apparently been persuaded that only a joint effort would be successful; each,
however, wishing the other to take the first step. Dupenloup,
the Bishop of Orleans, who had also joined this group, had
even gone so far as to suggest, 'though quite obliquely', that
the Powers actively join the minority bishops in their fight
against the Pope.[4] But, for all his zeal, even Arnim noted that
these were mostly empty phrases and not to be relied upon.
Only Dupenloup could be taken seriously in his determination
to fight for the rights of the minority. He too was dissatisfied
with the French Government's policy and its half-hearted
attempt to intervene in Rome. He wrote a letter to Daru in
which he made several suggestions on how to support the
minority bishops and advised him to replace Banneville, the
French Ambassador in Rome, and threaten the Curia with

---

[1] That Bismarck had suggested a conference is also mentioned by Lord Acton
in his letter to Doellinger of 12 Apr. 1870: Doellinger, *Briefwechsel*, ii. 304–9.

[2] Bismarck to Arnim, 25 Mar. 1870, *GW* vi*b*. 301; Busch, i. 15, 17–22.

[3] Bismarck to Arnim, 25 Mar. 1870.

[4] Arnim to Bismarck, 16 Mar. 1870; nos. 45, 46, 49, 51, of 18 Mar. 1870;
no. 51 in Doellinger, *Briefwechsel*, ii. 307, fn. 5. The minority bishops agreed with
Haynald, Archbishop of Kalocsa, who declared that they could, under no circumstances, ask for the intervention of the governments. If intervention did materialize,
the bishops as well as the Vatican must be equally taken by surprise. Friedrich,
Geschichte, iii. 817.

the recall of the French bishops and the non-recognition of the Council if it refused to change its policy. Arnim sent this letter on behalf of the Bishop, unsigned, to Paris by diplomatic pouch.[1]

Once more the attempt to arouse a secular Power against the Church failed. Daru claimed that his hands were tied by the Cabinet and that he could not depart from his policy.[2] Bismarck notified Arnim of Daru's position and instructed him to support the French Note. The Austrian and Bavarian representatives, who were to receive similar directives from their governments, would join him in this step.[3]

He advised Arnim that when carrying out this instruction he would have to avoid two pitfalls: he must not go beyond the policy expressed in the French Note, but he should, on the other hand, give his support to the extent that the French Government could not later declare that it had been ready for decisive action but had been prevented from carrying it out by the lack of support from the foremost Protestant Power on the continent. Prussia was supporting France, Bismarck explained, because the Government concurred in the views expressed in the French Note. While it did not intend to interfere in matters of faith of the Catholic Church, it could not forget not only that the German bishops in Rome were completely ignored but that the views expressed at the Council were in opposition to those of the majority of bishops from Germany, Austria, and Hungary. A pursuance of that policy might endanger the peace between Church and State and could be effected only over the objections of the bishops by a decision whose validity would not be generally recognized. There was no need to refer to individual points of dogma or specific instances, Bismarck advised Arnim; he should instead stress the general tendencies and consequences of such a procedure. These were general considerations rather than specific orders, Bismarck wrote, and it

---

[1] Arnim to Bismarck (private letters A and B) and tel. no. 10, 3 Apr. 1870; Friedrich, *Geschichte*, iii. 818 ff.; Doellinger, *Briefwechsel*, ii. 283–5.

[2] Werther to Bismarck, 7 Apr. 1870.

[3] Bismarck to Arnim (tel. no. 17), 8 Apr. 1870, *GW* vi*b*, 319–20; Bismarck to Arnim, directive no. 98, 8 Apr. 1870. See also E. Weinzierl-Fischer, 'Bismarcks Haltung zum Vatikanum und der Beginn des Kulturkampfes nach den oesterreichischen diplomatischen Berichten aus Berlin 1869–71', *Mitteilungen des oesterreichischen Staatsarchivs*, x (1957), pp. 309–13; Doellinger, *Briefwechsel*, ii. 205, 231, 309, fns. 6 and 7, 356, fn. 15.

was up to Arnim to use them according to his own judgement and in whatever form he considered best.[1]

Before taking any steps in that direction, Arnim saw the Cardinal State Secretary to inquire about the procedural details concerning the French Note. He was told that Banneville had requested an audience with the Pope to transmit the Note to him as head of the Council. The French Ambassador was informed, Antonelli told Arnim, that it was up to the Pope's discretion to submit the Note to the Council, because the Holy See did not recognize the right of the French Government to communicate with the Council directly.[2] When Arnim, at a subsequent conversation with the Cardinal State Secretary, inquired about the attitude of the British Government, Antonelli assured him that Odo Russell, the British representative, had declared that his government was not concerned with the affairs of the Council and was anxious to avoid any statements on this matter. Arnim, taken aback by this information, went to see Odo Russell to verify the Cardinal's story. Russell assured him that there must have been a misunderstanding, even though he had, for a whole hour, explained to Antonelli his government's support of the French Note. On Arnim's advice, Russell requested authorization from the Foreign Office to send a written note to the Holy See on Her Majesty's position.[3] This Clarendon, the British Foreign Secretary, refused. It was incompatible with the policy of Britain toward the Holy See, he declared to the Prussian Ambassador, who was unable to change Clarendon's mind.[4] The loss of effective British support, together with Banneville's uncooperative

[1] Bismarck to Arnim, 14 Apr. 1870; see also Friedrich, *Geschichte*, iii. 865 ff.

[2] Arnim to Bismarck, no. 78, 18 Apr. 1870.

[3] Arnim to Bismarck, no. 83, 28 Apr. 1870. In this report Arnim also explained that it was important to have England unmistakably lined up with Prussia and to demonstrate to public opinion that there were no gaps in the ranks of the Powers in their opposition to the Council. In Berlin, Arnim's proposal was approved by the King and the Foreign Ministry, and the Prussian Ambassador in London was advised to see Clarendon personally to discuss the matter with him and to support Odo Russell's request. Thile to Bernstorff, 5 May 1870. For Russell's report on his conversation with Antonelli, see N. Blakiston, *The Roman Question* (London, 1962), pp. 426–9, 439, henceforth cited Blakiston; and Doellinger, *Briefwechsel*, ii. 320, fn. 5, 337, fn. 3, 355, fn. 14.

[4] Bernstorff to Bismarck, 7 May 1870. As to Clarendon's attitude, see his letter to Lord Loftus, English minister in Berlin, as printed in Doellinger, *Briefwechsel*, ii. 306, fn. 4, and his note of 5 Apr. 1870 to Gladstone, ibid. 326, fn. 9.

attitude—he had neither called on Arnim nor kept him informed about the status of his *démarche*—raised Arnim's doubts about the advisability of supporting the French Note. He asked Bismarck for instructions and Bismarck replied that the French Note should be supported in any case.[1] The French leader of the minority bishops also asked Arnim to support the Note as vigorously as possible and begged him to request an audience with the Pope and to persuade Pius IX to prorogue the Council.[2] This Arnim declined. He was not at all certain that the Pope would want to listen to his opinion or accept his advice. Besides, he did not want to take such a step without authorization from the King. Instead he sent a memorandum to Antonelli in support of the French Note.[3]

His memorandum was, as Arnim himself remarked, pretty strongly worded.[4] The Prussian Government supported the Note, it stated, not only because the French Government had asked for this support but because Prussia's Roman Catholic subjects would welcome it if the resolutions of the Council favoured religious and social peace. There were serious apprehensions in German ecclesiastical circles lest the resolutions create dangerous conditions and struggles without end.[5] These resolutions were, furthermore, taken against the almost unanimous opposition of the German episcopate. The German bishops had fulfilled their duties, the memorandum continued, by warning the Holy See of the deplorable consequences if the Council proceeded with the issuing of decrees which would change the authority within the ecclesiastical hierarchy. This could not but alter the relationship between civil and ecclesiastical authorities.[6] These decrees seemed to have been intended

[1] Arnim to Bismarck, tel. no. 17, 20 Apr. 1870; Bismarck to Arnim, tel. no. 23, 22 Apr. 1870.

[2] Friedrich, *Geschichte*, iii. 869, 872.

[3] Arnim to Bismarck, tel. no. 19, 27 Apr. 1870, *Col. Lac.* vii/ii. 1601. When he received Arnim's telegram, Bismarck, ever suspicious of unauthorized moves, advised him not to do anything until he had received further instructions. The King wanted to see his Note to Antonelli first, Bismarck wired, before he would give his permission for Arnim to seek an audience with the Pope. Bismarck to Arnim, tel. no. 24, 28 Apr. 1870. Granderath, ii. 711–14.

[4] Arnim to Bismarck, no. 80, 28 Apr. 1870, with a copy of the Note of 23 Apr. 1870 enclosed. The text of the Note is printed in Friedrich, *Tagebuch*, 476–88, and in the *Presse*, Vienna, 18 Apr. 1874.

[5] Bismarck's marginalia on Arnim's Note to Antonelli: 'None of our business.'

[6] 'Not mentioned in the instructions', ibid.

to revive the ancient papal constitution and rights.[1] Their revival and proclamation would, it was feared, confuse the relationship between Church and State and bring about a crisis which the Holy See might not have foreseen. In Germany, Catholics and non-Catholics lived peacefully together and it was hoped that they would co-operate one day to combat the errors of the world.[2] Should the opinions of the German bishops continue to be suppressed, however, the German people would look upon this as a revival of old struggles. It would then not be pacified by the argument that the political behaviour of Catholics was supposed to be independent of their religious duties.[3] It was entirely possible that the Government of the North German Confederation would lose the freedom of action in religious affairs which it had exercised so far in the interest of its Catholic subjects. This could happen because the Government was accused, justly or unjustly, that it had not, in time, opposed the schemes of the Holy See. In submitting these thoughts, the Government was not being guided by enmity to the Holy See and there were no plans to weaken the sovereignty of the Pope. It was only as a friendly Power, trying to be of service to the Curia, that the difficulties of the situation were being discussed and the dangers of a religious crisis were being pointed out. In doing this, it might contribute to postponing all decisions of the Council which could compromise the satisfactory position of the Catholic Church in Germany.[4] If the Government of the North German Confederation, through its memorandum, contributed to such a solution, it could thank the Holy See for its wisdom and it would continue in its happy relationship with the Vatican.[5]

Arnim explained in a covering letter to Berlin that he had originally considered an oral presentation in support of the French Note, but had changed his mind when the Bishop of Orleans and the Archbishop of Paris had called upon him and had urged him to make as strong a representation as possible.

---

[1] 'Nothing of this in the instructions', ibid.

[2] 'Nothing in the instructions. Mentioned peace only', ibid.

[3] 'Nothing in the instructions', ibid.

[4] '!?! Nothing in the instructions; quite contrary to all previous instructions', ibid.

[5] 'Nothing in the instructions; the Roman Court can thank itself—not *we* it', ibid.

This he had done. He had considered the diplomatic situation as well as the desires of the bishops, because it was on their behalf that this action had been undertaken to begin with. He had not consulted the German bishops before writing the memorandum, because they were not among the leaders of the minority group and because they lacked all statesmanlike qualities and wisdom. He had later given a copy of the memorandum to the Bishop of Breslau. He, Arnim, had sent the memorandum to Antonelli on 25 April and had seen him the following day. He had told him that he personally was convinced of the uselessness of that kind of *démarche* because he was fully aware that the Vatican would not listen to the best meant advice. The Government of the North German Confederation did not want to let the occasion pass, however, without telling the Holy See that in this grave crisis all of Europe was against it. In closing his letter, Arnim stated that he had reason to believe that his presentation, which had come as a complete surprise to the Cardinal State Secretary, had not been without success and had made some impression.[1]

Arnim's memorandum to Antonelli was read at a meeting of German and Austrian bishops on 5 May and was received with great acclamation. It was said to be the best diplomatic document on that subject,[2] and Arnim was pressed by the bishops to have it published. 'It was impossible for a government to express justified objections in a milder form. The bishops had not at all been bothered by the references to them.'[3]

As soon as a copy of the memorandum was received in Berlin, Arnim was advised once more to refrain from any further steps in the matter. The Foreign Ministry considered its language exceedingly strong, and the King expressed his surprise that Arnim, contrary to previous instructions, had not consulted the German bishops beforehand to ascertain their approval.[4] Arnim defended himself by saying that he had

[1] Arnim to Bismarck, no. 80, 28 Apr. 1870.

[2] Arnim to Bismarck, tel. no. 20, 5 May 1870, *Col. Lac.* vii/ii. 1602. Friedrich, *Geschichte*, iii. 898, says the Note was read on 6 May. Odo Russell called it an 'able note of sound advice', Blakiston, p. 452. 'Without exception the best that has been addressed to the Papal Government on the subject of the Oecumenical Council', Doellinger, *Briefwechsel*, ii. 337, fn. 3. Doellinger himself called it 'very good, an honour to Arnim', ibid. 378.

[3] Friedrich, loc. cit.

[4] Thile to Arnim, tel. no. 25, 4 May 1870. Reporting to his Government on

acted exactly in accordance with his instructions.[1] That this was open to doubt is clear from his subsequent reports.

Arnim's explanations, though somewhat devious and involved—he asserted that he had discussed the memorandum with the Bishop of Breslau before sending it off, had informed the German bishops, and had transmitted one copy each to the Bishops of Cologne and Breslau[2]—were accepted in Berlin. As long as the German bishops were satisfied, Thile wrote to him, the apprehensions of the King and the Foreign Ministry were alleviated. He reminded Arnim that he should have assured himself of the bishops' approval beforehand and that he should not forget that the Government was only joining the French *démarche* and had no primary interest in this affair. It had certainly been in the interest of the French bishops to have him pull the chestnut out of the fire for them. That was why it was not intended in Berlin to publicize his action to any extent, but rather to preserve an attitude of watchful waiting.[3]

This should have been the end of the episode and anyone but Arnim would have been glad to accept it as such and let the matter rest. Not he. His vanity had been touched and his self-assurance had been questioned by constant reminders from Berlin to be on guard against the intrigues and machinations of the French bishops and diplomats.

Your Excellency will not consider this to be presumptuous [he wrote to Bismarck] if, after four months of official activities, I have confidence in my own judgement about certain persons, their ideas, and their motives. I fully appreciate the fact that I do not deal with partisans of the Prussian royal family and the North German Confederation. . . . I also may be permitted to point out that I do not remember ever having pulled chestnuts out of the fire for anybody else. . . . *My bishops*[4] will, however, have to get used to the idea of seeing me next to them, in front of them, or behind them, according

31 May 1870, Perglas, the Bavarian Minister in Berlin, discussed the reaction to Arnim's Note in the Prussian capital and noted the apprehensions in government circles. If this were true in the highest circle (*an maßgebender Stelle*), Perglas continued, it was not sincere. 'Because the Note of the Prussian Minister, based on carefully considered instructions, clearly reflects the understanding of events here. The representative of Prussia did in no way deviate from the spirit and letter of his instructions.' Doellinger, *Briefwechsel*, ii. 378, fn. 1.

[1] Arnim to Bismarck, tel. no. 20, 5 May 1870.
[2] Arnim to Bismarck, no. 85, 7 May 1870.
[3] (Thile to) Arnim, tel. no. 26, 6 May 1870, *Col. Lac.* vii/ii. 1602.
[4] Underlined by Arnim.

D

to circumstances; and if *they* are in the forefront, I too will be there ... that's how things are.[1]

The work that had to be done in Rome, Arnim continued, was of a rather delicate nature, and for him to do it properly, it was necessary that the Government allowed him complete freedom of movement and had confidence in his abilities. Should this view not be shared in Berlin and should it be more convenient for the Government to have an agent in Rome who would be personally disinterested in events, it might be better if a change in the person of the Prussian representative were to take place.[2]

This was, for all practical purposes, the end of the diplomatic activities connected with the French *démarche* in Rome. It was generally recognized that the fight of the minority bishops had become a lost cause.[3] In his preoccupation with the affairs of the Council, and apparently being kept in the dark by Bismarck about the worsening of Franco-Prussian relations, Arnim looked upon this episode as an utter defeat for French diplomacy.[4] He characterized the motives of Ollivier for withdrawing political pressure from the Holy See as those of a dilettante.

With the proclamation of the dogma of papal infallibility imminent, Arnim put forth still another suggestion to express the displeasure of the Powers with the policy of the Pope. 'It would be highly advisable,' he wrote to Berlin, 'and it would express the situation of the Powers correctly, if their representatives would, in a demonstrative fashion, take an extended leave from Rome without, however, giving the appearance of a diplomatic break.'[5] But Bismarck did not think much of this idea. This proposal might have been all right for ambassadors of Catholic countries, but for others this was a useless exercise, because the proclamation of the dogma was of no concern to them. 'To accept the fight over Catholic dogma on Roman

---

[1] Arnim to Bismarck, no. 85, 7 May 1870. See, however, Doellinger, *Briefwechsel*, ii. 219, on Arnim's lack of influence with the German bishops.

[2] Arnim to Bismarck, no. 85, 7 May 1870. There seemed to have been no reply to Arnim's report, and no indication of Bismarck's reaction could be found in the files.

[3] Friedrich, *Geschichte*, iii. 968.

[4] Arnim to Bismarck, 21 May 1870, and Bismarck's marginalia: 'War', 'Change'.

[5] Arnim to Bismarck, 11 June 1870, *Col. Lac.* vii/ii. 1607. This proposal had originated with Trauttmansdorff, the Austrian Ambassador. F. Engel-Janosi, 'Berichterstattung', p. 611.

soil, would mean for us to attack Leviathan in the water. We should let him come unto dry land; that means in the realm of practical application of the dogma, within the Prussian constitutional law. That is where we are superior to him.'[1]

Abeken notified Arnim that the King was in complete agreement with Bismarck's point of view and that he should not undertake a demonstration of any kind but should ignore the whole affair.[2]

More effective than his suggestion to stay away from the ceremony was a memorandum Arnim had written for the German bishops of the minority a month before the dogma was proclaimed.[3] In it he discussed the consequences that the decisions of the Vatican Council would have in the future on the relationship between Church and State, particularly in Germany. The day the infallibility of the Pope was announced, Arnim wrote, would mark the beginning of a new era. Not because of the dogma, for that by itself would hardly change anything that had not been in practice for the past thirty years. Rather because the Council would have furnished proof that there existed a power in Rome which, in opposition to the achievements of modern society, had decided to wage war against the political organization of the world. The deliberations at the Council had also publicly demonstrated that the German bishops were dependent on the Holy See to such an extent that they would, in the end, and against their own better judgement, accept Vatican views which the secular Powers could not recognize. There would not be a separation of Church and State but war. This war, to which Rome would be challenging the Powers, would be accepted by Germany, and the governments, especially Prussia's, would be assured of the whole-hearted co-operation of their subjects. The area over which this struggle would be fought was not difficult to determine, Arnim continued.

There will be interminable squabbles over the election of bishops, and, from that, prolonged vacancies of bishoprics. Jesuits will be expelled. The individual freedom of the monastic orders will be

[1] Bismarck to Abeken, 20 June 1870, *GW* vib. 333. H. Abeken, *Ein schlichtes Leben in bewegter Zeit* (Berlin, 1910), p. 375.

[2] Abeken to Arnim, 23 June 1870, *Col. Lac.* vii/ii. 1608.

[3] Arnim memorandum, 17 June 1870, ibid. 1604–7 and printed in the *Presse*, Vienna, 2 Apr. 1874, see pp. 129–30 below. Granderath, ii. 720 ff.

curtailed. Priests will be forbidden to study in Rome and, above all, there will be an end to all ecclesiastical influence on education.[1]

This was indeed remarkable perspicacity on Arnim's part. And when, at the height of the *Kulturkampf* in Germany and at the beginning of the Arnim affair, the memorandum was published in a Viennese newspaper, it created a sensation.[2] At the time of its writing, however, it went unnoticed. Arnim sent yet another report to Berlin pleading for last-minute action. His arguments were as of old; he now considered the dogma to be as dangerous as the Pope's increased powers, derived from the Council. Should the Pope prevail in this struggle, Arnim wrote, Prussia's future policy toward Rome would be more difficult. It should reply to a war of the Pope with a war of its own.[3] If he had previously suggested a demonstration by the diplomatic corps in Rome, it was because he felt that the gesture would show unmistakably that the European Powers were turning away from Pius IX.[4] He had not meant to impress the Pope but rather to show the German bishops and Catholics 'which way the wind was blowing'.[5] The time for that[6] would be especially favourable because the differences of opinions at the Council had come to the surface.[7]

When there was no reply to this report from Berlin, Arnim sent another directly to the King, telling of a discussion he had had with the Bishop of Breslau in which the Bishop had expressed views similar to his own.[8] This report too was apparently ignored. Two weeks later, on the eve of the public proclamation of the dogma, Arnim requested permission to go

[1] Arnim memorandum, 17 June 1870.

[2] See pp. 129–30 below.

[3] Arnim to Thile, no. 107, 24 June 1870, and Bismarck's marginalia: 'What does that mean in practical terms?' *Col. Lac.* vii/ii. 1608, without Bismarck's marginalia.

[4] 'Do they want that? Does France want that?', ibid.

[5] 'Every weather-vane does that already', ibid.

[6] 'For what?', ibid.

[7] At the end of the report, Bismarck noted: 'Empty talk without any practical proposals of *what* would be needed for warding off this arson. A silly report. It starts with *parturiunt montes* and not even a *ridic mus* is brought forth. Writer does not share my opinion but has none himself and does not ask for new instructions. Cheap bombast.' Arnim's report was shown to the King and he too, after careful consideration of Arnim's arguments, did not see any reasons for changing his views or to issue different instructions from those of the Chancellor. Abeken memorandum, 30 June 1870.

[8] Arnim to the King, 1 July 1870, *Col. Lac.* vii/ii. 1609–10.

on leave. Most of the bishops would leave on that day, he wrote, and so would the ambassadors of France and Austria.[1] But Bismarck could not be persuaded. He ordered Arnim to stay and to refrain from any demonstration.[2] To another report from Arnim, which told of a futile demonstration by some of the minority bishops, Bismarck noted, 'Refrain from any ostensible demonstration. The Infallibility is of no interest to us at the moment.'[3]

The end had come. The dogma of papal infallibility was proclaimed in Rome on 18 July 1870. The next day France declared war on Prussia. With the outbreak of the war the Council, its deliberations, and its resolutions were for the moment all but forgotten. Its implications and its consequences were not felt and received no attention until the war was over. Then the religious peace that had reigned in Germany since the end of the Reformation was rudely shattered and Arnim's predictions became reality.

That Arnim with all his foresight could not have prevented this development seems obvious. He was, after all and in spite of his own inclination, not a policy-maker but an observer. As such he reported and interpreted events as he saw them, and there is enough corroborating evidence to show that his dispatches were not wild guesses, figments of his imagination, or expressions of wishful thinking, but solid and well-founded reports of a shrewd eyewitness whose sympathies were on the side of the anti-papal party at the Council. That his language was flowery, his expressions occasionally ambiguous, and his recommendations sometimes vague and confusing was due to his personality. In spite of this it should be kept in mind that, Bismarck's pronouncements notwithstanding, Arnim consistently and over a long period had warned of the dangers that would ensue if the Pope and the majority party should carry out their plans. He persistently advocated a single policy: intervention by the governments in support of the minority bishops. His recommendations were often impractical, usually too complicated, and generally impossible to carry out. But none

---

[1] Arnim to Bismarck, tel. no. 29, 15 July 1870, ibid.
[2] Bismarck to Arnim, 16 July 1870, *GW* vi*b*. 387.
[3] Arnim to Bismarck, no. 113, 16 July 1870. Bismarck's marginalia and his telegram no. 38 of 20 July 1870 to Arnim, *GW* vi*b*. 409.

of this invalidated his basic ideas, and the fact remains that Bismarck rejected them. Against Arnim's view that something should be done *before* the Council adjourned, Bismarck insisted —and his policy prevailed—that there was ample time to take the necessary measures *afterwards*.[1]

[1] On 18 Oct. 1872, in the midst of the *Kulturkampf*, Odo Russell, at that time Ambassador in Berlin, wrote to Lord Granville: 'I fancy that Bismarck utterly misunderstands and underrates the power of the Church. Thinking himself more infallible than the Pope he cannot tolerate two infallibles in Europe, and fancies he can select the next Pope as he would a Prussian General. . . . Hitherto the anti-clerical measures have produced the very state of things the Vatican was working for through the Oecumenical Council, namely, unity and discipline in the clergy under an infallible head, or the Prussian military system applied to the Church.' Quoted by A. Randall, 'A British Agent at the Vatican. The Mission of Odo Russell', *Dublin Review* (1959), p. 44.

IV

THE OCCUPATION OF ROME

TERMINATION of the Vatican Council should also have ended Arnim's bustling activities. Instead there was only a pause. The crisis that foreshadowed the occupation of Rome by Italian troops provided once more an opportunity for his personal interference. Bismarck's instructions, on the other hand, called for a policy of non-interference.[1]

In September Arnim spent a few days in Florence, where he saw Visconti-Venosta, the Italian Foreign Minister, whom he urgently advised not to occupy Rome.[2] He based his advice on the curious contention that Prussia's position in Germany would suffer as a result of an occupation, especially if German soldiers of the Papal Army should become casualties in a skirmish with the Italian Army.[3] After Arnim left Florence, Brassier had to explain to the Italian Government Prussia's intentions in this matter, because the Italian Government, as a result of Arnim's remarks, had become highly suspicious.[4]

Back in Rome, Arnim found the Papal Government and the people in utter confusion. The Italian ultimatum requesting the dissolution of foreign regiments and the admission of the Italian Army into the city was curtly refused by the Papacy's Minister of War, and the Pope told Arnim that a defence of the city was necessary to satisfy military honour and to dramatize

[1] Bismarck to Brassier, 22 Aug. 1870, *GW* vi*b*. 455. It is not clear whether Arnim received a copy of these instructions.
[2] Brassier to Bismarck, 14 Sept. 1870, N. Miko, *Das Ende des Kirchenstaates*, 2 vols. (Vienna, 1962–4), ii. 370–1, henceforth cited Miko. See also S. W. Halperin, *Italy and the Vatican at War* (Chicago, 1939), p. 55, henceforth cited Halperin, *Italy*.
[3] Brassier to Bismarck, 14 Sept. 1870.
[4] On 26 Oct. 1870 a short item in the *Augsburger Allgemeine Zeitung* referred to this incident, commenting that Arnim's statements on this occasion were entirely his own and were not being supported by the Prussian Government. Arnim, who suspected Brassier as the source of this article, complained to Thile (Arnim to Thile, 29 Oct. 1870), but Brassier, when questioned about it, denied it (Brassier to Thile, 29 Nov. 1870). E. Schmidt-Volkmar, *Der Kulturkampf in Deutschland* (Goettingen, 1962), pp. 13–14, henceforth cited Schmidt-Volkmar.

the fact that force was being employed against it. Arnim pointed to the presence of 50,000 Italians around the city as sufficient proof of force and suggested that token resistance would hardly satisfy military honour. He proposed instead that of the two demands of the ultimatum the first be accepted under condition that Italian troops not occupy the city until peace had been restored and the European Powers had had an opportunity to express their views. The most important thing was to gain time. He knew with certainty, Arnim told the Pope, that it would be exceedingly embarrassing to the Italian Government to have its army fight German and French soldiers and that it would, most likely, accept a provisional solution to escape this unpleasant situation. But Pius IX thought little of these suggestions. All he wanted was for the Prussian Government to induce the Italians to withdraw their troops from Rome. The Pope seemed not to understand, Arnim wrote, that it was too late for such a move.[1]

After General Cadorna had issued the second summons to surrender the city, Arnim went to the Italian headquarters and asked the General not to force his way into Rome. The military elements were in control there, he said, and would defend themselves even despite the orders of the Pope. Respecting the wishes of the representative of the North German Confederation, Cadorna granted a delay of twenty-four hours, but stated that he would be unable to postpone occupation of the city beyond that limit.[2]

Meanwhile, the Italian Ambassador in Berlin, Count Launay, inquired at the Foreign Ministry about Prussia's policy regarding the occupation of Rome. It had been the

---

[1] Arnim to Foreign Ministry, 15 Sept. 1870, Miko, ii. 386–8. Schmidt-Volkmar, pp. 12–13.

[2] Brassier to Foreign Ministry, 17 Sept. 1870, Miko, ii. 427. In an instruction to Thile of 23 Sept. 1870, Bismarck, who had been informed of these events, asked that parts of the Brassier message be published in the newspapers as proof that only Prussian representatives had, in this difficult situation, done anything for the protection of the Pope. GW vib. 514–15. Wilhelm I to Augusta, 26 Sept. 1870, Die Vorgeschichte des Kulturkampfes, Quellenveröffentlichung aus dem deutschen Zentralarchiv (Berlin, 1956), pp. 30–1. Halperin, Italy, pp. 56–8. Another of Arnim's plans provided for a joint démarche by the diplomatic corps in Rome to persuade the Pope not to resist the imminent entry of the Italian troops. At a meeting Arnim's plan was explained to the diplomatic representatives by the Austrian chargé d'affaires—Arnim himself had accepted a dinner invitation that evening—but was rejected by them. Miko, ii. 429–39.

impression in Florence, Launay told Thile, that Prussia considered the Roman question a purely Italian affair and would not intervene in any form whatever. This, Launay said, was based on previous statements by Bismarck as conveyed by Brassier. Arnim's recent visit to Florence and his conversation with the Italian Foreign Minister made it appear, however, that Arnim was encouraging the Pope to resist at all costs. The Italian Government was anxious to know, Launay continued, whether Arnim had been authorized to do so. In his reply Thile pointed out that the only instruction Arnim had received was that he was accredited only to the Pope and should not leave him unless explicitly told to do so.[1]

When asked about these incidents, Arnim repudiated them. The inquiry about a change in Prussian policy by the Italian Government he attributed to a desire by Visconti-Venosta to find a pretext for his own dilatory policy.[2] His visit to the Italian headquarters near Rome he justified by his proper concern for the fate of German soldiers in the Papal Army. As to Brassier's report, it was based on a misunderstanding, Arnim said.[3]

But the impending occupation of Rome by Italy was not just a misunderstanding between Arnim and the Prussian Foreign Ministry or a dispute between Berlin and Florence; it was a European problem and concerned the future status of the Pope and the location of the seat of the Papacy. Pius IX began to consider himself a prisoner in the Vatican and the possibility of leaving Rome altogether was seriously discussed by his advisers. Austria had apparently offered him asylum and there were rumours that the British Government was prepared to take him to Malta.[4] Bismarck thought that it would be in the

---

[1] Thile to Bismarck, 18 Sept. 1870. In his reply from Ferrières of 23 Sept. 1870, Bismarck instructed Thile to 'tell Count Launay that Count Arnim had had no instructions whatever'.

[2] Arnim to Thile, no. 136, 19 Sept. 1870, Miko, ii. 472–4.

[3] Bismarck to Arnim, 24 Sept. 1870. Arnim to Foreign Ministry, 25 Sept. 1870. After having been informed by Abeken about the Thile–Launay conversation and of Brassier's report of 14 Sept. 1870 (Abeken to Arnim, 28 Sept. 1870), Arnim gave an involved explanation about this incident. Arnim to Thile, no. 137, 19 Sept. 1870, Miko, ii. 474–6.

[4] Arnim to Bismarck, no. 142, 24 Sept. 1870. Great Britain, Command Papers, C-247 Rome No. 1 (1871), *Correspondence respecting the affairs of Rome 1870–1*, nos. 8, 9. Halperin, *Italy*, pp. 59, 83–4. See, however, F. Engel-Janosi, *Oesterreich und der Vatikan*, 2 vols. (Graz, 1958), i. 177, fn. 86.

best interest of Germany if the Pope remained in Rome.[1] But, according to Arnim, there were some in the Curia who looked to Germany as the future seat of the Papacy.[2] He suggested, so as to forestall any eventualities, that the Prussian Government consult with the Italian Government on the position of the Pope without touching the territorial question and that the two governments should try to settle this question, at least temporarily, among themselves.[3]

But Bismarck, forever apprehensive of Arnim's unauthorized activities, ordered him to refrain from any discussions of this subject in Rome. He added, for Arnim's private information, that no suitable residence could be found for the Pope in Germany.[4] A few days later Antonelli asked Arnim whether the Pope, if he had to leave Rome, could count on the assistance of the King of Prussia. Arnim, with Bismarck's consent, advised him that he could.[5]

To Brassier, Bismarck explained that, though the Government did not intend to interfere in the internal affairs of Italy, the interests of its own Catholic subjects warranted its concern for the independence and dignity of the head of the Catholic Church.[6]

This attitude did not please the Italians, and Visconti-Venosta inquired once more in Berlin as to the real aims of Prussian policy in the Roman question.[7] Launay again approached Thile in this matter and complained that so far

[1] Bismarck to Foreign Ministry, 21 Sept. 1870, *GW* vi*b*. 513–14; Bismarck to Arnim, 3 Oct. 1870, ibid. 531.

[2] On 27 Sept. 1870 Odo Russell wrote to Archbishop Manning, 'I hear from Rome that Baron Arnim offered the Pope an asylum in Germany—Fulda, I think—and strongly pressed His Holyness to accept.' Quoted by Wallace, p. 131.

[3] Arnim to Foreign Ministry, tel. no. 64, 2 Oct. 1870, and Arnim to Thile, report no. 151, same date.

[4] Bismarck to Arnim, 3 Oct. 1870, *GW* vi*b*. 531.

[5] Arnim to Bismarck, tel. no. 65, 7 Oct. 70; Bismarck to Arnim, tel. no. 5, 8 Oct. 70.

[6] Bismarck to Brassier, 8 Oct. 1870, *GW* vi*b*. 537. When in January 1871 the Italian Government published certain documents pertaining to the occupation of Rome, among them the text of the Thile–Launay conversation, Bismarck advised the Foreign Ministry, by tel. no. 499 of 14 Jan. 1871, to publish Arnim's tel. no. 65 of 7 Oct. 1870 and his, Bismarck's, reply (tel. no. 5, 8 Oct. 1870) and his directive to Brassier of the same date, with 'the necessary changes'. The documents were published in the *Norddeutsche Allgemeine Zeitung* of 19 Jan. 1871.

[7] Thile to Bismarck, 27 Oct. 1870, and Bismarck's marginalia.

nobody in Berlin had given him a definite statement of Prussian policy.[1] Aside from the enigmatic policy of the Chancellor, there were the insidious interpretations of it by the Prussian representatives in Florence and Rome, who, each in his own way, appeared to pursue different aims. Of the two representatives, Launay stated, Brassier had always stressed the view that the temporal power of the Pope was an internal matter of the Italian Government and that Prussia would not interfere. With this his Government was in full agreement. Contrary to Brassier, however, Arnim had proposed to make Rome a free city on principles which were in accord with those of the Papacy.[2] This proposal, Launay concluded, would satisfy neither the Italians nor the Romans, and the free city would soon become a republic.

Informed of Launay's *démarche*, Bismarck pointed out to Thile that no harm had been done in not having expressed a definite policy in this matter so far. The different views proclaimed by the Prussian representatives in Florence and Rome appeared to the Italian Foreign Minister more divergent than they actually were. Neither of the two diplomats had been authorized to say what had been attributed to him and Arnim especially had had no instructions whatever for the statements he had made. It should be quite obvious that had the Prussian Government wanted to make an official communication to Florence, it would have done so through its accredited ambassador there. A clarification of the Government's policy in the Roman question would be inopportune at the time, Bismarck wrote to Thile, especially so because the attitude of the other Powers, which were more intimately concerned with the problem, was not as yet known.[3]

Another consideration, which the Chancellor did not mention, but which probably was on his mind, was the Franco-Prussian War. Because of it he dared not offend Italy, for she might come to the aid of France. Neither did he dare to offend the Pope, because German Catholics might oppose his plan for a united Germany once the war was over. Far from being annoyed by the divergent and, to the Italians, confusing statements

[1] 'No reason for me to comment', ibid.
[2] 'I was not aware of this', ibid.
[3] Bismarck to Thile, 3 Nov. 1870, *GW* vib. 575–7. Schmidt-Volkmar, p. 19.

made by Arnim and Brassier, Bismarck clearly relished the situation they caused. It enabled him to support either of the two ambassadors at will and he was not obliged to choose sides in this difficult and fluid situation.

The last period of Arnim's stay in Rome coincided with the termination of the temporal power of the Pope. The stage was all set. The decisions had all been taken. When the final act would be played was merely a matter of time. Arnim's role was not, and, indeed, could not have been, a decisive one. It was solely a question of details, of protocol, and of petty intrigue. Still, he seemed satisfied as long as he was among the principal actors and on the centre of the stage. There was the problem of the audience of the King of Italy with the Pope, about which Arnim was apparently being consulted.[1] There was also the question of Arnim's personal conduct toward the King and the royal family, which, when not carefully regulated and tactfully handled, could and did bring him into conflict with his official duties at the Vatican.[2] His frequent visits to the Italian Crown Prince caused some annoyance at the papal Court and gave rise to some scandalous rumours.[3] But these things seemed not to matter any more.[4] Political developments in Germany as well as in Italy called for a reappraisal and change of the relationship between the two countries and between them and the Vatican.

In his last major report from Rome, Arnim summarized the events of the past, examined the new situation that had arisen, and appraised its implications. The diplomatic world, he wrote, had increasingly become accustomed to seeing in the amiable relationship between Rome and Berlin the result of a policy of particular wisdom and adroitness. Anybody who knew the details had to realize, however, that the intimate relationship between Prussia and the Holy See was only a misleading mirage.

[1] Arnim to Bismarck, tel. no. 73, 14 Nov. 1870; report no. 182, 16 Nov. 1870. Bismarck to Arnim, 15 Nov. 1870, *GW* vi*b*. 589.

[2] Arnim to Thile, no. 190, 29 Nov. 1870. Bismarck to Arnim, tel. no. 53, 9 Dec. 1870.

[3] The rumours were caused by Arnim's association with the Duchess of Rignano, who supposedly was a former mistress of the Italian Crown Prince. Arnim to Bismarck, 19 Feb. 1871.

[4] There were at that time also discussions and diplomatic exchanges about papal mediation in the Franco-Prussian War and about the attitude of the Curia toward the new German Empire. *GW* vi*b*. 620, 623, 624, 632, 638, 641, 643.

According to Arnim, two main considerations determined Prussia's relationship with the Vatican. The Prussian Legation in Rome was to be, first of all, the outward symbol and guarantee for its Catholic subjects which would safeguard the delicate relationship between them and their Protestant sovereign. The good offices of the Holy See would, in turn, prevent any serious crisis. Secondly (and this had become the main factor in the last decade before the Vatican Council) through the repeated demonstrations of respect and deference by the Prussian Government to the head of the Catholic Church it had been hoped to win the sympathies of the Catholic population throughout Germany. At the same time, the Government had believed that the Pope could be convinced of the soundness of its ecclesiastical policy at home and that his influence, in turn, could be used in exceptional cases by the Government in Prussia. In reality, Arnim wrote, these endeavours had been in vain. The internal policy toward the Catholic Church in Prussia had been conducted independently and without regard to the diplomatic relationship with Rome. Far from getting any concessions from the Pope in internal ecclesiastical affairs, the Holy See had in general created more difficulties, not fewer.

The hope too that Catholics in Germany and perhaps throughout Europe would support Prussian policy because of its deference to the Pope had met with disappointment. At no time had a relationship been established with Rome which was based on mutual support and assistance. The development of the past fifty years should be convincing enough that one could expect nothing from the Holy See in the future. This, together with the recent changes in Italy, might provide an opportunity for the Prussian Government to reshape its policy toward the Vatican. It was to be expected, Arnim continued, that as soon as peace with France had been restored the Vatican would ask Prussia's help in the restoration of the temporal power of the Pope. In view of the general European situation and the particular circumstances dominating the domestic scene in Germany, a sympathetic approach to this request would greatly burden the Government's policy in all respects. Reorganization of the political structure in Germany might, however, provide a solution to this problem. According to

Arnim, this would involve transfer of the representation of the Reich at the Vatican from Prussia to Bavaria. (This was made possible by a provision in the negotiations between Prussia and Bavaria regarding the future of the Reich, according to which, in case of impediments, Bavaria could take over imperial embassies.) There would be numerous advantages to this step; not the least would be considerable freedom for German foreign policy and avoidance of a nuntius in Berlin.

The danger that Bavaria would use its position at the Vatican to advance its particularistic tendencies in Germany could be foreseen and taken into account. The arrangement should therefore be temporary and subject to immediate change. It could be assumed that Bavaria would be very glad to accept this proposition, for it would be flattering to its great-power ambitions, 'and would enable it to practise an innocent form of diplomatic indoor gymnastics in an area which had been set aside exclusively for its own use'.[1]

Arnim's recommendations were accepted, though because of the peculiar circumstances prevailing they lasted only a short time.[2] On 17 February Bismarck informed Arnim that the King wanted to talk to him about the Roman and the Italian situation and he asked him to come to Berlin for this purpose. Tauffkirchen, the Bavarian Minister, who took Arnim's place, arrived in Rome on 24 February. Arnim left two days later.[3] His Roman assignment had come to an end.

[1] Arnim to Bismarck, 19 Jan. 1871.
[2] After Arnim had left Rome in Feb. 1871, the Bavarian Minister became representative of the Reich at the Holy See. When the King of Italy moved to Rome, Brassier was again put in charge of the German Legation. Bismarck justified this change because the Holy See had not restrained the agitations of the Centre Party in Germany. Thile to Arnim, tel. no. 3, 18 Feb. 1871. E. Deuerlein, 'Bismarck und die Reichsvertretung beim Heiligen Stuhl', *Stimmen der Zeit*, vol. 164 (1958-9), pp. 203-19. Georg Franz-Willing, *Die Bayerische Vatikangesandtschaft 1803-1934* (Munich, 1965), pp. 63-5.
[3] Arnim to Bismarck, tel. no. 94, 25 Feb. 1871.

V

THE PEACE NEGOTIATIONS WITH FRANCE

THE preliminary peace between Germany and France was signed at Versailles on 26 February 1871.[1] The war had been brought to an end, France had been defeated, and the German Empire had come into existence. Brussels had been chosen for the final peace conference, scheduled to begin toward the end of March.

The principal German negotiators were Hermann von Balan, Prussian Minister in Brussels, and Count Harry von Arnim. Representatives from the lesser German states were Lieutenant-General von Fabrice (who had been appointed military governor of France) for Saxony, Baron Quadt for Bavaria, and Count Uxkuell for Wuerttemberg.[2] France was represented by Baron Baude, French Minister in Brussels, Goulard, a member of the French Assembly, de Clerq, from the French Foreign Ministry, and General Doutrelaine of the French Army.[3] Arnim's appointment as one of the two chief delegates to the Peace Conference was something of a surprise.[4] There was some confusion about his position and his relationship with Balan. Balan was Arnim's senior in both age and service but it was Arnim who had participated in the two decisive meetings of the Prussian ministerial council of 14 and 15 March which had considered the peace negotiations and it was he who had received Bismarck's personal instructions at that time.[5]

In Dresden the Saxon Minister of State, Friesen, told

---

[1] *Die Große Politik der europaeischen Kabinette 1871–1914*, 40 vols. (Berlin, 1924–7), i. 3–6, henceforth cited *GP*.

[2] Hugo Graf Lerchenfeld-Koefering, *Erinnerungen und Denkwuerdigkeiten 1843 bis 1925* (Berlin, 1935), p. 81, henceforth cited Lerchenfeld.

[3] Hans Goldschmidt, *Bismarck und die Friedensunterhaendler 1871* (Berlin, 1929), p. 20, henceforth cited Goldschmidt.

[4] There are no indications, either in the archives or in the memoir literature, as to why Arnim was chosen.

[5] Goldschmidt, pp. 8–9; Robert I. Giesberg, *The Treaty of Frankfort* (Philadelphia, 1966), p. 128, henceforth cited Giesberg.

Eichmann, the Prussian Minister, that Arnim had been appointed chief delegate and Balan his assistant.[1] Bismarck, on the other hand, in a directive of 2 April, referred to Arnim as the second representative.[2] Still, the relationship between the two men must have been ill defined, for Balan did apparently consider Arnim a possible rival; and to forestall any future conflict, or perhaps merely to clarify their respective positions, he expressed, in a report to Bismarck, his gratification at having as his colleague in Brussels 'an experienced junior assistant'.[3]

On 17 March, when Bismarck was informed that the French representatives had left for Brussels, he requested permission from the Emperor to send Arnim there.[4] Arnim left Berlin two days later.

The peace negotiations in Brussels were much more difficult than originally expected. This was partly due to the confused conditions in France—the insurrection of the Paris Commune lasted from mid March to the end of May—and partly to Bismarck's distrust of French policies.[5] This in turn led to protracted conferences between the German and French representatives and to an extensive correspondence between Bismarck and Balan and Arnim. Whatever the causes—preoccupation of the French with the suppression of the Commune and their desire to strengthen the Government, or their conscious attempts to use the insurrection to extract more favourable peace terms from the victors—the negotiations soon bogged down in a mass of unconnected details and trivia.[6] By the end of March Bismarck advised Balan that unless the negotiations in Brussels proceeded more speedily in the future, he would request their transfer to Berlin. The situation in France did not permit long-drawn-out negotiations, he wrote, and either a definite peace settlement would be speedily decided on, or the war would be continued. In that case, Bismarck threatened, an ultimatum would be issued to the French.[7] When, as a result

[1] Eichmann to Bismarck, 15 Mar. 1871.
[2] Goldschmidt, p. 59.
[3] Balan to Bismarck, 15 Mar. 1871.
[4] Bismarck to the Emperor, 17 Mar. 1871. The Emperor's marginal comments on this report were: 'Agreed; [I] would like to see Arnim and be informed beforehand as to what has been discussed at the ministerial meeting.'
[5] Goldschmidt, pp. 20 ff.; Hans Herzfeld, *Deutschland und das geschlagene Frankreich* (Berlin, 1924), pp. 22–37, henceforth cited Herzfeld.
[6] Goldschmidt, pp. 40 ff.   [7] Ibid., pp. 48–9.

of this directive, Arnim expressed his intention to threaten the French with breaking off the negotiations—after having been told by Baude that the French Government expected Germany to take over the debts of Alsace-Lorraine—Bismarck restrained him.[1] He did follow Arnim's suggestion, however, and authorized him and Balan to avoid formal conferences until agreement on their proposals had been reached by prior confidential conversations with the French delegation.[2] Likewise, again on Arnim's suggestion, he approved individual reporting by the German representatives.[3] This last provision seems to have aroused Arnim's vanity and provided him with an opportunity for intrigue. Never a person to conceal his own achievements, he soon discovered and reported to Berlin that his Prussian colleague, 'whose experience and patriotism were unquestionable and highly valued', lacked the temperament to carry on private conversations with the French delegates. This necessarily put the burden of the work on himself, Arnim concluded.[4]

To be entirely fair, it should be noted that according to the official record Arnim did carry the greater burden of work in Brussels. Most of the joint reports were drafted by him and, in addition, he sent more than twice as many individual reports to Berlin as did Balan. While some historians, notably Goldschmidt, accuse him of harbouring the desire to appear as the real peacemaker (*der eigentliche Friedensmacher*), there was some solid work on Arnim's part to substantiate this claim.

Arnim seems also to have attempted to blame Balan exclusively for the failure of negotiations and to have him recalled. Arnim planned to accomplish this through Count Lerchenfeld, secretary to the Bavarian representative, Count Quadt. Lerchenfeld was to prevail upon his chief to write to Munich that Balan was of no use in the negotiations and that as long as he was a member of the delegation no peace treaty would be signed. This report would presumably be forwarded from Munich to Berlin, where it would be seen by Bismarck. The plot failed, however, when Quadt refused to play his part.[5]

Arnim's reports during this period showed his characteristic

---

[1] Ibid., pp. 57–9.
[2] Ibid., p. 73 and fn. *.
[3] Ibid., pp. 84–5. *GP* i. 19–20.
[4] Goldschmidt, pp. 88–9. Lerchenfeld, p. 82.
[5] Ibid.

style: straight facts laced with wit and irony, salted with shrewd observations and unconfirmed rumours. There were no noticeable inconsistencies of opinion in his reports, possibly because the negotiations in Brussels were comparatively brief. The suggestion advanced later that Arnim, at this stage, actively favoured and worked for a return of the monarchy in France is not borne out by the available evidence.[1] He reported, like many of his contemporaries, the widespread Bourbon and Orleans intrigues and the strength of the monarchists and suggested that the chances of a monarchical restoration seemed good.[2] The idea that a return of the monarchy in France was imminent was widely held at the time and it is no great credit to Arnim's perspicacity to assert that he noted this trend or foresaw its consequences.[3]

After another month of fruitless discussions, Arnim submitted to the Chancellor a twenty-four page memorandum which serves well to illustrate his views and ideas on the peace negotiations.[4] From the way the negotiations had proceeded, Arnim began, the attitude of the French Government seemed to be influenced by the hope that a more favourable interpretation of the peace preliminaries could be attained. Achievement of a definite peace seemed further away than ever, and it would appear that it was the Germans, rather than the French, who were now anxious for its conclusion. It would be far more logical for Thiers to try to achieve a speedy settlement rather than to dwell on trivia and to haggle over minute details. Why, then, did he do this? There were several theories, Arnim thought. Some believed that, by waiting for the subjugation of Paris, Thiers would be able to confront the Germans with such a formidable army that the Reich would rather concede more

---

[1] Goldschmidt, pp. 24, 28.

[2] H. O. Meisner (ed.), *Denkwuerdigkeiten des General-Feldmarschalls Alfred Grafen von Waldersee*, 2 vols. (Stuttgart, 1922), i. 131–2, 161, henceforth cited Waldersee. S. M. Osgood, *French Royalism under the Third and Fourth Republic* (The Hague, 1960), pp. 1 ff., henceforth cited Osgood.

[3] Goldschmidt, pp. 124–5. Lord Newton, *Lord Lyons*, 2 vols. (London, 1913), ii. 2, henceforth cited Newton; H. Rogge, *Friedrich von Holstein, Lebensbekenntnis* (Berlin, 1932), p. 111. See also H. von Petersdorff, 'Das Friedenswerk 1871', *Neue Preußische Kreuzzeitung*, 25 Apr. 1929, who, in a review article of Goldschmidt's book asserts that 'Fabrice's opinions, e.g. on Thiers, strikingly coincide with those of Arnim'.

[4] (Arnim) memorandum, 1 May 1871, partially printed and summarized by Goldschmidt, pp. 115–18.

lenient peace terms than reopen hostilities. Another explanation could be found in that France would not be relieved of the considerable burden of foreign occupation by concluding a speedy peace settlement, especially because she had no means, at that time, to pay the half billion francs which would have to precede the first stage of the evacuation by German troops. A third theory, according to Arnim's information, maintained that Thiers was purposely retarding negotiations and payment of the war indemnity so as to be forced by French patriots to demand speedy termination of the occupation, because the presence of German troops provided Thiers with a certain measure of support.

It was difficult to ascertain, Arnim continued, which of these theories influenced French diplomacy. The fact, however, remained: the delaying tactics of the French Government, even if not consciously planned, placed into their hands a number of troops which, though no danger, could constitute a real discomfort for Germany. This all the more because the significance of the troops would probably be greatly exaggerated by the French Government as well as by the nation after victory over the Commune had been achieved. The real motive of French behaviour, Arnim concluded, was probably a mixture of all these considerations. It would seem logical that Thiers would not want to conclude a final peace treaty without having at least attempted to procure better conditions for France. At the moment, military operations in Paris restrained his action; as soon as these were terminated he would be able to meet the German Chancellor on an equal footing, as a leading statesman of a great Power. 'He [Thiers] wants to draw a diagonal line between the opposing views and this will become the path on which the German armies will march stumbling home.'[1] The President seemed to have no doubt about the success of his endeavours. Faced with this situation, the problem of German policy toward Thiers was of some importance, Arnim continued. Among other things, it depended on the degree of confidence placed in Thiers's willingness to fulfil the promises of the peace preliminaries even after his attempt to soften them should have failed. Should this confidence exist, there could be no objections to following the French procedure and for

[1] Ibid.

allowing Thiers to proceed unhindered in his fight against the Commune.

The task of the German negotiators in Brussels, in this case, would be to tie the opponent to the chess board and to play the game so skilfully and in such a way that at the decisive moment, i.e. immediately after the conquest of Paris, the queen can be checkmated in a few moves. It would then be important not to let the thread be broken off, however taut it might have been stretched; to establish the differences in regard to the important questions; neither to give, nor to accept an ultimatum and, at the same time, to do nothing that would deprive the French in advance of the hope that leniency might in the secondary questions be useful to them and, in the end, lead to concessions on the main points.[1]

This procedure, Arnim went on, might have one important flaw—it could be based on a wrong assumption: that Thiers would remain master of the situation after the subjugation of Paris. In the opinion of most Frenchmen this was highly problematic. The consensus seemed to be rather that the President would not survive the victory. It was not considered impossible, Arnim thought, that immediately after the destruction of the Commune a new fight among the royalist parties would occupy France to such an extent that the settlement with Germany would assume a minor role in the minds of most Frenchmen.

The difficulties of governing France and finding a suitable regime for her were considerable. It would seem that the country had finally found it in the person of M. Thiers. But what if this supposition turned out to be a myth? Arnim asked. What would the situation be if, without having concluded a final peace, the President would have to wait for the uncertain result of a new crisis to find a French Government which would recognize the peace preliminaries and be ready to conclude a final settlement with Germany? These considerations and apprehensions made a continuation of the present procedure seem careless and dilatory. No proper account was being taken of all the possibilities which might arise and which might demand new sacrifices from Germany. Even the eventual consolidation of M. Thiers's Government would not offer adequate guarantees in this respect. From whichever angle

[1] (Arnim) memorandum, 1 May 1871, partially printed and summarized by Goldschmidt, pp. 115–18.

one approached these problems, one always would arrive at the same result: the speedy conclusion of a definite peace was a goal toward which one should strive with the greatest energy. Against this it could be argued that a peace treaty signed by M. Thiers would lose in value as the position of the French President deteriorated; but those objections were not valid, Arnim asserted. No government could exist in France without German approval; and any government which did not accept the peace terms in their entirety would be denied this approval. It went without saying that the German position would be much stronger if any new French Government could be confronted with a ratified peace treaty which it would have to accept within twenty-four hours than if Germany should have to renegotiate its acceptance.

In conclusion, Arnim summarized the situation as follows: from the material on hand, it was clear that the French Government:

(1) either openly denies the commitment to pay five billions in gold or silver within three years, or it declares definitely to be unable to fulfil it at all,

(2) considers the question of the division of the state debt as not settled,

(3) supports the Eastern Railroad in its completely untenable demands,

(4) will not renew the commercial treaty and will not grant Germany most-favoured-nation treatment.

Diplomatic action, Arnim continued, would have to concentrate, first of all, on these four problems and on ways and means to bring about their speedy solution. This might best be done by confronting the French Government with an ultimatum and then with an 'ultimatissimum'.

The ultimatum would have to demand that France, in the shortest possible time, should recognize:

(1) that the French Government is bound by the preliminary peace to transfer to the German treasury five billion francs in gold or silver within three years;

(2) that the question of debts in regard to Alsace-Lorraine has been settled;

(3) that we have the right to expropriate the Eastern Railroad.

If this ultimatum should meet with the expected opposition,

Arnim continued, a stronger one would have to be presented which would concede a longer period of payment but, on the other hand, would set new conditions for France which were not included in the preliminary peace.

The 'ultimatissimum' would demand:

(1) that France should pay the five billions in gold or silver in four, or perhaps, five years, if there are no objections and if guarantees can be found;

(2) that France agrees to give up the division of debts [regarding Alsace-Lorraine]:

(3) that France hand over the Eastern Railroad against a compensation of 70 million thalers;[1]

(4) that in regard to trade and navigation treaties we will be accorded a most-favoured-nation treaty;

(5) that the agricultural and industrial products of Alsace-Lorraine will keep those advantages in transit that we demand for them.

It would be advantageous, Arnim added, if these demands could be formulated in such a way so as to leave no room for misinterpretation by the French delegates at Brussels and stipulate a brief period during which the discussion of minor questions and the signing of the treaty would have to be accomplished.

Should M. Thiers not agree to these demands, it would be reasonable to assume that it would be much more difficult to treat with him later on, when his self-esteem would be greatly enhanced by successful military operations. Concluding his memorandum, Arnim wrote:

According to the character which the negotiations have assumed here from the beginning, nobody could doubt for one moment that the question of peace and war will have to be posed once more. The way matters have developed recently, the assumption that this possibility has diminished would be premature.[2]

What is the importance of this memorandum and what does it reveal of its author? Did Arnim really attribute to Thiers 'quite fantastic' designs, and are there no proofs at all for these

---

[1] Bismarck's marginalia: 'Vessels', ibid.

[2] Ibid. Balan expressed his disagreement with Arnim's views in a short note to Bismarck, ibid., p. 119.

allegations?[1] Does it contain only idle speculations and figments of his fantasy? Or is it a sound evaluation of events and a useful working-paper on which German policy could have been based?

The memorandum is composed of two parts. The first is an appraisal of the situation as it presented itself to Arnim at Brussels; the second, a plan of action to be taken on the basis of this appraisal.

As to the first part, the dilatory tactics of the French negotiators in Brussels were an established fact. Arnim's explanations for the motives behind these tactics were as sound and accurate as they could have been under the circumstances.[2] His recognition that Thiers's position in France and the German attitude toward the President's position were of prime importance to the future development of German–French relations was equally well founded. His opinion that the French President might not remain in office after the Government's victory over the Commune proved to be wrong. His view was not based on personal preferences, however, but rather on contemporary opinions common throughout Europe. Arnim's further observation that a speedy conclusion of the peace negotiations was of paramount importance was also sound.

In his recommendations, Arnim proposed that pressure be put on the French by an ultimatum, to be followed, should this be of no avail, by an 'ultimatissimum'. This typical piece of Arnimiana, written no doubt to impress the reader, left Arnim open to ridicule. Pressure was, however, used successfully by Bismarck himself in his negotiations with Favre in Frankfurt.[3] It should also be noted that, aside from the linguistic cartwheels, the provisions in the memorandum were, by and large, the same that were finally embodied in the Treaty of Frankfurt.[4]

While the negotiations in Brussels were stalled, General Frabrice, the German Governor-General in France, and Jules Favre, the French Foreign Minister, discussed French policy

---

[1] Ibid., p. 28.

[2] Arnim's contention that the French hoped to get better peace terms later on, when they had increased their army, was also expressed by Bismarck on 24 Apr. 1871 in his speech before the Reichstag (*GW* xi. 159 ff.). See also Busch's entry for 2 May 1871 (Busch, ii. 239–40). The arguments Busch used in an article for the *Koelnische Zeitung* resemble those used by Arnim. See also Herzfeld, pp. 37 ff.

[3] *GW* viii. 4–5.   [4] *GP* i. 38–43.

in connection with the suppression of the Commune.[1] When these talks failed and when Bismarck, impatient and frustrated by the long-drawn-out negotiations in Brussels, threatened to resume war operations, Favre told Fabrice that Germany could have peace if she would accept the preliminary treaty as the final one.[2] Favre also suggested that he meet with Bismarck to negotiate the final peace treaty.[3] When Bismarck was informed of these proposals he replied that he was ready to meet with Favre at Frankfurt or Mainz.[4] Favre agreed and the two men met at Frankfurt on 6 May. Arnim, at Bismarck's request, joined the meeting.[5]

The negotiations dealt with additional guarantees which France would have to give Germany in connection with the payment of a French indemnity and the withdrawal of German troops from the occupied territories: the question of 'most-favoured-nation' status to be granted to Germany; an exchange of territories regarding the French request to enlarge the area around Belfort; and, finally, the fixing of an indemnity for the Eastern Railroad. After three days of hard bargaining the negotiations were concluded and the peace treaty was signed on 10 May 1871 by Bismarck and Arnim for Germany, and Favre, Pouyer-Quertier, and Goulard for France.[6]

Following the signing of the treaty, Arnim remained in Frankfurt as the principal German representative for the subsequent negotiations with France which dealt with the railroad question, the regulation of customs duties between France and Alsace-Lorraine, and lesser problems arising from the treaty. These negotiations were nearly as protracted as the earlier ones at Brussels.[7] Arnim's part in them was neither brilliant nor distinguished, though his general attitude was somewhat more conciliatory. From this otherwise rather uninteresting period, one incident alone is worth preserving because it sheds a light on Arnim's character and because it provides a counterpart to

[1] Herzfeld, pp. 31 ff.; Busch, ii. 232 ff.
[2] Giesberg, p. 151.
[3] GP i. 31, 32.   [4] Ibid. 31.
[5] Bismarck to Arnim, 2 May 1871. It is not clear why Arnim was chosen and not Balan, of whom Bismarck said, 'I feel especially sorry for poor Balan . . .', Busch, ii. 244. Bismarck to Rosenberg, 31 May 1871.
[6] For details of these negotiations see Giesberg, pp. 158–67. Text of the Treaty of Frankfurt in GP i. 38–43.
[7] Goldschmidt, p. 145. For details see Giesberg, pp. 178 ff.

the Balan episode of the previous April.[1] It too involved Arnim and one of his colleagues, this time the representative of Wuerttemberg, Count Uxkuell.

The arrival of the representative of the Bavarian Government at the negotiations at Frankfurt opened the question of the rights and privileges of the lesser German states to send representatives of their own to peace negotiations between the Reich and foreign powers. To clarify this situation Arnim and Uxkuell asked the Foreign Ministry in Berlin for a decision.[2] In a private letter to Arnim, Thile, the State Secretary, noted that the negotiations at Frankfurt were not concerning the conclusion, but rather the execution, of a peace treaty. Admission of a representative of one of the lesser German states was therefore a privilege, rather than a right. Arnim alone was plenipotentiary of the Reich and Thile left it to Arnim's good judgement how to convey this delicate matter to his colleagues.[3] This put Arnim on the spot. He had expected, he replied to Thile, that the demands of Bavaria in this matter would be rejected and had therefore had no scruples about informing Weber, the Bavarian representative, accordingly.[4] In the case of Uxkuell, the situation was more awkward. When first notified of the latter's appointment he had asked Balan what position Uxkuell would have and had suggested that he should be 'somewhat higher than a counsellor' and attached to his, Arnim's, staff.[4] Balan had replied that Count Uxkuell was definitely equal in rank to him and also a plenipotentiary of the Reich. Since the arrival of this letter, Uxkuell had been upheld in his position and several directives from the Foreign Ministry had been addressed to both him and Uxkuell. In this situation, Arnim concluded, it would be difficult to communicate to the representative of Wuerttemberg the current view of the Government in Berlin concerning his position without offending Uxkuell and his king. It might be better if Uxkuell were advised about his new position either directly or through the Government of Wuerttemberg.

Before closing this letter, Arnim must have had some second thoughts. In a postscript he noted that he had not welcomed Balan's information that Uxkuell was to be equal to him in rank

---

and position, adding his famous comment, 'My requirement for colleagues is always satisfied, even if I don't have any.' ('*Mein Beduerfnis an Kollegen ist immer gedeckt, auch wenn ich keine habe.*') But, now that things had developed so far, it was better to leave them as they were. Uxkuell was a good man, in his work as well as in his attitude and outlook. He would, therefore, Arnim concluded, break the embarrassing news to Uxkuell himself, should this still be necessary.[1]

This turn seems to be as complete a reversal as could be expected of Arnim. The situation was not dissimilar to that at Brussels. Whereas there he had tried to get rid of his colleague by all sorts of intrigues, if Lerchenfeld's account can be relied upon (and from what is known of Arnim's character there are many reasons why it should be), in this particular case, where the downgrading of his colleague was made possible by an official directive, he declined to accept it. Why? It could be that Uxkuell never represented a challenge to Arnim as Balan had. Arnim *was* chief negotiator in Frankfurt, though Uxkuell was nominally equal to him in rank. This had not been true in Brussels. Inasmuch as Arnim's eminence had been established and had been confirmed officially, it was perhaps to his advantage to be generous in this case.[2]

[1] Arnim to Thile, 17 July 1871.
[2] The incident was finally settled when Uxkuell was recognized as second imperial plenipotentiary and Arnim was advised to inform him accordingly. Thile to Arnim, 28 July 1871.

VI

THE APPOINTMENT OF ARNIM TO PARIS

FRANCO-GERMAN negotiations in Frankfurt were making little headway, but in France Manteuffel, Commander-in-Chief of the German occupation army, was busy negotiating an agreement over the evacuation of French territory by German troops with Pouyer-Quertier, the French Minister of Finance.[1] Having concluded and signed this agreement without Bismarck's knowledge, Manteuffel wrote to the Emperor and asked for his and the Chancellor's approval.[2] Bismarck, as could have been expected, was furious about this unauthorized incursion by the military into his exclusive domain of foreign affairs; particularly so in this case because Manteuffel's activities had seriously upset negotiations with the French at Frankfurt. To get these going again and, at the same time, to forestall any further meddling by the military in diplomatic negotiations, Bismarck decided to send an experienced man from the Foreign Ministry on a special mission to Paris. He chose for this post Count Harry von Arnim.[3]

The question of why Arnim was chosen to go to Paris is a vexing one. The immediate reasons for his appointment are easily understandable; the underlying causes and fundamental considerations, however, are difficult to explain. An accurate interpretation of Bismarck's motives for his choice is important for the understanding of the relationship between Bismarck and Arnim; it would also put the subsequent conflict between the two in its proper perspective.

The question is this: Why was Arnim appointed to one of

---

[1] *GP* i. 61–2; *Occupation et libération du territoire 1871–1873*, 2 vols. (Paris, 1903), i. 36–8, henceforth cited *OLT*; Herzfeld, pp. 72 ff.

[2] Goldschmidt, pp. 206–7.

[3] Bismarck to Thile, 12 Aug. 1871; Thile to Arnim, 12 Aug. 1871, *GP* i. 60–1; Waldersee, i. 153; see also St. Vallier's letter to Thiers of 15 Aug. 1871, according to which Manteuffel considers Arnim a moderate who will be more conciliatory than Waldersee, *OLT* i. 54.

the most important posts in the German foreign service when Bismarck himself had expressed distrust of Arnim on numerous occasions?[1] There was, in addition to the pronouncements of the Chancellor—which may or may not be taken at face value—Arnim's own behaviour as recorded in the official correspondence, his intrigues and independent actions during his appointment to Rome and Brussels. These alone should have disqualified him for Paris.

Curiously enough, this problem is generally not contemplated by writers on the subject. One of the few who deal with it blames the lack of trained and experienced officials.[2] This, at best, is only partially correct. While Hatzfeld and Radowitz may have been too young, and Reuss and Schweinitz were perhaps then indispensable at their posts at St. Petersburg and Vienna, there were, after all, Buelow and Hohenlohe, Bernstorff and Solms.

There is some indication that Bismarck himself was most reluctant to make the appointment. On two later occasions he reminded the Emperor that he had hesitated to appoint Arnim because, as he wrote in December 1872, of the Ambassador's inability to separate his personal impressions from his political judgements.[3] Four months later he recalled,

how at the appointment of Count Arnim to his present post I expressed myself in a respectful letter to Your Majesty . . . to the effect that it was only my complete assurance of having Your Majesty's confidence that encouraged me to attempt a political co-operation with an ambassador of such doubtful and untrustworthy character and perhaps to have to renew the struggle which I had to carry on for years with Count Golz.[4]

Count Beust, the former Austrian Chancellor, was present when Arnim met Bismarck at Gastein. On that occasion Bismarck, according to Beust, was supposed to have said contemptuously of Arnim, 'and with such a man one is supposed

---

[1] See, among others, his conversations during the Franco-Prussian War, in Busch, i. 243, 390–1, 564.

[2] Goldschmidt, p. 27.

[3] Bismarck to the Emperor, 5 Dec. 1872, and p. 101 below.

[4] Bismarck to the Emperor, 14 Apr. 1873, printed, with omissions, in the *Reichsanzeiger*, 24 Jan. 1876, in *Brief des Grafen Harry von Arnim an den Fuersten Bismarck* (Zuerich, 1876), and in *GW* vic. 36–7. Bismarck's letter to the Emperor at the time of Arnim's appointment has not been found. See also pp. 114–15, below.

to conduct higher politics'.[1] Beust thought that the relationship between the two men was strained even then.

If Bismarck was so reluctant to appoint Arnim, powerful pressure must have been exerted on Arnim's behalf. The most common explanation along this line is Arnim's alleged influence at the Prussian Court and Empress Augusta's admiration for him. Although there are many references to this in the literature of the period,[2] there is no detailed factual evidence to connect Arnim's appointment with his influence at the Court. What then were the reasons? The obvious ones are to be found in the peculiar circumstances of the moment. The negotiations at Frankfurt were deadlocked.[3] At Compiègne, Manteuffel was negotiating independently with the French to the detriment of German national interests. While this had to be stopped, the main negotiations had to be pushed ahead and put on a more regular basis. These things were to occur simultaneously and were to be brought about as speedily as possible by someone who had the necessary knowledge and who belonged to the permanent staff of the Foreign Ministry. Considering these factors, the choice of man and place to accomplish this task was not too difficult. It was Arnim in Paris.

So much for the immediate circumstances. As to other considerations, there were at least three. (1) Bismarck needed a man with experience, initiative, and a quick mind to deal with the French. (Balan had the first qualification but not the other two.) (2) He wanted Arnim removed from Berlin because he was apparently afraid that his presence would reinforce the opposition to him, the Chancellor, at Court. (3) He was confident that he could control any aberrations of Arnim, while still making use of his talents.

Upon receiving the news of his appointment, Arnim suggested to Bismarck that he be allowed to come to Gastein, because it would give his mission greater prestige to arrive in Paris after having been previously received by the Emperor

---

[1] Beust, ii. 482.

[2] Philipp zu Eulenburg-Hertefeld, *Aus 50 Jahren* (Berlin, 1923), pp. 36–7; N. Rich and M. H. Fisher, *The Holstein Papers*, 4 vols. (Cambridge, 1955–63), i. 103, henceforth cited Rich and Fisher; O. von Mohl, *Fuenfzig Jahre Reichsdienst* (Leipzig (1920)), p. 60.

[3] It should be noted, however, that Bismarck was considering Arnim's appointment as early as 8 June; see Waldersee, i. 137.

and the Chancellor.[1] Bismarck agreed and asked him to come immediately.[2] No details of Arnim's stay at Gastein are known, except Beust's short observation. It can be presumed that he was briefed on his assignment and familiarized with the Chancellor's views. Arnim left for Paris on 22 August and arrived there about a week later.[3]

[1] Arnim to Bismarck, 14 Aug. 1871.
[2] Bismarck to Arnim, 18 Aug. 1871.
[3] Abeken to Delbrueck, 22 Aug. 1871; France, Ministère des Affaires Étrangères, Commission de publication des documents relatifs aux origines de la guerre de 1914, *Documents diplomatiques français 1871–1914*, 31 vols. (Paris, 1929–59), i. 71, henceforth cited *DDF*; Waldersee, i. 154.

VII

VIEWS AND ATTITUDES ON FRENCH AFFAIRS

Arnim's reception at Paris was mixed. The French were none too happy about his appointment.[1] Thiers especially regretted it because of the Count's 'morose nature'.[2] That Arnim had taken a by and large anti-French attitude at the Vatican Council might have also played a part. The impression Arnim made on Waldersee, the German chargé d'affaires in Paris, is interesting. He found the rumour that Arnim had not much courage confirmed by his behaviour. He was surprised to find him somewhat embarrassed during his first encounter with Thiers, and this the more so because Arnim was known to be quite overbearing. Arnim himself admitted to Waldersee that 'he has the misfortune that people consider him everywhere impolite'.[3] Waldersee, in turn, thought that Arnim's severe near-sightedness might at least be partly the cause of his attitude.[3]

Arnim's first negotiations with the French dealt primarily with payment of the indemnity and the problem of the customs-duty rebates for Alsace-Lorraine.[4] His conversations with Pouyer-Quertier gave him the impression that, while it would not be difficult to fix the financial arrangements concerning

[1] Waldersee, i. 153–4; *Denkwuerdigkeiten des Generals und Admirals Albrecht von Stosch* (Stuttgart, 1904), pp. 262, 264, henceforth cited Stosch; N. Rich, *Friedrich von Holstein*, 2 vols. (Cambridge, 1965), i. 71–3. On 29 Oct. 1872 St. Vallier, the French representative at General Manteuffel's headquarters at Nancy, wrote to Thiers this characterization of Arnim which was given to him by two highly placed German officers: 'Il [Arnim] n'est nullement l'homme qu'il nous faudrait à Paris; il ne saura jamais s'y faire une bonne position; c'est un ambitieux malade et hypocondre; il a persécuté son cousin Bismarck pour obtenir de lui le poste de Paris; il le poursuit aujourd'hui pour en avoir un autre; il est mécontent; il l'a été toute sa vie; il le sera toujours et désirera toujours autre chose que ce qu'il a.' *OLT* ii. 123.

[2] *Memoirs of M. Thiers 1870–1873* (London, 1915), p. 184, henceforth cited *Thiers*.
[3] Waldersee, i. 154.
[4] *GP* i. 66, fn. ***, 75–7.

the current payment of the indemnity instalment by France, the problem of the customs duties would prove more intractable. In his report of 2 September to the Chancellor he asked that, in view of this situation and so that the negotiations could be kept going, Germany's demands in this respect not be set too high. To this Bismarck agreed.[1]

Between 2 and 14 September there was no indication that Arnim was busily concluding an agreement with Thiers, despite several reports on other topics. But this, in fact, was the case. On 14 September Arnim informed Bismarck that he had negotiated an agreement with Thiers whereby France would make certain concessions concerning the duty-free entry of goods from Alsace-Lorraine. 'The financial arrangements cause no difficulty', he added cryptically.[2]

News of this agreement evoked surprise in Berlin. The cause for the surprise, which, with Bismarck, quickly turned into indignation, was not so much the conclusion of the agreement itself, but rather that Arnim had gone ahead without the knowledge or the approval of his superiors. The Chancellor liked initiative in his subordinates only within reach of his own close supervision. His famous expression that he and he alone made foreign policy, and that it was the duty of his ambassadors to fall in line at his command like well-drilled soldiers, was more than just a *bon mot*. It fully expressed Bismarck's notion of the role he expected German diplomatic representatives to play. Under these circumstances it was sometimes difficult, as Arnim and others before and after him had learned to their regret, to know exactly when and how far a German diplomat could venture on his own initiative. Aside from that, however, Arnim's unilateral procedure in this particular case would have tried the patience even of a Foreign Minister less autocratic than Bismarck.

Arnim's motives are not difficult to guess. He wanted to inaugurate his mission to Paris with a great and shining success. He wanted to show, no doubt, what he alone, given a free hand,

---

[1] Arnim to Bismarck, no. 97, 2 Sept. 1871. This document, as printed in the *Große Politik*, i. 77–8, is incomplete; for the text of the passage that has been omitted, see Appendix I.

[2] Arnim to Bismarck, 14 Sept. 1871, *GP* i. 79. For details of the Arnim–Thiers negotiations, see Giesberg, pp. 193 ff.

could achieve in a short time, where others during a much longer period had failed.[1] That in concluding this agreement he had not exceeded his instructions was probably true but was hardly to the point. The main issue was that he had committed the Reich without the consent or even the knowledge of the Emperor or the Chancellor. Bismarck was, of course, not slow in pointing this out. Even before Arnim's detailed report reached him, the Chancellor expressed his strong disapproval and voiced his doubt whether Arnim was familiar with the procedure regarding the conclusion of a treaty. The fact that the contents of a treaty were in line with the instructions a negotiator had received from home, Bismarck wrote, did not justify the negotiator in signing such a treaty without its having been submitted previously to the Foreign Ministry for examination. (This was not fair to Arnim, inasmuch as he had not signed a treaty; he had only concluded an oral agreement with Thiers.) This was common practice in business, among lawyers, and in court. 'Even at places and times where railroads and telegraph communications did not exist, it would be difficult to find an example of a Prussian representative concluding an international agreement without submitting the text of it first to the Minister of Foreign Affairs and obtaining his approval.' From this it was not difficult to imagine, Bismarck continued, that the Emperor was shocked and painfully surprised to learn from the newspapers that an agreement, concluded in the name of the German Emperor, the contents of which were unknown to him, had been submitted to the French National Assembly. In conclusion Bismarck asked Arnim to keep in mind that

---

[1] That Arnim succeeded in his negotiations to some extent, i.e. won concessions from Thiers regarding the customs duties, can be shown by comparing Thiers's statement to Manteuffel with the final settlement (Goldschmidt, pp. 223–5). Manteuffel's message to Arnim of 10 Sept. 1871 was as follows: 'Thiers has informed me that he can agree to Prince Bismarck's demands regarding customs concessions only to the extent of half the amount of duties to 1 Jan. 1872 and two-thirds to 1 Jan. 1874. Even if he could win a speedier evacuation of the departments by further concessions, he could not do so against his conscience and against [the will of] the Assembly. I pass this on for your information only. von Manteuffel.' Against this, Arnim was able to obtain duty-free imports to 1 Jan 1872; one-quarter duty to 1 July 1872; and one-half to 1 July 1873. It is also interesting to note that the agreement that was finally reached and ratified between Bismarck and Pouyer-Quertier on 12 Oct. 1872 follows the Arnim–Thiers negotiations with the exception that half-duty is granted by France only to 31 Dec. 1872. *GP* i. 91–5.

F

repetition of such a procedure would severely endanger the authority of the German Government.[1]

Of interest here are Arnim's extensive reports of 24 September, in which he tried to justify his behaviour and to pacify the Chancellor.[2] He attempted, first, to reassure Bismarck that there had been no written agreements between himself and Thiers, and that only oral discussions had taken place. Next, he asserted that the bill submitted by Thiers to the Assembly was only an authorization to negotiate with the German Government regarding the Alsatian customs duties, because Thiers did not believe that he could negotiate without the Assembly's consent.[3] The Assembly was about to adjourn and ratification could only have been accomplished after it had reassembled in December. This would have made any agreement between France and Germany valueless: Thiers therefore decided to ask for an authorization to conclude as well as to ratify an agreement with Germany. For this he had to demonstrate to the Assembly certain advantages which France would derive from the negotiations. To this end, Arnim had given to the President certain assurances regarding the evacuation of some of the department. 'For us', Arnim explained to Bismarck, 'the dealings between Thiers and the Assembly were interesting only to the extent that from them would emerge a person sufficiently authorized [by the Assembly] with whom we could finally sign a treaty.' He did have apprehensions about Thiers submitting the bill to the Assembly, Arnim continued, and he did express them to the President. The resulting complications were, however, much greater than he had foreseen. They were further increased by the Assembly's printed report, which gave a lopsided version of the bill. This, in turn, was picked up by

[1] Bismarck to Arnim, no. 85, 21 Sept. 1871: see *GP* i. 83, fn. *; Goldschmidt, pp. 232–3.

[2] Arnim reports, nos. 128, 129, 132, 24 Sept. 1871.

[3] Arnim to Bismarck, no. 132, 24 Sept. 1871; regarding this report Abeken made the following notation: 'His Majesty has known from the very beginning that the National Assembly "had not been presented with an agreement in the name of the German Reich, but only with a draft law which would authorize the President to conclude negotiations with the German Government." His Majesty's astonishment always referred to the fact that he had not been informed of the *arrangements* of Count Arnim with von Thiers, which enabled and justified the latter to submit such a draft law to the Assembly. This, in turn, had to raise the definite expectations of the Assembly and of the whole world that on this basis the Convention would be concluded. Abeken' (Memorandum, 30 Sept. 1871).

Reuter, distributed by the agency to all newspapers, and in this version created a sensation in Berlin. 'The whole affair was dominated by a peculiarly unlucky star', Arnim concluded his report.[1]

In the next report (No. 129) he pointed out that, while he was ready to assume full responsibility for his part in the negotiations at Paris, it was Counsellor Herzog who had conducted the economic aspects of the negotiations there. He had been under the impression that Herzog was familiar with the economic policies of the Reich Chancellory under Delbrueck and that his concessions in this sphere would be approved by this department.

Arnim's excuses, like many before, sound sincere to a point, but there are, as always, too many misunderstandings, wrong interpretations, and misapprehensions to make them really authentic. Withal, the controversy between Bismarck and Arnim seemed to have been factual rather than personal on this occasion. For Arnim came to Berlin and together with Bismarck signed the agreement with France.[2] Arnim had, at that time, an audience with the Emperor and afterwards a talk with the Chancellor.[3] The content of these conversations is not known; that they took place at all would indicate, however, that this episode did not constitute the beginning of the Bismarck–Arnim struggle as has been claimed by the editors of the *Grosse Politik*.[4] Later, under similar circumstances, Arnim was not asked to come to Berlin and did not sign the Franco-German agreement of 15 March 1873.[5]

After Arnim had returned to Paris, Thiers and many members of his Government expressed their gratitude and appreciation on the successful conclusion of the convention. It meant an increase of French prestige and a strengthening of the Government's position throughout the country. It was precisely on this latter point, however, that Arnim voiced his doubts.[6] In a subsequent conversation, Pouyer-Quertier, who had recently returned from an extensive tour of the provinces, admitted to Arnim that Thiers's Government could easily be overthrown by

---

[1] Arnim to Bismarck, no. 128, 24 Sept. 1871.
[2] *GP* i. 91–6.   [3] Arnim (to Bismarck), 18 Oct. 1871.
[4] *GP* i. 83, fn. *.   [5] See p. 113 below.
[6] *GP* i. 97–8.

a *coup d'état*.[1] The Bonapartists might have lost sympathy temporarily because of Napoleon III's unsuccessful trip to Corsica, but the small businessmen and tradespeople of Paris longed for the return of the Empire for purely selfish economic reasons. To these could be added the socialists in the suburbs, where Bonapartist propaganda had been highly successful and where the Platonic advances of the arid republicanism of Thiers had fallen on barren ground.[2] Among conservative circles too the Government was steadily losing adherents.[3] It was generally accused of having shown too much leniency toward the democratic republicans and the communards. There seemed to be no one aside from the President and his immediate friends who believed in the continuation of the provisional arrangements.[4] The Count d'Aumale and his brothers and nephews had pledged themselves to assume the leadership of the army in case of a Bonapartist uprising, but it was questionable whom the army would follow in such an emergency. According to other reports, the Count of Chambord was in Lucerne, and a number of monarchical deputies had gone there to persuade him to accept the tricolour as an essential condition for his return to France. Should he accept, the Count of Paris would submit to him; otherwise the deputies would recognize the Count of Paris as the representative of the traditional monarchy in France.

In a private letter to Bismarck, Arnim told of a dinner party to which he had been invited by Thiers, where all the guests, including a well-known lady of legitimist leanings, had been more or less of the same opinion. Thiers's internal policy apparently was meant to establish the Republic permanently rather than to prepare the country for the monarchy. But the respectable Republic would not last in France, Arnim wrote, and time was being lost with experimentations which were only to the advantage of the Bonapartists. The newspapers of that faction were adopting the most provocative tone against Germany and there were many people who, though anti-Bonapartist before, seemed to have changed their minds in

[1] Arnim to Bismarck, no. 144, 30 Oct. 1871.
[2] Ibid.; Newton, ii. 17.
[3] Arnim to Bismarck, no. 155, 13 Nov. 1871, and Bismarck's marginalia: 'Never had any.'   [4] Ibid.

favour of the former Emperor. The appointment of Count Orloff as Russian Ambassador in Paris was being fully exploited by the chauvinists, and many saw in it the beginning of a Franco-Russian alliance. As a result of these developments it would become much more difficult to calm the excitement of French public opinion.[1]

Bismarck's reply was quick and decisive. He pointed out that the lack of confidence among monarchist circles toward Thiers was not new and that it was the German Government's, and particularly Arnim's, task to strengthen Thiers's position. Arnim should let it be known, especially through private conversations, that Germany would have to ask for stronger guarantees for the execution of the peace treaty, particularly for the right to reoccupy recently evacuated territory, in case a change of government occurred. Further measures might also have to be taken. Official pronouncements should not be made for the time being, because the time for them had not yet arrived. 'I should like to ask your Excellency', Bismarck continued, 'not to consider indications about the situation which come from legitimist circles, especially from ladies of that party, as reliable and, in case of background reports, to indicate exactly their source of origin.'[2] The directive which followed this telegram was even more explicit. The Chancellor expressed in it his apprehension that Arnim attached too much weight to the atmosphere of the social circles in which he moved and had given too much credence to the local witticisms against the established government. He noted that the republican as well as the royalist parties were minority parties and that it was in their common interest not to upset the existing order so as not to endanger once more the existence of the State. This feeling for peace and consolidation should be especially prevalent among the politically indifferent classes in the provinces, and this had been expressed in the election to the General Council. A united action by the different parties to overthrow Thiers would presuppose agreement on his successor. Since, as Arnim himself had reported, such a person did not

---

[1] Arnim to Bismarck (private letter), 13 Nov. 1871. While Bismarck assured Arnim of Orloff's pro-German sympathies (Bismarck to Arnim, no. 16, 21 Jan. 1872) Arnim's original impression to the contrary was confirmed by Lord Lyons, British Ambassador in Paris (Newton, ii. 28–33).

[2] Bismarck to Arnim, tel. no. 81, 16 Nov. 1871.

seem to exist, the chances in favour of Thiers should not be underestimated.

However that may be, it is in our interest to support him [Thiers] in any way we possibly can and, as I have stated repeatedly—for example in my directive No. 87 of 22 September 1871[1]—I ask your Excellency to adopt these ideas without reservations and to use all opportunities which may present themselves to you, in your social intercourse and conversations, to give expression to them. I also ask you that you do not keep it a secret that, for the time being, we consider any change of government a threat to the execution of the peace treaty and that, if the need arises, we will intervene quickly and decisively to guard our own interest. . . . The entire subject, your observations and activities, should be treated in such a way in your reports that the Emperor, who will read them, should be convinced that your Excellency does not deviate, because of impressions gained from your social gatherings, from the strict execution of the directives which you receive.[2]

Acknowledging this instruction, Arnim was as devious and vague as ever. He expressed appreciation for Bismarck's directive, because it provided him with a much-needed official view and because it conveyed to him the apprehensions of the Chancellor. There was no need for anxiety because, he wrote, 'I am convinced I did not deviate in my attitude one iota from the direction which your Excellency's opinion and the present situation have made it my duty to maintain.'[3] As to the sources of information, which the Chancellor had criticized as being too much influenced by society gossip, Arnim maintained that, apart from the few persons Thiers had introduced to him, he did not move in Parisian society at all, because no private house had been opened to him.

The occasion of a by-election for the Paris municipal council gave Arnim another chance to discuss the political future of France and the chances of a republican regime under Thiers. In the municipal election the candidates of the radical left wing of the republican party had won the majority and dominated the council. This created general consternation among the public and was exploited by Bonapartist journals. The feeling was widespread that a restoration of the Empire

[1] Goldschmidt, pp. 229–31.
[2] Bismarck to Arnim, no. 112, 18 Nov. 1871.
[3] Arnim to Bismarck, no. 164, 27 Nov. 1871.

was unavoidable. To buttress his views Arnim cited the opinion of an English businessman, who was in touch with all classes of society and had lived for a long time in Paris, and Count von Henckel-Donnersmarck, a leading German industrialist. Both men believed that those groups previously opposed to the Empire were now in favour of restoring it and considered the political trends highly favourable to a royalist regime. Count Henckel gave the present government in France no more than six months. But Arnim was not willing to support this prophecy entirely. In his opinion there were two alternatives in the development of the political scene in France: the restoration of the Bourbon monarchy or the return of the Empire. The situation was such, however, that it was too early to tell, 'and neither the proper moment nor the opportunity had arrived as yet . . . to abandon . . . neutrality'.[1] The means to support Thiers were insignificant, Arnim thought, especially after the verdicts of Melun and Paris had made the amnesty for French prisoners of war so much more difficult.[2] It was their liberation which was so important to the President in the interest of his position. The French were apparently unaware that a fundamental change in their government could not be brought about without the consent of Germany. At the decisive moment they would become aware of this fact and the more Germany had kept an open choice in this matter the more favourable her position would then be.[3]

The views expressed by Arnim on Thiers and his Government completely disregarded Bismarck's directive (No. 122) of 18 November.[4] They were certainly at variance with Arnim's previous statement that he was convinced that he did not deviate one iota from the directives of the Chancellor as set forth in his most recent report.[5] These exchanges between Bismarck and Arnim constitute the opening round of their struggle over the form of government in France and the maintenance of Thiers as its head. It provided the main theme of Arnim's appointment in Paris and was one of the major causes for his subsequent recall.[6]

---

[1] Arnim to Bismarck, no. 165, 29 Nov. 1871.
[2] At Paris and Melun French juries found two Frenchmen innocent of murdering and attempting to murder German soldiers. Herzfeld, pp. 101 ff.
[3] Arnim to Bismarck, no. 165, 29 Nov. 1871.
[4] See p. 70 above.   [5] See p. 70 above.   [6] See p. 122 below.

Bismarck's views and statements on this subject are well known. He favoured a moderate republican government in France because, in his opinion, this form of government would make it difficult, if not impossible, for the country to contract alliances with any of the great monarchical powers in Europe.[1] Furthermore, it would keep France weak and divided internally for a considerable period of time.[2]

These two statements have been repeated so often and for so long that by now they are generally accepted as the cornerstone of Bismarck's policy toward France. But were these propositions in conformity with the facts and events of the period? As to the first statement, it should be remembered that France, from the end of the Franco-Prussian war onward, enjoyed a great deal of sympathy in Great Britain. And this despite or perhaps even because of her republican form of government. The earliest concrete sign in this direction was the Anglo-French negotiations for the renewal of a trade treaty in the summer of 1872.[3] The relationship to Russia was also quite friendly and in no way adversely influenced by political theories. Russia, after 1871, looked to France as a counterweight to German preponderance and, because of the liberal reforms under Alexander II, its sympathies, outside the circles around the Court, were with a democratic France rather than with a conservative Prussia and Germany.[4] The final and conclusive proof of Bismarck's miscalculation came, of course, in the famous war crisis of 1875, when both Britain and Russia backed France against Germany. As to the second premiss—that

[1] Like in many other instances, Bismarck's views on which type of Government would be best suited for France had changed over a period of time. During the siege of Paris, when he was looking anxiously for a partner with whom he could conclude a lasting peace, he expressed the opinion that 'Napoleon or a Republic is a matter of indifference to us' (Busch, i. 220) *GW* vib. 503–4; see also H. Geuss, *Bismarck und Napoleon III* (The Hague, 1959), pp. 280–1, 303–6. And, on the subject of contracting alliances, he considered England equally unfit, because she was 'unpredictable and revolutionary' (*GP* iii. 401).

[2] *GW* xv. 360–1; Wahl, *Deutsche Geschichte*, 4 vols. (Stuttgart, 1926–36), i. 22, henceforth cited Wahl; E. Eyck, *Bismarck*, 3 vols. (Zuerich, 1941–4), iii. 33–4, henceforth cited Eyck.

[3] W. Windelband, *Bismarck und die europaeischen Grossmaechte 1879–85* (Essen, 1940), pp. 39–40, henceforth cited Windelband; Newton, ii. 3–4, 33.

[4] Windelband, pp. 33–4; W. Taffs, *Ambassador to Bismarck. Lord Odo Russell* (London, 1938), p. 55; Herzfeld, p. 175; A. J. P. Taylor, *The Struggle for Supremacy in Europe 1848–1918* (Oxford, 1954), pp. 222 ff., henceforth cited Taylor; *DDF* i. 182, 184–8; *OLT* ii. 27 ff.

a moderate republican form of government would weaken France internally and keep the nation divided—this too proved to be a serious misconception. The best indication that exactly the contrary was the case was provided by the speed and facility with which the war indemnity was being paid off, the rapid economic recovery of the country, and the quick and thorough rearmament and reorganization of its armed forces.

What then were Bismarck's reasons for opposing a monarchical restoration in France? The clue can be found in Germany's domestic policies rather than in French internal affairs. It was the *Kulturkampf* and the Chancellor's fight against Catholics at home and his fear of a Catholic alliance and conspiracy abroad that dictated his attitude toward the governmental system in France. A French-Austrian coalition was not an impossibility, as events have shown, though it probably was the change in Austrian foreign policy (and especially the replacement of Beust by Andrassy) rather than the republican form of government in France that made an alliance between these two countries most unlikely in this period. Bismarck's fear of a Catholic conspiracy, real as it might have been in his own mind, was baseless, or, at least, greatly exaggerated.[1]

Arnim's views of the French political scene have by now also emerged quite clearly. He favoured a monarchical restoration, both because of his own personal preference for this type of government and (and this should not be overlooked) because many signs in France pointed to this development.[2] Contrary to Bismarck's idea, Arnim saw in the Republic a potential source of unity and strength and feared, especially in its more radical form, a spread of republicanism to other parts of Europe, particularly to Germany.

The Chancellor and the Minister thus found themselves in complete disagreement on the vital question of which governmental system in France would be most advantageous for German foreign policy. This situation, as far as the Prussian foreign service was concerned, was not unique, especially not

---

[1] J. B. Kissling, *Geschichte des Kulturkampfes im Deutschen Reich*, 3 vols. (Freiburg, 1911–16), i. 386; for a different opinion, see G. Franz, *Kulturkampf* (Munich, 1954), pp. 211–12, henceforth cited Franz; W. N. Medlicott, *Bismarck, Gladstone and the Concert of Europe* (London, 1956), pp. 12–13; Taylor, pp. 223–4; Bismarck to the Emperor, 4 Jan. 1874.

[2] Newton, ii. 17, 20–2.

before 1870.[1] After the unification of Germany, most of the Prussian governmental institutions and departments underwent considerable expansion and with it arose the necessity for better organization and tighter control. This applied to the Foreign Ministry and the foreign service to a greater extent than to any other governmental agency. The problems that confronted Bismarck in this sphere were considerable. While primarily responsible for the conduct and execution of foreign affairs of the Reich, he lacked the necessary powers to enforce his directives. For, while in France and in the United States the country's representatives abroad were constitutionally and legally under the supervision and disciplinary powers of the Foreign Minister, in Germany they were still agents of the Emperor and had direct access to him.[2] To secure uniformity of policy and compliance with his instructions under these circumstances, Bismarck had to rely on persuasions and threats.[3] When these failed, he could enlist the support of the Emperor by presenting his case in person and, if the need arose, he could threaten to resign. If all these measures failed, or if it was inopportune or impolitic to apply the last one, he could set in motion a campaign of public pressure and intrigue to eliminate the recalcitrant diplomat. In the case of Arnim, he employed all these measures.

Thus the official relationship between Bismarck and Arnim was not at all simple and clear-cut. It was further complicated by the personalities of the two men. Bismarck, in his attempt to centralize and unify the German foreign service and to concentrate foreign policy in his own hands, demanded absolute compliance with his directives and instantaneous execution of his orders.[4] That he carried his concept too far and beyond any reasonable and, for the foreign service, practicable limit is clear from some of his directives. He asked, in many instances, that the reports from abroad be similar in contents to the instructions received from Berlin regardless of any factors or

[1] Of interest here is Bismarck's account of his own attitude while Ambassador in St. Petersburg and Paris under Schleinitz, *GW* xv. 396.

[2] In Great Britain this right existed in theory but was not exercised in practice.

[3] See Muenster to the Emperor, 30 Dec. 1886; Bismarck to Muenster, 4 Jan. 1887, *GP* vi. 160–6.

[4] G. A. Craig, 'Bismarck and his Ambassadors', (U.S.) *Foreign Service Journal* (June 1956), pp. 20 ff.

events that might have led to different views or other conclusions.[1] It was this attitude that led Arnim to suggest on one
occasion that it might be simpler and more natural, under the
circumstances, 'to compose the reports of the ambassadors in
Berlin'.[2]

Under this autocratic regime, where a premium was put on
obedience and submissiveness as against initiative and independence, Arnim proved intractable. He considered himself
the ambassador of the German Emperor and the Prussian King,
a servant of his sovereign to whom he had sworn fealty, just
as the Chancellor had. It was his duty, as Arnim saw it, to
report to his emperor and king any developments in France
that were detrimental to his dynasty and to his interests just
as much as it was the Chancellor's and Foreign Minister's duty
to do so about affairs at home and abroad.

In view of these fundamental differences between the two
men, it is difficult to understand why Bismarck did not attempt
to clear up this most unsatisfactory situation between himself
and Arnim or, failing that, ask for his recall. But, aside from
several admonishing directives, Bismarck made no attempt to
rectify the situation at any time during this period. It may be
that he considered no attempt along these lines worth the
effort and that he felt his own position with the Emperor was
not strong enough nor the issue important enough to ask
for Arnim's recall. He might also have thought it inopportune
to pick a fight when most of his attention was concentrated on
the *Kulturkampf* and other internal difficulties. He might have
wanted to give Arnim more time and rope to hang himself.
This Bismarck did, and it proved successful.

Bismarck had not replied to Arnim's report of 29 November;[3]
thus the controversy over the governmental system in France
was set aside, at least for the time being, and the immediate
problems came once more to the fore. First among these were
the incidents of Paris and Melun,[4] where French juries found
two Frenchmen innocent of murdering and attempting to

[1] See Bismarck to Arnim, no. 112, 18 Nov. 1871, p. 70 above.

[2] *Pro Nihilo. Vorgeschichte des Arnim'schen Prozesses* (Zuerich, 1876), p. 37, henceforth cited *Pro Nihilo*. The copy used for this study is the one preserved in the
Foreign Ministry Archives with the marginal comments by Bismarck.

[3] See above, p. 71.

[4] p. 71, fn. 2.

murder German soldiers.[1] The German counter-measures taken in this connection by Manteuffel and his staff were deemed insufficient by the Chancellor, and he advised Arnim to discuss the matter with Remusat, the French Foreign Minister. Arnim in turn pointed out that the whole affair had been handled by Manteuffel and St. Vallier from the start and that he had been neither informed nor consulted in the matter by the chief of the occupation army. He also noted the irregularity and duplicity of French diplomatic practice as demonstrated in this particular incident by the employment of St. Vallier at Nancy.[2] The position of St. Vallier was that of a French representative of the Foreign Ministry with the commander-in-chief of the occupation army, and, as such, another and (so it was believed in Paris) more profitable channel of communication between Paris and Berlin.[3] The closing of this channel, which, as previous experience had indicated, seemed to run from Manteuffel directly to the Emperor, had been Bismarck's intention as early as September 1871.[4] With the approval of the Emperor, he directed Arnim once more to urge the French Government to terminate this unsatisfactory state of affairs, inasmuch as the 'French Ambassador was still functioning at Nancy, where no diplomatic business was being transacted, after regular diplomatic representation had been established in Paris, which alone was competent to deal with these affairs'.[5]

This, however, was only a minor disturbance in the storm which the incidents at Paris and Melun had brought about. Bismarck, and with him public opinion throughout Germany, demanded satisfaction from the French Government. When this was not forthcoming but when, instead, the culprits went unpunished and were set free, the Chancellor dispatched a strong note to the French Government, condemning French policy and justice and threatening reprisals.[6]

---

[1] Bismarck to Arnim, tel. no. 82, 21 Nov. 1872.

[2] Arnim to Bismarck, no. 166, 29 Nov. 1871.   [3] Herzfeld, pp. 70 ff.

[4] Bismarck to Arnim, tel. no. 13, 3 Sept. 1871. It should be noted that Bismarck himself made use of this channel when it suited his purpose. See pp. 98, 107 below.

[5] Bismarck to Arnim, 6 Dec. 1871. In his directive of 21 Dec. 1871 Bismarck reaffirmed these views and pointed out that the French Government, even in its dealings with Manteuffel, could only do so through regular diplomatic channels, i.e. through the German Embassy in Paris.

[6] GP i. 103–5; Herzfeld, p. 108.

Charged with the tasks of getting rid of St. Vallier and obtaining satisfaction from the French Government, Arnim was unsuccessful in both. Concerning St. Vallier, Remusat denied that diplomatic exchanges had taken place between Paris and Nancy and called St. Vallier an administrative official. Regarding the more serious incidents at Paris and Melun, the French Foreign Minister complained about the violent language in the German press.[1] Bismarck's reply was to publish the directive of 7 December in the *Kreuzzeitung*.[2]

The year ended with the appointment of Arnim as Ambassador of the German Reich to the French Republic, and Gontaut-Biron French Ambassador to Berlin.[3]

The normal diplomatic relationship of the two countries having been re-established, it was hoped that the problems and difficulties between France and Germany would be solved more speedily and amicably than heretofore. This did not prove to be the case. The recovery and recuperation of France continued unabated at an ever-increasing pace and with it Germany's anxiety and apprehension.

In January of the new year Bismarck informed Arnim of the Emperor's growing misgivings about the rearmament in France and of the increased military and political importance he placed on German occupation of French territory in view of these developments.[4] Arnim, in turn, reporting on the various financial schemes that were being discussed in Paris to pay off the French indemnity, considered the situation less alarming. In his view Germany had to protect two vital points of interest in her relationship with France: her military superiority and her financial demands. Should the French Government find it necessary to request Germany's indulgence in regard to its financial obligations, the Reich could safeguard its military preponderance without undue hardship and without increasing its occupation forces. Should France be able, on the other hand, to pay off the remaining three billion, or offer acceptable securities in their place, Germany would, indeed, have to give

[1] Arnim to Bismarck, no. 180, 17 Dec. 1871.
[2] Of 22 Dec. 1871; Herzfeld, p. 109, fn. 1.
[3] Thile to Arnim, 29 Dec. 1871; Arnim to Bismarck, 9 Jan. 1872; Gontaut-Biron, *Meine Botschafterzeit am Berliner Hofe 1872–7* (Berlin, 1909), pp. 8 ff., henceforth cited Gontaut-Biron.
[4] Bismarck to Arnim, tel. no. 18, 25 Jan. 1872.

up its dominating military position. But in this case Germany's military preponderance would no longer be necessary, Arnim thought, because France, poorer by three to four billion, would find herself in a greatly weakened condition during which the rearmament plans of M. Thiers would have slim chance of being put into effect.[1]

Arnim's prediction proved only partly correct. The economic recovery of France was more solidly founded and longer-lasting than he seemed to have realized, and French rearmament plans, though perhaps on a slightly reduced scale from their original concept, were put into effect in the following years.

There were numerous indications in late January and early February 1872 that the French were ready to enter into preliminary negotiations on the payment of the remaining three billion of the war indemnity. There were differences of opinion among members of the French Government on methods as well as on the timing of payments. Thiers was more reluctant to proceed, whereas Pouyer-Quertier wanted to start payments as soon as practicable. Arnim advised, and Bismarck agreed, that Germany's attitude in this matter should be one of reserve and that the different opinions within the French Government should be resolved before official discussions were entered into.[2] These were to be held in Berlin. Until then Arnim was directed to proceed to Rome and to present to the Pope his letter of recall.[3] His absence from Paris would indicate to the French Government that Germany was in no particular hurry to start negotiations, and this, together with the pressure of public opinion, would speed up the deliberations on this problem within the French administration.[4]

Before his departure from Paris, Arnim had a talk with the President, who told him of his latest plan regarding payment of the three billion. Thiers did not believe that France could pay the full sum by 1 May 1874, as stipulated by the peace treaty, but he hoped that two billion could be paid before this date, and one billion afterwards. The most important point, as

[1] Arnim to Bismarck, no. 18, 30 Jan. 1872.

[2] Arnim to Bismarck, no. 22, 6 Feb. 1872.

[3] Bismarck to Arnim, tel. no. 23, 25 Feb. 1872; E. Schmidt-Volkmar, *Der Kulturkampf in Deutschland 1871–1890* (Goettingen, 1962), pp. 96–8, henceforth cited Schmidt-Volkmar.

[4] Bismarck to Arnim, 19 Feb. 1872.

far as Thiers was concerned, was to terminate the occupation of French territory as soon as possible. He wanted to be reassured on this before he started financial negotiations. In his talk with Arnim, Thiers also reaffirmed his desire for peace and justified the increase and reorganization of the army by his apprehension lest France be reduced to the level of power and prestige of Belgium. Arnim thought that the President's proposals should be considered favourably.[1]

He left Paris for Berlin at the end of February and went to Rome in early March. The timing of his journey coincided with the initial phase of the *Kulturkampf* and gave rise to a host of speculations, making his trip appear of much greater importance than it actually was. It was rumoured that Arnim's trip was a political mission of the first order and closely connected with Bismarck's attempt to subdue the political opposition in the Reichstag. When Odo Russell, the British Ambassador, asked the Chancellor about these rumours, 'he was told by Bismarck that the object of the visit was only to deliver letters of recall and to attend to private affairs. He [Bismarck] did not consider that direct negotiations with the Pope were likely to lead to any good results, nor did he think them at all necessary. Direct legislation could regulate future relations between the clergy and the state without interference from Rome.'[2] A dispatch from Sir Robert Morier, British Ambassador in Munich, to Lord Granville, however, told a different story.

In a long conversation with Arnim, Sir Robert had suggested that the German Ambassador was charged to offer advantageous terms to the Pope, and that Bismarck's attitude was determined by the fact that he had in his hands the threads of a tangible ultramontane conspiracy. Arnim agreed that he was not far wrong. He had been instructed to offer the Pope the friendship and alliance of Prussia if he would exert his influence to detach the clerical party from coalitions hostile to the Empire, so that it would be no longer identified with the Guelphs, Poles and French revengists. Papal refusal meant war to the knife—no compromise was possible. Arnim did not share Bismarck's brooding suspicion of a secret conspiracy. The connection of ultramontanism with all the elements hostile to the Empire was common knowledge, but Bismarck was carried away by passion. The real danger of the situation was Bismarck's

---

[1] Arnim to Bismarck, 3 Mar. 1872; for details see Giesberg, pp. 211 ff.
[2] Taffs, p. 14; see also Schmidt-Volkmar, pp. 96–9.

position of prime minister of a state with Protestant traditions and chancellor of an empire with Catholic traditions. His own mission, he thought, would not be entirely fruitless; by it the zeal of the ultramontanes would be restrained.[1]

What, in view of these conflicting statements, was the truth? There is no indication in the archives that Arnim went to Rome for any purpose other than to present to the Pope his letter of recall. On the other hand, the documents might not tell the whole story. If Arnim did go to Rome to discuss German internal affairs with the Pope, his instructions and his reports might not have been recorded or, if they were, might not have been filed in the Foreign Ministry's archives. But it seems most unlikely that he was sent on such a mission. It can be assumed that the conversation with Morier was for Arnim an opportunity to enhance his own prestige and to expound his views on the subject rather than to confide state secrets to the British Ambassador. In any case, he mentioned nothing of the sort in his two reports from Rome. In the first, to the Emperor, Arnim told of his audience with the Pope. He noted in great detail the habits and preoccupation of the papal Court, the Pope's financial situation, and his attitude toward the recent events in Italy and Germany.[2] His second report, to Bismarck, dealt primarily with Germany's representation at the Holy See. Arnim saw the time when it might be better for the Reich to be without a permanent representative; for the time being, however, he suggested that a German churchman of independent attitude and an opponent of the Jesuits might be the best person to be accredited to the papal Court.[3]

Returning from Rome, Arnim came to Berlin, but, instead of proceeding to Paris, remained in the German capital during most of April. The reasons for his delay are not quite clear. All sorts of rumours were circulating in Paris[4] as well as in Berlin, and were reinforced by an article in the *Daily Telegraph* of 18 April, which asserted that Arnim would be carrying an

[1] Taffs, p. 15; Hohenlohe, ii. 77–8.
[2] Arnim to the Emperor, 26 Mar. 1872.
[3] Arnim to Bismarck, 30 Mar. 1872. It is interesting to note that both these predictions did in fact come true later on. According to Gontaut-Biron, however, Hohenlohe's appointment had nothing to do with Arnim's report: Gontaut-Biron to Ministère des Affaires Étrangères, 1 May 1872, *Correspondance politique, Allemagne*, vol. vi.
[4] Wesdehlen to Bismarck, tel. no. 60, 20 Apr. 1872.

ultimatum to Paris regarding the expansion of the French Army and the belligerent speeches of the President.[1] To Abeken, who queried Bismarck about these rumours, the Chancellor replied that 'these were pure inventions. Count Arnim is still here and there are no indications that he will return to his post with other than the usual instructions.'[2] It might well have been Bismarck's plan to demonstrate in this way his annoyance with the increase and reorganization of the French Army and his reluctance to evacuate French territory. At the same time he put pressure on the French Government to hasten its decision about starting negotiations for payments of the three billion.[3]

Arnim left Berlin on 27 April and with his arrival in the French capital most of the rumours subsided. Negotiations about the future payments of the French war indemnity began almost immediately.

[1] Gontaut-Biron, p. 91; Taffs, p. 8.
[2] Abeken to Bismarck, 19 Apr. 1872, and Bismarck's marginalia.
[3] *DDF* i. 140 ff.; *OLT* i. 274–6; Giesberg, pp. 214–16.

VIII

THE CONVENTION OF JUNE 1872

THE negotiations which culminated in the Franco-German agreement of 29 June 1872 were complicated. They were influenced to a considerable degree by the domestic policies of the two countries.

Reorganization and increase of the French military establishment and the debates on this subject in the French Chambers of Deputies left a lasting and deep-seated suspicion in German governmental and military circles. The reluctance of the Emperor and the Chancellor to consider the French view more sympathetically during these negotiations and the final outcome of the conference bear eloquent testimony to this attitude of suspicion.[1]

On the German side, preoccupation with the *Kulturkampf*, especially Bismarck's attempt to persuade the major European Powers to take common action at the next papal election,[2] tended to overshadow the negotiations that were going on in Paris and made the Chancellor appear hesitant in his directives and reluctant in his decisions. Arnim carried the main burden of the negotiations, which, contrary to Bismarck's original intention, were taking place in Paris. Count Henckel-Donnersmarck came to the French capital to assist the Ambassador unofficially and, at the same time, as a private citizen, to offer his 'unselfish' and 'disinterested' advice to the French Government.

Count Henckel [Bismarck informed the Emperor] will have to operate carefully and adroitly, so as to maintain his role as an expert *private citizen*, in view of the fact that he had conferred with me and has had an audience with Your Majesty; as soon as he appeared

---

[1] The French expected to achieve an immediate or, at least, a greatly accelerated evacuation of the occupied territories as soon as they had given firm or definite commitments regarding the payment of three billions. Instead they were offered only partial evacuation against partial payments. For details, see Giesberg, pp. 211–27.

[2] See pp. 86 ff. below.

as an official negotiator from our side, he would put us into the disadvantageous role of a seller who is offering his goods—the evacuation—instead of waiting for the covetousness of the buyer.[1]

Henckel's double role could not, however, be concealed. Thiers may never have been completely aware of the Count's true status, but he certainly realized that he was not a disinterested private citizen.[2]

The negotiations between Thiers and Arnim were complicated, tedious, and lengthy. Arnim's role, except for when he answered a French note on his own authority without previously consulting Berlin,[3] seemed little different from any he had played in previous, similar, negotiations. There were the usual delays in transmitting directives, obscure passages in overlapping and outdated reports, and the changes of opinions so characteristic of Arnim's work. The picture that emerges from the published official documents, both French and German, is not entirely sharp and clear, but detailed enough to convey a general impression of what was going on in Paris in May and June of 1872.

For the more discerning observer, however, discrepancies remain which apparently cannot be explained.[4] One of these is Arnim's conversation with Thiers on 15 May, as reported by the President on one hand, and by the Ambassador on the other.[5] Another, the accusation that Arnim was involved at that time in illegal financial operations, repeatedly voiced by Bismarck later on but never proved, cannot be dismissed altogether and may go far toward explaining some of Arnim's actions.[6] Bismarck's accusation derived support from a letter

[1] Bismarck to the Emperor, 23 May 1872.   [2] *Thiers*, pp. 242 ff.
[3] Arnim to Bismarck, no. 79, 20 May 1872.
[4] Herzfeld, pp. 140 ff.
[5] *GP* i. 120–21; *Thiers*, pp. 238–40.
[6] *GW* vic, 36–7; viii. 132; ix. 274. Stock-market speculations were fairly common among high government officials at that time and both Holstein and Bismarck were involved at one time or another. About Holstein, see H. Rogge, *Holstein und Hohenlohe* (Stuttgart, 1957), pp. 215–16; N. Rich, *Holstein*, i. 49–59; Trotha, *Fritz von Holstein* (Berlin, 1931), pp. 21–2. About Bismarck, J. Pindter, the grand-nephew of E. Pindter, editor of the *Norddeutsche Allgemeine Zeitung* from 1872 to 1894, writes, 'according to these notes [of E. Pindter] Bismarck used at times even the organization of the Foreign Ministry to advance the business profits of his financial adviser [Bleichroeder], without any state interests being involved at the particular time'. *Der Spiegel*, 30 Oct. 1957, p. 9; a request by the author of this study for further information on this matter brought no reply.

written by Henckel-Donnersmarck to Arnim which was found in Berlin at the time of Arnim's arrest in the autumn of 1874.[1] The letter is undated, but from the events it describes, it must have been written toward the end of August or the beginning of September 1872.[2]

Henckel, recalling his activities in Paris earlier in the year, maintained that he had

predicted the uncanny success of the loan, but once again nobody here would believe me. I showed my confidence in the transaction very profitably in my country-bumpkin way by participating in the loan to the extent of six millions and within eight days selling at a profit of five francs. One should not allow French securities to cool off in one's safe.

Bleichroeder as usual behaved foolishly, which did not astonish me.

My best wishes for the purchase of Nassenheide. I was certain that Leo Henckel would behave as a gentleman and not withdraw. But it has been a bitter affair for him.

The mysterious undertaking with a great future has not yet been born. If anything should come of it you will be informed in good time.

I am sincerely glad that my financial advice has agreed with you. I will add to-day that unless you need ready cash, do not sell Laura, Plessner and Zinkhuetten preference shares (to-day at 115). I would put a limit on Laura of 210 and on Zinkhuette of 120. I firmly believe in this course. If anything, I would get rid of Plessner. . . .[3]

Despite these intrigues and delays, the convention with France was signed by Arnim and Remusat on 29 June 1872.[4]

[1] See p. 181, n. 2 below.

[2] In May 1876, when Arnim was prosecuted for treason and his stock-market speculations were investigated, Henckel-Donnersmarck testified that the date of this letter was 30 Aug. 1872; Lueck to Foreign Ministry, 15 May 1876.

[3] Rich and Fisher, iii. 457-8, where the date is given as 30 Aug. (1874).

[4] *GP* i. 144-6.

IX

PLANS FOR A PAPAL ELECTION

ARNIM'S recall from Rome left a vacancy there which Bismarck was not over-anxious to fill immediately.[1] Political events at home made it soon desirable, however, to restore more normal relations with the Vatican. As a result, Cardinal Hohenlohe was designated German Ambassador at the Holy See, but the appointment was rejected by the Pope.[2] Rebuffed in his attempt to make peace with the Vatican, Bismarck now tried to organize a coalition of European Powers against it.

Commenting on these events after his return to Paris, Arnim suggested to the Chancellor that Germany should try to exercise its influence at the next papal election.[3] Inasmuch as new Vatican decrees had given the Pope the right to intervene directly in the administration of any German bishopric, and since no bishop could occupy an episcopal see without the Pope's approval, Germany should likewise interfere in the papal election and, like Austria, France, and Spain, should claim the right to exercise its veto. Arnim foresaw a general outcry against these 'unjust' pretensions on Germany's part, but this did not matter.

If any Pope or priest does something which he is not supposed to do, the objections of the Government are being rejected [by the Church, by declaring] that natural, divine, and canonical law are on the side of the priest and, therefore, he need not pay any attention to the law of the land, the constitution, or any similar devilish nonsense. These tactics of the ultramontanes can be copied and imitated by us with profit. If they tell us that the pretensions of a Protestant Emperor to take part in the creation of a pontifex are uncanonical

---

[1] See p. 46 above. Since Arnim's absence from Rome, a chargé d'affaires, von Derenthal, had been the German representative in the Vatican: F. Hanus, *Die preussische Vatikangesandtschaft, 1747–1920* (Munich, 1954), p. 314.

[2] Hohenlohe, ii. 79, fn. 1; Franz, p. 227; Augusta to Wilhelm I, 9 May 1872, *Die Vorgeschichte des Kulturkampfes*, pp. 243–4.

[3] Arnim to Bismarck, 7 May 1872.

and unheard of, we, on our part, can justifiably appeal to state, divine, and natural law, according to which it is unthinkable, nonsensical, and highly dangerous to leave to a herd of impotent Italian oldsters the production of the Dalai Llama, who exercises the most important governmental rights in our country.[1]

Arnim went on to suggest that Germany would not recognize a Pope elected against its will or without its approval. Should this be ignored, so much confusion could be created in the Church and in the world that the Catholic-political conspiracy would be ruined. A new Council of Constance, rival popes, and national churches could be summoned and used, 'and before a decade had passed the Roman intriguer either will lie impotent in sulphur, or will meekly request our help'.[1] It would be most important to have an emissary ready to proceed to the conclave in Rome at a moment's notice, Arnim believed, because directives seemed to have been issued to the college of cardinals to proceed with the election of a new Pope immediately after Pius IX's death and before the termination of the usual nine-day waiting-period. And, somewhat presumptuously, Arnim assured Bismarck that he would have been more restrained in his expressions had he not been ready 'to assume the responsibilities for all consequences of a policy which would liberate Germany from its most dangerous enemies'.[1]

Arnim's report of 7 May arrived in Berlin on the 10th. Four days later a circular directive was sent to the major Prussian missions abroad, inquiring whether the governments would be willing to exchange views and, later, enter into an agreement concerning steps to be taken at the next papal election.[2] In this directive Bismarck, like Arnim before him, pointed to the basic interests which any government with a sizeable number of Catholic subjects must have in the election of a Pope. This the more so because the powers of the head of the Church were far-reaching and assumed almost sovereign rights in the various countries in which they were being exercised. 'A Pope to whom all or the majority of the European sovereigns would deny recognition because of formal or material reasons would be as unthinkable as a bishop who would want to exercise his

---

[1] Arnim to Bismarck, 7 May 1872.
[2] Circular directive, 14 May 1872, printed in *Staatsarchiv* vol. 24/ii. 266.

rights in a country whose government did not recognize him.'[1]
These basic considerations were made more important and
assumed greater significance by the pronouncements of the
Vatican Council because they gave the Pope the power to
take over the rights of a bishop in each diocese and to exercise
papal authority in each local bishopric. Thus, in principle, the
Pope took the place of the bishop and it only depended on the
Pope when he wanted to occupy the place of the bishops against
the wishes of the government. 'The bishops were only his tools,
his subordinates, with no responsibility of their own; toward
the government they have become officials of a foreign sovereign,
of a sovereign who, because of his infallibility, has become an
absolute one—more absolute than any absolute monarch in the
world.'[1] Before any man could assume this post, the governments should ask themselves if this person offered sufficient
guarantees against any abuse of power on his part. In addition,
there were the usual uncertainties about the safeguards at
a papal election and the ineffectiveness of the right of veto by
Spain, France, and Austria. For all these reasons, the directive
concluded, it would seem desirable for the governments concerned to consider these problems in due time and, if possible,
to consult with each other on how to deal with them.

The replies were disappointing.[2] The British and Russian
Governments pointed out that their position was quite different
from other countries in this respect. In the case of Britain,
neither the Pope nor the bishops were officially recognized,
although the bishops were not being restricted in the exercise
of their functions. Under these circumstances Britain could not
claim any influence at a papal election. The Russian Government declared that it had no trouble with its Roman Catholic
bishops. The publication of the papal dogma of infallibility
had been prohibited and the officials of the Church were fully
aware of the ruthless punishment they would suffer if they came
in conflict with the laws of the State. For these reasons there
was very little interest in a papal election in St. Petersburg.

Reaction from the other states that had been approached in
this matter was favourable. The Vienna cabinet expressed its
willingness to discuss ways and means of preventing abuses
at a future election of a Pope. Bavaria welcomed Prussia's

---

[1] Ibid.   [2] Unsigned memorandum, Berlin, 10 July 1872.

initiative and looked forward to a speedy agreement. The Government of Portugal let it be known that it shared Prussia's views about the significance of the next papal election and considered negotiations among the Powers very desirable. Madrid too approved of the Chancellor's scheme, and the Italian Government was reported to have already considered the implications of a papal election and welcomed Prussian initiative.[1]

These replies, however, had little significance. What mattered was that Britain and Russia had declined and France, for obvious reasons, could not be expected to take the same side as Prussia.[2] This was recognized by Bismarck, who, through a newspaper article by Busch, tried to hide his disappointment and to minimize the failure of his diplomatic action.[3] As far as the papal election of 1878 was concerned, no measures suggested by Bismarck were taken by any of the Powers and his circular of 14 May 1872 had been all but forgotten.

[1] Unsigned memorandum, Berlin, 10 July 1872.
[2] Arnim to Bismarck, 28 June 1872.
[3] Busch, ii. 265–6.

X

EARLY CLASHES AND DIFFERENCES
OF OPINION

ARNIM, after signing the convention with France on 29 June, went on leave to Germany and stayed there throughout the summer and part of the autumn. In September he went to Berlin to gather information and to familiarize himself with the Chancellor's views, particularly in regard to the outcome of the September (1872) meeting of the three emperors. But Bismarck had left for Varzin without receiving Arnim, although Arnim had reported his presence to the Foreign Ministry and had requested a meeting with the Chancellor. Thile, the State Secretary, had just been dismissed from his position because of the famous decoration incident following the three emperors' meeting, and Arnim had to leave for Paris with no briefing at all.[1]

The reasons for Bismarck's behaviour are difficult to ascertain. It could not have been a mere oversight, because Arnim had reported his presence in Berlin several days before Bismarck's departure. It is equally difficult to believe that the Chancellor deliberately avoided a meeting, because there was, at the time, no apparent reason for doing so. Be that as it may, some of Arnim's misguided activities in Paris in the following months can be attributed to his lack of instructions, and Bismarck can be blamed for this at least in part.[2] It was not without justification that Arnim could write later on: 'The fact that Prince Bismarck refused to see Count Arnim in September 1872 became disastrous for later developments. . . . As a result, the Ambassador was deprived of the possibility to inform himself

---

[1] *Pro Nihilo*, pp. 6–7.

[2] In *Pro Nihilo*, p. 7, Arnim writes that he intended to resign because of this incident, but that he had changed his mind. To this Bismarck wrote on the margin, 'Too bad, I had hoped so.' It is, however, questionable whether this was Bismarck's feeling at the time (Sept. 1872) or whether it was his view in 1876 after the Arnim affair had run its full course.

of the attitude of the Chancellor. This could have changed, for the situation in France had become completely different.'[1]

After his return to Paris, Arnim sent a long report to the Foreign Ministry which contained many significant features.[2] It reviewed the political situation in France, the temper of the country, its military and economic strength, and its position in Europe. Considering these factors, Arnim concluded that France's recovery was all but complete. The French believed that their standing among the Powers of Europe was better than it had been in 1870; this might be based on self-delusion, Arnim commented, but their new confidence was a fact one had to accept.

The President of the French Republic [he wrote] does not believe in an Austro-German intimacy. Just as little as in a Russo-German [one]. . . . The general impression which the French public receives and the interpretations which it feels justified to make from the official and non-official Russian pronouncements are not in accordance with the intentions of Emperor Alexander. Every means is being used from here to make the Russians aware of [their] solidarity of interests [with France]. . . .[2]

The one man who had brought about this state of affairs in France was Thiers. And with the signing of the convention of 29 June Thiers's usefulness for Germany had come to an end, Arnim believed. Were he allowed to stay on, his facility for procuring large sums of money would be employed in forging armaments against Germany which, in the end, would be used by Gambetta if Germany did not intervene beforehand. The easiest and best way to alter this development—which Arnim believed inevitable—was to effect a revolution while part of France was still occupied. It could be a repetition of the Paris Commune on a larger scale and a change of government under German supervision and sponsorship.

Arnim's evaluation of France's position on the morrow of the three emperors' meeting was valid and fair.[3] Whatever arguments could be marshalled against it, the fact remained

[1] *Pro Nihilo*, p. 8.

[2] Arnim to Bismarck, 3 Oct. 1872; see *GP* i. 150–3, where this report is printed with some omissions. For the parts that were left out there, see Appendix II of this study.

[3] For other contemporary opinions, see *DDF* i. 182–3; Taffs, pp. 52, 55; E. Wertheimer, *Graf Julius Andrassy*, 3 vols. (Stuttgart, 1910–13), ii. 75; Newton, ii. 34.

that France was no longer as isolated as Bismarck had wished or had made it appear.[1] It was also an undisputed fact that the country's internal position was strong and secure. Gambetta's chances of coming to power were difficult to assess, but in any case, and from the German point of view, the situation was sombre enough. Arnim's recommendations were radical and extreme, but no more so than some of Bismarck's own schemes in the past.[2]

The Chancellor's reaction appears in a letter to the Emperor.[3] In it he rejected Arnim's ideas completely—his premisses as well as his conclusions, which, he said, were wrong and contradictory. 'What would Europe say to such a policy?' he exclaimed. He, who not so long ago had ridiculed the idea of a public opinion in Europe. Besides, Bismarck said, Arnim had spent only a few days in Paris during the last months, not enough to form a sound opinion on the situation there. Arnim was again in Germany, Bismarck reminded the Emperor, and under the circumstances would do better to return to his post.[4]

Arnim's presence in Germany so soon after an extensive leave deserves special attention. It seems that he desired an appointment to the Upper House of the Prussian Diet in order to take part in the deliberations on the rural district organization (*Kreisordnung*)[5] in which the conservative elements opposed any attempts by the Government to change the existing order. Arnim had apparently decided, in view of the Chancellor's refusal to receive him during his previous stay in Berlin, that his employment in the foreign service was no longer possible.[6] As a member of the Upper House he would be independent

[1] This does not appear very clearly from the report as printed in the *Grosse Politik*, for the passage pertaining to it has been left out. Thus Arnim's report appears to be much worse and disjointed than it actually is, and Bismarck's attack on it (Bismarck to the Emperor, 14 Oct. 1872, *GP* i. 153–4) seems justified. This latter document (Bismarck to the Emperor, 14 Oct. 1872) is also incomplete as printed in the *Grosse Politik*. For the text of the last paragraph, that was left out, see Appendix III of this study.

[2] Such as the creation of a Hungarian Legion during the Austro-Prussian War of 1866, and the plan to employ a force of southern Slavs to threaten Austria during the Franco-Prussian War.

[3] Bismarck to the Emperor, 14 Oct. 1872.

[4] Arnim had left Paris for Baden-Baden on 8 Oct.; he left Berlin on 24 Oct.; Gontaut-Biron to Ministère des Affaires Étrangères, 24 Oct. 1872, *Correspondance politique, Allemagne*, vol. vii.

[5] Bismarck to the Emperor, 14 Oct. 1872, Appendix III of this study.

[6] See p. 89 above.

and could oppose the Chancellor's policy as he saw fit.[1] But Bismarck was not anxious to have Arnim in the Upper House. In his letter to the Emperor he expressed the opinion that Arnim was indispensable from his very important post, and although there were 'serious shortcomings by which the value of the unusual talents of this gifted statesman is being injured and the weight of his reporting and of his judgement are being weakened . . . taken with caution, his reports will not only be interesting but also useful'.[2] For these reasons he asked the Emperor not to appoint Arnim to the Upper House.

Bismarck's arguments and his characterization of Arnim are interesting. Why this sudden praise? The most obvious explanation would be that the Chancellor wanted Arnim away from Berlin because he did not want him to join the Opposition and stir up more trouble in the Upper House. The best way to accomplish this was to praise Arnim's abilities to the Emperor, who, having received Arnim in audience, might have been influenced by him.[3] Bismarck's scheme is revealed by the closing sentence in his letter to the Emperor. 'As long as Your Majesty's confidence allocated to him [Arnim] a post of such fateful importance, he will have to be asked to devote his undivided efforts to it.' Bismarck was successful and Arnim returned to Paris, having failed to get the desired appointment.

It might have been reasonable to assume that Arnim would have drawn the logical conclusions from his experience in Berlin. His opinion that Thiers was unsuitable had met with definite disapproval and opposition from the Chancellor and no great encouragement from the Emperor. His desire to be appointed to the Upper House had been thwarted, and, since he had no intention of leaving the foreign service, the only thing to do, under the circumstances, would have been to toe the line. But for this Arnim had too much self-confidence and pride and was too foolhardy to boot. He apparently believed that he could, in time, and even from abroad, exert enough

---

[1] Wahl, i. 126 ff.

[2] Bismarck to the Emperor, 14 Oct. 1872, Appendix III of this study.

[3] In a note to Bismarck of 4 Dec. 1872 the Emperor informed the Chancellor that he had seen Arnim before the Ambassador's return to Paris. At that time Arnim had said that he felt compelled always to express his conviction in his reports, though he realized that he might have gone too far, because it had never been his intention to *bring about* a conflict with France.

influence to change the Emperor's views regarding German policy toward France.

Arnim's first step in this direction was to talk with Manteuffel almost immediately after his return from Germany, when he visited the General's headquarters in Nancy. He must have counted on Manteuffel's dislike of and opposition to Bismarck and on the General's influence with the Emperor, which had been so apparent on the occasion of his negotiations with Pouyer-Quertier in August 1871.[1] But many things had happened since then and Manteuffel had given up his opposition to the Chancellor, which, in any case, had never been very deep-seated. At Nancy, Arnim talked to St. Vallier and Manteuffel and freely expressed to them his opinion of Thiers, the dangers of a republican regime in France, and his own preference for a monarchical restoration. Hearing this, St. Vallier was disturbed,[2] Manteuffel plainly bewildered. Following Arnim's visit, Manteuffel wrote to Bismarck and asked for an explanation.[3] In his reply Bismarck disavowed Arnim and assured Manteuffel that the Government's policy and his own views had not changed.[4] When the Chancellor asked Arnim to present his side of the story, Arnim replied evasively. Manteuffel's letter was based on a misunderstanding, he wrote. He had discussed the political situation with St. Vallier; the restoration of the monarchy he had mentioned only to Manteuffel, who had agreed with this whole-heartedly, aside from some minor reservations concerning the French payment of the indemnity. Arnim implied that Manteuffel had fabricated most of the conversation which he had ascribed to him and St. Vallier, and he complained that the General should have written first to him before reporting this incident to Berlin.[5]

[1] See p. 59 above.
[2] St. Vallier to Thiers, 29 Oct. 1872, *OLT* ii. 119–24.
[3] Manteuffel to Bismarck, 1 Nov. 1872. Later on, at the trial, Arnim indicated that this letter was the beginning of his conflict with Bismarck. *Darstellung der in der Untersuchungsache wider den Wirklichen Geheimen Rath Grafen von Arnim vor dem koeniglichen Stadtgericht zu Berlin im Dezember 1874 stattgehabten oeffentlichen Verhandlungen* (Berlin, 1875), p. 111, henceforth cited *Darstellung*. See also Herzfeld, p. 232.
[4] Bismarck to Foreign Ministry (Manteuffel), 5 Nov. 1872; Manteuffel to Foreign Ministry (Bismarck), 5 Nov. 1872; St. Vallier to Thiers, 6 Nov. 1872 *DDF* i. 190–1.
[5] Bismarck to Arnim, 8 Nov. 1872; Arnim to Bismarck, 12 Nov. 1872.

This explanation made it difficult for Bismarck to pursue the matter further and he decided to let it go at that. He wrote to Manteuffel, however, to tell St. Vallier, 'whatever Count Arnim may have said [on that occasion], if he had given any indication of a hostile attitude toward Thiers and his Government, he had done so [on his own] and had not expressed His Majesty's nor my own opinion'.[1]

In his report of 3 October Arnim had expressed certain opinions and had made allegations regarding the attitude of the press toward Thiers and Gambetta.[2] He had been asked by Balan to be more specific[3] and after his return to Paris had complied with this request. The most significant part of this report, which he now sent to Berlin, was his complaint about German newspapers attacking legitimist circles in France and the effects of these attacks in Germany. This 'derision of the monarchical tendencies of a respectable part of the French nation', he wrote, 'will not add to the strengthening of monarchical principles in Germany'.[4] He stressed once more that his conviction as expressed previously (i.e. in his report of 3 October) had not changed and that nothing had happened in France in the meantime to invalidate his views that '(1) the contagious quality of French democracy increased every day, and (2) the Government of M. Thiers was more dangerous to us and to a definite peace, than any form of monarchical government'.[4] This is Arnim's first open avowal of the royalist cause and of a monarchical restoration in France. It could have been that the conversation he had had with the Emperor during his recent stay in Germany had encouraged this view, because he mentioned in the same dispatch that the Emperor had asked him to report further details on these matters. This he did two days later. He reaffirmed his views but suggested less violent measures to deal with French problems and was careful not to offend the views and prejudices of the Emperor.[5] He used the customary arguments and well-worn phrases in describing the political situation in France and the dangers to Germany. He characterized the President and his policies and, to illustrate

[1] Bismarck to Manteuffel, 17 Nov. 1872, *GW* xiv/ii. 842–3.
[2] See p. 90 above.
[3] Balan to Arnim, 21 Oct. 1872.
[4] Arnim to Balan, 10 Nov. 1872.
[5] Arnim to Bismarck, 12 Nov. 1872.

the threat which Thiers constituted to Germany, he para-
phrased one of his slogans as 'La Republic est ce qui me permet
de diviser le plus', to which Bismarck noted on the margin,
'Tant mieux pour nous'. And, when Arnim, again to disparage
Thiers, mentioned that the President's policies were full of
contradictions and were disuniting all Frenchmen, Bismarck
wrote, 'Should *we* work for their unification?'

Arnim's other arguments were equally ineffective and ill
chosen. He stressed the dangers of republicanism to Italy and
Spain but considered Germany immune to it; he favoured the
conservative elements in France, but admitted that they too
were full of hatred and revenge toward Germany. As to the
policy that should be pursued by Germany, Arnim, contrary
to his earlier views, now found it impossible to advocate any
radical measures or extreme steps. He recommended that the
German press should not take Thiers's part as much as it had
at the time of the President's conflict with the conservative and
monarchical parties. Otherwise, everything should remain as
before.

A caustic directive by Balan contained Bismarck's reply.[1]
The Chancellor neither shared Arnim's views nor agreed with
his conclusions. He insisted that his policy prevail, 'and that the
representatives of His Majesty the Emperor outwardly refrain
from expressing any contrary opinions abroad'.[2]

Unlike the sarcastic and deprecating remarks of the Chancellor, the Emperor was favourably impressed by Arnim's
report and noted on the margin: 'These explanations of the
Count are very relevant. The idea of utilizing the press requires
careful wording, however, and should be well considered.
There is no doubt much truth in these arguments. W 17/10/72.'

[1] Balan to Arnim, 23 Nov. 1872, *GP* i. 155–6. Omitted there are Arnim's
marginalia: 'Dann instruirt doch Eure Kosaken' (page 155, middle of second paragraph); 'Ganz meiner Meinung' (page 155, lines 7–8 from bottom); 'Das versteht
sich wohl von selbst' (page 156, last paragraph). Of interest too is the last sentence
of Bucher's instruction to Balan for the preparation of his directive to Arnim
(Bucher to Balan, Varzin, 19 Nov. 1872), 'Der Bericht vom 12. widerlegt durch
den ersten Theil den zweiten und erschuettert den Glauben des Fuersten [Bis-
marck], dass der Berichterstatter [Arnim] sich je zu objectiver, von Persoenlich-
keiten und fixen Ideen befreiten Beurtheilung der Zustaende erheben koenne.'

[2] Balan to Arnim, 23 Nov. 1872, *GP* i. 155–6.

XI

THE GOVERNMENTAL CRISIS IN
FRANCE, NOVEMBER 1872

THE governmental crisis in France in November 1872[1] was
a severe test for Arnim's political sagacity, power of
observation, and insight. At the beginning of the crisis,
when a deadlock between the President and the Assembly
seemed imminent and Thiers's defeat a possibility, Arnim
exulted over the turn of events which he maintained he had
predicted freely and frequently.[2] When, after some time,
Thiers's defeat did not materialize, and no solution to the crisis
seemed in sight, Arnim became uneasy and more cautious. The
President might still outwit his opponent, he thought, but the
outcome was impossible to foresee. But, even if the President
should still stage a comeback, he would have lost a great deal
of authority and would never again be the central power in
France. According to Arnim, this was a victory for Germany;
a victory which would be lasting and which he had predicted.[3]

Far from being a victory for Germany or for Arnim, it was
rather an attempt by the Ambassador to cover up his erroneous
assumptions and foolish predictions. When Thiers's continuation in office seemed assured, Arnim used his old arguments and
tried to discredit the President and his policies.

Because Thiers had brought about this crisis by his own
stubbornness and vanity, and because this was not the first
time he had let his emotions override reasons of state, he could
no longer be trusted, Arnim reported.[4] All parties were deserting
Thiers, he wrote. Gambetta and the radicals were ready and
waiting in the background. But should Thiers remain in power

[1] For details on the crisis, see G. Hanotaux, *Contemporary France*, 4 vols. (London,
1903–9), i. 530–3.
[2] Arnim to Bismarck, no. 139, 14 Nov. 1872; Arnim to Foreign Ministry, tel.
no. 59, 19 Nov. 1872; Arnim to Foreign Ministry, tel. no. 61, 21 Nov. 1872.
[3] Arnim to Bismarck, 24 Nov. 1872.
[4] Arnim to Foreign Ministry, 25 Nov. 1872.

he would become a source of serious disturbance for the monarchical governments of Europe.[1]

Arnim's prediction was in clear contradiction to his earlier prophecy that Thiers would have no influence if he remained as the head of the Government, and it completely ignored Balan's directive of 23 November.[2]

When, by the end of the month, the crisis had been resolved and Thiers was still President of the Republic, his power and influence intact, Arnim found himself in a difficult position. His fears had been exaggerated, his prophecies had been false, his prejudices exposed. But he did not recant; he admitted neither faults nor mistakes. In his single-minded and stubborn opposition to Thiers and the republican Government, he carried on as usual.

Recapitulating the events of the past fortnight, Arnim repeated most of his previous clichés. The settlement was only temporary and a new crisis would follow. Everything would collapse. France had suffered a terrible blow and great loss of power through the crisis and would be unable to recover for some time to come.[3]

Going over those of Arnim's reports which had arrived in Berlin during the crisis in France and comparing them with some German newspaper reports for the same period, Bismarck believed that he could detect similar anti-Thiers tendencies. To clarify the matter, he requested an investigation by his press chief, Aegidi. Aegidi explained that, on previous orders from the Chancellor, he had instructed various papers—such as the *Spenersche*, the *Koelnische*, and the *Norddeutsche Allgemeine Zeitung*—that the German Government observed an attitude of strict non-interference regarding French internal affairs.[4] During the crisis, the officially inspired press in France, in order to intimidate the opposition, let it be known that Germany would intervene should Thiers be defeated. Following

---

[1] Arnim to Balan, 29 Nov. 1872; see also T. E. Mullen, *The Role of Henri de Blowitz in International Affairs 1871–1903* (University Microfilm, no. 59–6950), pp. 34–8.

[2] Balan to Arnim, 23 Nov. 1872, *GP* i. 155–6.

[3] Arnim to Balan, 30 Nov. 1872; Bismarck's marginal comments to the last part of this report were: 'Simply not true! Why the earlier pessimism. If *we* should burden ourselves with the thankless and stupid task to consolidate France and to give it a monarchical order, the country will, to our detriment, soon recover.'

[4] Aegidi to Bismarck, 3 Dec. 1872.

Aegidi's instructions, some papers, especially the *Spenersche* and the *Norddeutsche Allgemeine Zeitung*, maintained and reiterated the view that the German Government would do nothing of the sort. The effect of this was none too favourable for Thiers, however, and, as these charges and countercharges were repeated several times, opposition to the President increased. This anti-governmental tendency was further heightened by the reports of the Paris correspondent of the *Spenersche Zeitung*, Herr Landsberg, who maintained close contact with the German Embassy, and by those of the *National Zeitung*, written by Dr. Beckmann, who was employed by the Embassy and was paid out of special funds. This unsatisfactory arrangement in Paris would be rectified shortly by sending to the French capital a pro-Thiers correspondent, Herr Lindau.[1] The over-all picture that emerged, Aegidi continued, was as follows: the *Norddeutsche Allgemeine Zeitung* took the position of a calm observer and objected to the continuous annoyances of the French press; the *Spenersche Zeitung*, which in general was neither for nor against Thiers, showed through its Paris correspondent some slight tendencies against the policies of the President.[2] Only the *National Zeitung* was completely opposed to Thiers. In closing, Aegidi noted that, although the editor of the *Spenersche Zeitung*, Dr. Wehrenpfenning, was a personal acquaintance of Arnim, he was not under the Ambassador's influence, but was, on the contrary, very anxious to obtain official guidance and directives.[3]

Aegidi's report made no visible impression on Bismarck. To Manteuffel he deplored the anti-Thiers attitude of the German press, which, he wrote, he had no means of bridling or directing from Varzin. He asked that Thiers be informed confidentially through St. Vallier that no change had occurred in the German Government's attitude. The King shared his opinion, he said, and any recent misunderstandings would be cleared up in short order.[4] To Balan too the Chancellor expressed his disapproval

[1] On Beckmann, Landsberg, and Lindau, see pp. 135, n. 4, 142–3, 152, n. 4, 170, 172–3. below.

[2] According to Aegidi, Landsberg had been one of those detractors of Thiers who was inclined to presuppose an understanding between the French President, Gambetta, and the radicals. To this, the Emperor noted: '[A fact] which has been completely confirmed.' See also Gontaut-Biron, p. 179.

[3] Aegidi (to Bismarck), 3 Dec. 1872; (Aegidi) memorandum, 9 Dec. 1872.

[4] Bismarck to Manteuffel, 3 Dec. 1872, *GW* xiv/ii. 844; St. Vallier to Thiers, 6 Nov. 1872, *DDF* i. 190–1.

of the attitude of the official press and the pernicious tendencies in Arnim's reports, which he said were against the interest of the State, and asked Balan to inform the Emperor accordingly. Arnim should be ordered to cease this kind of policy forthwith.[1]

The Emperor, however, did not share his Chancellor's views. There were, he wrote, two aspects in Arnim's political views which had to be noted:

(1) The dangers he describes if the republic consolidates itself in France and the dangers which will arise from it for the monarchical principle in Europe.

(2) The steps My Government will have to take in view of these dangers.

ad 1 I have to support Arnim's view. We cannot conceal the fact that the threefold proclamation of the republic in France has found supporters throughout Europe; that it admits, for the past eight years, all liberal ideas and that its goals are republican tendencies and their realizations.

ad 2 Naturally I cannot condone those measures which would involve us in an open fight with the republic of Thiers. I believe, however, with Arnim that it is not a good thing if our official organs put up Thiers as an idol and that only he can govern France. How insecure his position is has been demonstrated during the past two weeks; if he falls, nobody will know what will happen. Therefore, we must not do anything to remove him, especially as long as he pays regularly. But he must not be idolized either. Wilhelm[2]

The Chancellor's reply was essentially a defence of his policy and a reiteration of his belief in the *Buendnisunfaehigkeit* of a republican France.[3] According to him, Thiers's position in the recent crisis, none too secure to begin with, had been further endangered by attacks in the press which came from persons close to the German Embassy in Paris. The German press too had contributed to these attacks and along the very same lines which Arnim had followed in his report of 10 November.

While Bismarck did not say so explicitly, he strongly implied that Arnim had been behind this action and had been using Embassy press funds to oppose his policy. This was in clear contradiction to Aegidi's reports of 3 and 9 December, which

---

[1] Bismarck to Balan, 3 Dec. 1872, *GP* i. 156–7.
[2] The Emperor (to Bismarck), 4 Dec. 1872.
[3] Bismarck to the Emperor, 5 Dec. 1872.

had stated that the only anti-Thiers articles that could be charged to Arnim were those written by Beckmann in the *National Zeitung*.

Bismarck now justified his support of Thiers to the Emperor by asserting that any other French Government would, after a token payment, cease to fulfil its financial obligations; in this, the Chancellor wrote, it would most likely be supported by several of the European Powers. The responsibility for such a contingency would be difficult to bear for any German minister; still, it would not be the greatest danger resulting from a change of governments. The greatest danger would be when France would be able once more to contract alliances with the monarchical powers of Europe. This ability it lacked for the time being, because as a republic it was insecure and divided and it would continue in this state, perhaps even to a greater extent, under Gambetta or a similar government.[1] For the united monarchical states of Europe, this present government was quite safe. By its warning example it demonstrated how a country under a republican form of government would weaken and isolate herself. In Germany republican sympathies had declined ever since the Paris Commune. This trend would be reversed, however, if Germany were to assist in the establishment of a monarchy in France; for the first step of this new government would be to seek allies against the Reich, and it would become clear to the German people that this dangerous result had been brought about by the policies of its own government.

Having thus intimidated the Emperor with the prospective loss of the French indemnity—to which Wilhelm attached very great importance—and with the curious argument of a rise of republicanism in Germany should a monarchy be established in France, Bismarck further confused the issue by allowing that a restoration of the Bonapartes would not be quite as bad as that of the House of Orleans or the Bourbons. It should be made known in France, Bismarck continued, that Germany would request fresh guarantees and safeguards for the maintenance of peace from any new government in France.[2]

---

[1] See, however, Bismarck's memorandum to the Emperor of (19) June 1873, after the fall of Thiers, p. 121 below.

[2] *GP* i. 156, fn. *.

To this report the Chancellor added a handwritten note in which he reminded the Emperor of his hesitations at the time of Arnim's appointment to Paris because of the Ambassador's inability to separate his personal impressions from his political judgements.

I had, however, not counted that in Paris too his political judgement would be suppressed to the extent that his tendentious and factually contradictory reports actually bear witness to. I had hoped that the importance of the position and the seriousness of the situation would weigh more heavily with him. For the time being, and in view of the confidence which Your Majesty has granted me in this matter so graciously for so many years in the past, I would like to ask Your Majesty not to ascribe any importance to the reports of Count Arnim which an objective and conscientious presentation might otherwise require.[1]

But the Emperor seemed unimpressed by the Chancellor's arguments. For the time being, at least, he held to his own convictions and repeated his previous opinion. There should be no attack against Thiers, but neither should he be made an idol. 'An old monarchical state like Prussia, now at the head of Germany, must *never favour* a republic as such; but, *faute de mieux*, it might tolerate one.'[2]

Bismarck was not pleased with the Emperor's attitude. Together with his ill health and the reverses he had suffered in the field of domestic policy, to be rebuffed in his own department of foreign affairs was difficult to bear. He felt that the Emperor's confidence in him was on the decline and that he was out of favour with every member of the royal house. It was hard and degrading for him to argue, before the King, with such an unscrupulous and frivolous egoist as Harry von Arnim about his rights as Minister.[3]

Meantime, while defending his policy at Court, the Chancellor directed Arnim to curtail the press activities of the Embassy. As a first step in this direction, Arnim was informed that the subsidy to Beckmann would be discontinued.[4] This was

---

[1] Bismarck to the Emperor, 5 Dec. 1872.
[2] The Emperor to Bismarck, 12 Dec. 1872.
[3] Bismarck to Roon, 13 Dec. 1872, *GW* xiv/ii. 844–5.
[4] Buelow II to Arnim, 30 Nov. 1872. On Arnim's relationship with German journalists in Paris, see Rich and Fisher, *Holstein*, iii. 32–3.

in retaliation for the alleged press activities of the Embassy during the governmental crisis in France. Arnim strongly objected and asserted that because Beckmann was the only man on his staff who had contacts with journalists and politicians in Paris he was indispensable.[1] Told that there were no funds for press purposes and that Beckmann would have to go, Arnim replied that no funds were being spent for such purposes and that Beckmann was being paid for intelligence services.[2] Bismarck was unrelenting. Sums spent on dissemination of news in Paris, which were allotted from secret funds and the *Welfenfond*, and for which he had to account, Bismarck wrote, had not been used for their intended purposes. Beckmann's activities during the recent crisis had been in opposition to the policies of the Government. As for intelligence services, they were of little use and money spent for them was usually wasted.[3]

The after-effects of the crisis, which began with Thiers's speech in the Assembly on 13 November, continued throughout most of December. Arnim's reports during this period were more balanced and in a calmer vein than those he had submitted during the previous month. He noted with satisfaction the consolidation of the rightist Opposition and the possibility of Thiers's dissolving the Assembly. Failing that, the President would have to rely more on the conservative parties in the future.[4] In any event, even should a new government take over Germany would not suffer appreciably as far as its financial demands were concerned, though continuous political upheavals would have a detrimental effect on the final stages of the war-indemnity transactions, which Thiers intended to accelerate.[5]

Aside from this somewhat laboured exposition, Arnim's observations were sound. Following the demands of the Assembly, Thiers reshuffled his cabinet and did take some conservatives into his Government.[6] Arnim also reported that it was believed in Paris that there existed a connection between

---

[1] Arnim to Buelow II, 3 Dec. 1872.
[2] Arnim to Buelow II, 11 Dec. 1872.
[3] Bismarck to Arnim, 20 Dec. 1872.
[4] Arnim to Balan, nos. 160, 161, 6 Dec. 1872.
[5] (Arnim to Foreign Ministry, 12 Dec. 1872), Balan to Bismarck, 13 Dec. 1872.
[6] For a comparison of Arnim's views with those of other observers during this period, see Gontaut-Biron, pp. 181–2, 193; Radolinsky to Bismarck, 22 Dec. 1872.

Gambetta and the German Government and between Gambetta's followers and democratic circles in Germany. This observation, probably meant to draw the attention of the Emperor, provoked the Chancellor's wrath. Once again he expounded his views and policies toward France, repeating in essence what he had told the Emperor two weeks previously.[1]

Of interest here are Arnim's marginalia on Bismarck's directive, which were omitted by the editors of the *Grosse Politik*. To Bismarck's statement that he considered Arnim's conviction that any French Government would fulfil its financial obligations an error and a very risky assumption, the Ambassador noted, 'Not at all, Henckel [Donnersmarck] is entirely of the same opinion'. To the Chancellor's view that Germany might have to draw the sword again to satisfy its demands if a new government should come into power by force, Arnim noted, 'Really'. To the statement that France's enmity forced Germany to keep her weak and that it would be acting against her own interest to allow her to consolidate herself under a monarchy, Arnim wrote, 'Nothing would be weaker than Henry V'. When the Chancellor alleged that he might be prosecuted if he pursued such a treasonable policy to make France strong, united, and able to conclude alliances by allowing her to become a monarchy, Arnim remarked dryly, 'On the basis of what law?'

At Bismarck's exclamation of what a horror a republican anarchy would be in Germany, Arnim, in a neat exchange of roles, put on the margin, 'The republic is by no means an anarchy! Thiers as the suppressor of the anarchy is stronger than most of the royal governments.'

To the statement that a French Republic would find it extremely difficult to have a monarchical ally against Germany, Arnim noted, 'I beg your pardon'.

Bismarck's regret at finding himself in disagreement with the Ambassador on fundamental points of his policy is answered by Arnim's exclamation, 'What horrible exaggeration!'

To Bismarck's admonition that he should examine his impressions of French and German conditions more carefully because his dispatches were being incorporated into official reports and presented to the Emperor, to official bodies, and

[1] Bismarck to Arnim, 20 Dec. 1872, *GP* i. 157–62.

even to other cabinets, Arnim noted, 'I have really written only to you' and 'Indeed'.

To the Chancellor's reproach about Arnim's use of the indirect pronoun in his remarks about connections between the German Government and Gambetta, Arnim wrote, 'One, is Monsieur Humbert' (King of Italy?).

To Bismarck's insinuation concerning the dubious connections which the Embassy in Paris was maintaining, Arnim noted, 'What is the meaning of this? Obviously there must have been some gossip.'[1]

Arnim elaborated his marginal comments into a lengthy reply.[2] Bismarck had Arnim's statements checked and compared with similar previous ones and had these noted on the margin. Arnim's reply to Bismarck's many and various charges centred on only one point: the Chancellor's assertion of the different points of view that existed between them on fundamental aspects of policy. Arnim steadfastly maintained that there were none; that he and the Chancellor were in agreement on the main issue, which was to keep France isolated, and that they differed only on the means of achieving this.

Returning to Paris last October, Arnim wrote, he had found Thiers's power and stature considerably increased. He had become capable—so it had seemed to Arnim—of concluding alliances.

In his report of 12 November, however, the Ambassador had written—and this is quoted on the margin—'the continuation of the present regime is only useful to wild radicalism, the programme of which goes hand in hand with revenge and with the fight against all monarchies and the entire order of Europe'. It was under that impression, Arnim continued, that he had written his report of 3 October. Quoted here is the following sentence: 'It is questionable even today if Thiers, who is believed to have concluded a pact with the agitator [i.e. Gambetta], is still a match for him.' Upon his second return to Paris in October 1872, Arnim had found Thiers still more powerful and those Powers in Europe which were unsympathetic to Germany well pleased. Under these circumstances he

---

[1] See also *Pro Nihilo*, pp. 11–13.

[2] Arnim to Bismarck, 3 Jan. 1873; this was printed, with minor changes, in *Pro Nihilo*, pp. 23–6.

regarded the President's attempts to secure his powers for several more years not without misgivings, especially because Thiers endeavoured to organize the vital forces of the country by shifting them once toward the government parties, then toward those of the revolution, for a fight against Germany. Noted here is, 'This he did not really see according to [his] reports?' and the quotation, 'The total amount of power which he [Thiers] accumulates will pass into other hands [Gambetta's]. Report of 3 October.' From this point of view, Arnim went on, he had recommended that Thiers's position should not be supported by the inspired German press as unconditionally as it had been in the past. And on the margin:

In the report of 3 October Count Arnim recommends to *bring about* a crisis, out of which there would emerge either Gambetta or a government depending on Germany. We would be justified . . . in crushing Gambetta. He [Arnim] advises us to withdraw our support from Thiers.

Report of 29 November: The Ambassador adheres to his opinion that the Government of the President will have to be, from now on, a source of serious disturbance for monarchical Europe.

Report of 9 December: One can assume that it will be very difficult for the President to govern if he does not simply decide to govern with a conservative majority.

This was the last of the marginal notes with quotations and summaries from previous reports by Arnim. Obviously it was not difficult to show that there were contradictions in his reports and that his expressions were not always clear and precise. But what did this prove? These facts could have been established several years previously through an analysis of his Roman reports. At this point it could hardly have been news to Bismarck. It is difficult to guess what the Chancellor's real purpose was, but it may have been that he was already compiling a dossier on Arnim's activities in Paris.

The rest of Arnim's report of 3 January dealt with the press activities which Bismarck had castigated, and Arnim repeated that he had no influence whatever on the press. The conservatives would not have opposed Thiers as strongly as they had done had they not read in the official *Norddeutsche Zeitung* and the *Correspondance de Berlin* that the German Government would, under no circumstances, intervene to support Thiers.[1] The situation at the time was such, Arnim concluded, that Thiers was strong enough to carry out the provisions of the peace treaty but too weak to prepare for any military adventures in the near future.

Aside from the fact, which goes without saying, that the political attitude of all diplomatic agents has to follow unconditionally and completely the directives from their authoritative quarters, I believe that I may assume that in the situation as it has developed today the nuances have disappeared from the picture which gave rise to the apprehensions of Your Excellency, that I would come in opposition with the intention about which Your Excellency had given me the honour to advise me in such unequivocal way. Arnim.[2]

It is hard to understand why, after the directive of 20 December, Arnim did not hand in his resignation and why, after Arnim's letter of 3 January, Bismarck kept him in his post. It is difficult to assume that the Ambassador considered himself in the confidence and trust of the Chancellor, as it is unlikely that the latter believed the declarations and protestations of the former. It could have been that Arnim thought that his ideas on the policies to be pursued in France might, in the end, prevail, especially with the silent backing of the Emperor. He might also have believed that time was on his side and the developments he favoured inevitable. In this he was at least partially right. There were probably several reasons for Bismarck's reluctance to dismiss this exasperating subordinate, or at least to transfer him to a lesser post. The Chancellor was not absolutely certain of the Emperor's support, which he would have needed in any move against the Ambassador. He might also have believed that the worst of the crisis in France was over and that in normal and quiet times Arnim might again behave properly. Then, too, there was the *Kulturkampf* at home. But, most of all, there were at that time no real, clear-cut offences, as there were later, with which Arnim could be charged.

---

[1] Marginal note: 'They finally came around as soon as Thiers was encouraged.'
[2] Arnim to Bismarck, 3 Jan. 1873; see also Busch, ii. 392–4. By 'authoritative quarters' Arnim meant the Emperor and not Bismarck.

XII

THE CONVENTION OF MARCH 1873

THE year 1873, the last full year of Arnim's ambassadorship in Paris, was conspicuous for two events—the signing of the convention between France and Germany in Berlin on 15 March for payment of the last instalment of the French war indemnity, and the fall of Thiers on 24 May.

Preliminary negotiations between Thiers and Arnim started early in February.[1] Preparing for them, Arnim advanced a most elaborate scheme, including provisions for the speedy evacuation of French territory and, at the same time, the right of reoccupation for the German Army as a final safeguard against French defaults. This plan was turned down by Bismarck.[2]

On 19 February Arnim reported to Berlin that, according to a rumour making the rounds in Paris, negotiations between France and Germany concerning the evacuation had been completed in Berlin.[3] Bismarck replied that 'there are no negotiations whatsoever going on, except those [conducted] by you since 4 February, which have been suggested from here but [which have been] without results so far. I have not seen the French Ambassador since then as I do not get out because of my health. The rumours are inventions without any foundation. Bismarck.'[4]

This was essentially untrue. As early as January Bismarck had corresponded with Manteuffel about the problem of French payments and German evacuation, and, through St. Vallier and Manteuffel, Thiers had addressed his views to the Chancellor, who replied through the same channels.[5] Thus,

[1] Arnim to Bismarck, 5 Feb. 1873, *GP* i. 166–8; Thiers to Gontaut-Biron, 9 Feb. 1873, *DDF* i. 204–6; *Thiers*, pp. 310–11; Giesberg, pp. 228–43.
[2] Arnim to Bismarck, 7 Feb. 1873, *GP* i. 168–74.
[3] Arnim to Foreign Ministry, tel. no. 4, 19 Feb. 1873.
[4] Bismarck to Arnim, tel. no. 4, 19 Feb. 1873.
[5] St. Vallier to Thiers, 5 Feb. 1873, *DDF* i. 203–4, 208, fn. 1; Herzfeld, pp. 242 ff.; *Thiers*, pp. 311 ff.

before Arnim had even a chance to start negotiations, discussions were going on behind his back and without his knowledge.

Despite rejection of his earlier plan, Arnim recommended that Thiers's proposals for the complete evacuation of French territory on receipt of payment of the last billion be accepted, because he said this was also in Germany's interest. He considered the financial guarantees sound and the political situation stable. Neither the proclamation of a red republic nor the outbreak of civil war in France was likely for the rest of the year.[1]

While Arnim forwarded this report to Berlin, Thiers outlined his proposal to St. Vallier and this was passed on to Bismarck through Manteuffel.[2] Bismarck, in turn, submitted Thiers's proposals to the Emperor on 1 March and they were approved at a conference with Moltke and Roon the next day.[3] The only changes made in the French proposals concerned the stipulation that Belfort and the district surrounding it would remain occupied until the last instalment, together with the accrued interests of the indemnity, was fully paid.

On 2 March Arnim and Manteuffel, and, through Manteuffel, St. Vallier and Thiers,[4] were notified of the main points of the German plan, and Arnim was authorized to negotiate with Thiers on that basis. The more detailed directive, together with the draft of the proposed convention, was sent to Paris the following day.[5] Before this communication had reached him, Arnim telegraphed Berlin requesting that Gontaut-Biron not be informed of the German proposals; otherwise the hopes of M. Thiers would be raised to such an extent that any further negotiations would become more difficult, and he, Arnim, wanted to start negotiations by offering the President less than was proposed.[6] (Arnim had, of course, no idea that Thiers was

[1] Arnim to Bismarck, 22 Feb. 1873.
[2] Thiers to St. Vallier, 23 Feb. 1873, *DDF* i. 209–10.
[3] Bismarck to the Emperor, 1 Mar. 1873.
[4] Bismarck to Arnim, tel. no. 6, 2 Mar. 1873; Bismarck to Manteuffel, tel. (no no.), 2 Mar. 1873; St. Vallier to Thiers, 3 Mar. 1873, *DDF* i. 211–12.
[5] Bismarck to Arnim, 3 Mar. 1873, *GP* i. 174–8.
[6] Arnim to Foreign Ministry, tel. no. 8, 2 Mar. 1873. Later on, Arnim claimed that he had sent this telegram to prevent Bismarck from carrying on negotiations behind his back. See *Brief des Grafen Arnim an den Fuersten Bismarck* (Zuerich, 1876), p. 14.

already in possession of the German proposals through Manteuffel.) Bismarck advised Arnim that the German proposals
were not secret and that it was only a matter of accepting or
rejecting them. The French Ambassador in Berlin had been
informed and there was little doubt that the German proposals
would be accepted by the French. 'If not, not. We can wait',
Bismarck wrote.[1]

From here on, the negotiations between Arnim and Thiers,
and Arnim's part in them, become unclear.[2] And so, too, the
role of Bismarck. Complications surrounding the negotiations
were due to several factors. First, Bismarck used two main
channels of communications: Arnim and Manteuffel. And he
did so *before* there were any indications of irregularities on
Arnim's part. Next, Arnim proceeded in a vague and dilatory
fashion in his discussions with Thiers and seemed to complicate
and prolong these negotiations unnecessarily. Finally, Bismarck's suspicion of Arnim was aroused for no apparent
reason, and his vacillation between Belfort, Toul, and Verdun
seemed strange. Altogether there are too many unknown factors
to derive a clear-cut picture of this episode. While Arnim's
behaviour must be suspect and, judging from previous incidents, cannot be above reproach, the Chancellor's is not as
transparent and trustworthy as most historians have claimed.

According to Arnim, he went to see the President on 3 March,
but Thiers did not feel well and became really ill the following
day. On 5 March Arnim went again to Versailles, not knowing
that Thiers was still ailing. He saw the President for a few
minutes but could discuss nothing with him. Thiers asked the
Ambassador to say nothing about this illness, neither in Paris
nor in a report to Berlin, lest disquieting rumours be spread;
he also requested that nothing be published about the negotiations; otherwise he could not defend himself from uncalled
advisers.[3] Before withdrawing, Arnim left with the President
a translation of the German proposals.[4]

[1] Bismarck to Arnim, tel. no. 7, 2 Mar. 1873, *GP* i. 179, fn. *.
[2] Thiers's version is given in his *Memoirs*, pp. 313 ff.
[3] Arnim to Foreign Ministry, tel. no. 9, 5 Mar. 1873.
[4] Arnim to Foreign Ministry, tel. no. 16, 13 Mar. 1873, in which he reported
that 'the translation was *almost* verbatim, as far as it contained new proposals;
those articles which repeated stipulations from previous conversations were
summed up'.

A comparison of Bismarck's directive of 3 March[1] with Arnim's translated note that he had left with Thiers reveals several disparities.[2] In article five of the proposed convention, Arnim inserted the date of 1 March 1874 for the end of the demilitarization of the provinces evacuated by German troops, while the directive, without a specific date, stipulated that it coincide with the evacuation of Belfort. Arnim justified this arbitrary action on the basis of the directive's authorization to ask, if possible, for a prolongation of the period of demilitarization of the evacuated departments.[3] In this connection, a curious difference should be noted between the text of the directive of 3 March as printed in the *Grosse Politik* and in *Pro Nihilo*. In the former the pertinent part of the sentence reads, '. . . and I do not hesitate to authorize Your Excellency to *demand* [*verlangen*] those [obligations], if you think it possible to obtain this concession'.[4] In the latter this passage reads, '. . . and I do not hesitate to authorize Your Excellency to *prolong* [*verlaengern*] these . . .'.[5]

It is impossible, of course, to say with absolute certainty if the substitution of 'prolong' for 'demand' [*verlaengern* for *verlangen*] was a typographical error or a falsification. The latter assumption could explain the insertion of the date in article five of the draft convention. Another reason for this date— and further proof that his was not a mere slip-up—was that Arnim's draft nowhere mentioned the occupation of Belfort, a fact stressed repeatedly in Bismarck's directives. As a result, the time of evacuation of this fortress could not be given as the termination of the demilitarization of the evacuated provinces, but a specific date had to be given instead. There are further gaps in the Arnim draft, all concerning the occupation of Belfort. Article three, for instance, stipulated in the official version that the evacuation of Belfort would take place after

---

[1] *GP* i. 174–8.
[2] The draft of Arnim's translation could not be found in the files; a memorandum by Wilke of 30 Nov. 1875, which was used during the Arnim trial, deals extensively with it.
[3] *Pro Nihilo*, p. 51.   [4] *GP* i. 176.
[5] *Pro Nihilo*, p. 50. In January 1876, when Arnim's activities during these negotiations were reviewed by the court in connection with the publication of *Pro Nihilo*, Manteuffel informed the Foreign Ministry that on his copy of this order the term used was 'demand' (*verlangen*). Manteuffel to Foreign Ministry (21 Jan. 1876). The original order, which is in the files, also has 'demand'.

the payment of 250 million francs and interests, due on
1 September 1873. Arnim's draft completely ignored this
clause. Article four in the official version mentioned again the
troops in the territory of Belfort, and again no reference was
made to this in the draft. Arnim's justification for this summary
omission of Belfort was that there had already been complete
agreement between him and Thiers on the occupation of
Belfort until the final payment was made.[1] If this were true, it
still was odd that Arnim should have omitted these passages,
because, even had there been agreement on this point, its
renewed mention would have done no harm. Deliberate
omission of the Belfort clause, on the other hand, meant
jeopardizing this item, because it would have been difficult to
return to it later on during the negotiations. Arnim's motives
in omitting Belfort in his draft are not known. It was a fact,
however, that after Arnim's visit to the President on 5 March
Thiers did not seem to have accepted the occupation of Belfort.
On the contrary, from that date onward, there was a continuous search by the French for ways and means to circumvent
this clause.[2]

When Arnim reported Thiers's apprehensions about Belfort,[3]
Bismarck became suspicious and admonished the Ambassador
to act exactly according to his instructions.[4] On the same day
the Chancellor asked Manteuffel to discuss the matter confidentially with St. Vallier, and to find the cause of the difficulties.[5]
Manteuffel replied that he was convinced that if the German
demands persisted Thiers would give in.[6] Bismarck, in return,
stated that Toul could be substituted for Belfort, if Thiers were
really afraid that Germany would break the peace treaty over
Belfort and not evacuate the city in the end.[7]

This sudden and entirely unexpected change from Belfort
to Toul, when only two days previously Bismarck had advised
Manteuffel that if the French made difficulties over the very
lenient German proposals everything would remain as before,

---

[1] *Pro Nihilo*, p. 51.

[2] Thiers knew about the Belfort clause from St. Vallier and Gontaut-Biron.
Thiers, pp. 312 ff.   [3] Arnim to Bismarck, 8 Mar. 1873, *GP* i. 178.

[4] Bismarck to Arnim, 8 Mar. 1873, *GP* i. 178–9.

[5] Bismarck to Manteuffel, 8 Mar. 1873, *GP* i. 179.

[6] Manteuffel to Bismarck, tel. (no no.), 9 Mar. 1873.

[7] Bismarck to Manteuffel and Arnim, 10 Mar. 1873.

is difficult to explain. Manteuffel, apparently also taken by surprise, reiterated his conviction that Thiers would accept the German proposals with sufficient pressure. He asked Bismarck not to change anything until St. Vallier had received further information and he expressed his conviction that stock-market speculations were behind all the manœuvres.[1]

Arnim again reported that Belfort was a sore point with the French but that he would not give it up. He suggested that Verdun might be a more suitable fortress than Toul because it was less exposed.[2] But Bismarck insisted that Arnim should remain firm on Belfort and, if the French did not accept the German proposals, everything would remain as before.[3] On the same day the Chancellor sent these instructions to Arnim, he had a conversation with Gontaut-Biron in which he offered to substitute Toul or Verdun for Belfort and, alluding to stock-market speculations in Paris, hinted to the French Ambassador that the convention could be concluded and signed in Berlin.[4]

Bismarck stated repeatedly then and later during the trial that Arnim had purposely delayed the transmittal of the German proposals to Thiers.[5] But was this really true? Arnim reported as early as 5 March that he had seen the President regarding the draft convention and, from that day on, he reported fairly regularly, by telegraph and courier, on the progress of the negotiations. It was true that he had altered the draft which he had left with Thiers and that his reports were sometimes vague. Bismarck's accusation that Arnim did not notify the President of the draft convention seemed singularly misplaced and his insistence on it very odd. This the more so, because he was kept fully informed by Manteuffel on the progress of the talks in Paris. That Arnim's procrastinations were not as bad as Bismarck made them out to be was also supported by a note by the Emperor of 12 March, appended to Arnim's report of 8 March.

[1] Manteuffel to Bismarck, 10 Mar. 1873.
[2] Arnim to Bismarck, tel. no. 13, 10 Mar. 1873.
[3] Bismarck to Arnim, tel. nos. 11, 12, 11 Mar. 1873, no. 12, *GP* i. 182.
[4] Gontaut-Biron to Thiers, 11 Mar. 1873, *DDF* i. 216–17.
[5] When Arnim's role in these negotiations was examined in court in 1876 no proof, other than the documents mentioned here, was submitted by the Government and no connection with alleged stock-market speculation was found. In spite of this lack of evidence, Arnim was accused of treason for his part in these negotiations. See pp. 180–1 below.

From the enclosure I understand that the delay of Arnim has not been so important after all as it has been made out to be. The dispatch of the third, he received on the evening of the fourth; on the fifth he had the first superficial talk with Thiers because the latter was still ailing. On the eighth Thiers called for Arnim; the matter is being discussed in detail and Thiers makes the remarks and states his demands as contained in the enclosure. On the eighth therefore Thiers knew everything: when did the latter declare that he *did not* know *anything* of our project? This is all that has to be found out. Wilhelm[1]

That Thiers did in fact know almost everything about the German draft convention from Arnim is clear from the President's own memoirs.[2] The only thing that Arnim did not disclose at the beginning was Bismarck's original insistence on the occupation of Belfort, and that Thiers learned from Manteuffel by way of St. Vallier.

Bismarck's reply to the Emperor's note of 12 March was a lengthy document, in which he took note of Arnim's reports concerning the draft convention.[3] Conspicuously absent in this report was Bismarck's communication with Thiers through Manteuffel and St. Vallier. His two telegrams of 10 March to Manteuffel and Arnim (in which he substituted Toul for Belfort), and his talk with Gontaut-Biron on 11 March, were also missing. He informed the Emperor that he could find in Arnim's 'procrastination no recognizable political disadvantage so far; but certainly a curtailed reliability for a prompt and effective execution of clear instructions which was necessary for the direction of the Foreign Ministry'.[4]

On 15 March Bismarck and Gontaut-Biron signed the convention in Berlin.[5] The Chancellor's action in transferring the negotiations from Paris to Berlin at the last minute and concluding them there was a sign of disapproval and lack of confidence, and could only be interpreted as such by Arnim and the French Government. Arnim's usefulness as the representative of the German Emperor had been severely impaired by this action. It is surprising that Arnim did not submit his resignation immediately. Instead, he wrote a complaining letter to the

---

[1] *GP* i. 179–82, without the Emperor's note, however.
[2] *Thiers*, pp. 313 ff.
[3] Bismarck to the Emperor, 18 Mar. 1873.   [4] Ibid.
[5] *GP* i. 186–8; *DDF* i. 220–7; *Thiers*, pp. 316–18.

Emperor and requested an investigation of the whole matter.[1] Arnim maintained that he had informed Thiers of the German proposals on 5 March, but was hampered in his further negotiations with the President by the communications and discussions going on behind his back between Versailles and Nancy, and Nancy and Berlin.

The Emperor sent Arnim's letter to Bismarck at Varzin with the request that the Chancellor state his views of the incident.[2] Bismarck flatly asserted that Arnim's letter to the Emperor had presented an incomplete picture of the negotiations and, if one had to decide who spoke the truth, Arnim or Thiers, it was the latter who should be considered more reliable.[3] He reminded the Emperor that he had been most reluctant to agree to Arnim's appointment to Paris and had done so only because he was fully convinced of the Emperor's trust in himself. For the time being, and until he had had a chance to consult the official files, Bismarck requested that Arnim be directed by the Emperor to send his complaint through official channels. This was necessary for the maintenance of discipline in the foreign service.

Should this not happen, I would stand with my subordinate on the same level of two disputing parties. It would be impossible for me, according to my present state of health, after the fights in the imperial and provincial diets, in the ministry, and with the foreign cabinets, against social influences and against attacks by the press, to have to conduct a paper war for the official authority which I need for the conduct of affairs. However gladly I would like to dedicate to Your Majesty's service the last ounce of my strength, I cannot conceal that this would be used up very quickly, if I am to suffer under the painful feeling that I have to fight with a man like Count Arnim for Your Majesty's confidence, after I possessed this confidence undiminished for so many years and without ever having deceived it to my knowledge.

For years I have never made a secret to Your Majesty of my impartial opinion of the personality of Count Arnim. I had hoped that this high and, for the fatherland, important position in Paris would perhaps put him beyond petty intrigues; otherwise I would

---

[1] Arnim to the Emperor, 8 Apr. 1873, partly printed in *Pro Nihilo*, pp. 58–60.

[2] The Emperor to Bismarck, 14 Apr. 1873.

[3] Bismarck to the Emperor, 14 Apr. 1873, *GW* vic. 36–7; also published in the *Reichsanzeiger*, 24 Jan. 1876, where it was printed incompletely, and in the pamphlet *Brief des Grafen Arnim an den Fuersten Bismarck*, pp. 3–5.

have had to request Your Majesty most earnestly and in consequence of the Roman experience not to entrust him with this position, in spite of all his qualifications. I understand that after this nomination he has no other ambition but to become my successor and that for these reasons he keeps in close touch with persons and parties in the Upper House and at Court who are hostile to me.[1] I, and not only I, am suspicious that occasionally he subordinates his official duties to his personal interests; it is impossible to prove this; but it is difficult with such a suspicion in mind to continue to be responsible for the way in which this high official is discharging his instructions. I took the liberty of informing Your Majesty of my suspicion; Your Majesty knows already how little confidence I have in the objectivity of his reports. So as not to make Your Majesty angry, I have avoided to express officially my official misgivings.

The step of Count Arnim to which he had been encouraged from Berlin, and which has been expected there already in the past week, does not leave me any other choice. Your Majesty will kindly remember that I talked about the attempt to lessen the dangers which Paris poses for Arnim's character, by transferring him to London; that from there, however, the strongest protests were expressed after the very first feelers because of Arnim's inclination for intrigue and untruthfulness. 'One could not believe one word he would say.'[2] Against the accusations of a man of such a reputation, my respectful request is only that Your Majesty may direct him to submit his official complaint through official channels.[3]

The Chancellor's request was granted, and, after considerable delay, Arnim was advised to submit his complaint through official channels.[4] This was the end of the incident for the time being. No decision had been reached either way, and, outwardly at least, things between Bismarck and Arnim went on pretty much as before.

For Arnim it should have been a warning. The Emperor's reaction to this episode should have left Arnim with no doubt

[1] See G. Ritter, *Die Preussischen Konservativen und Bismarcks deutsche Politik 1858–76* (Heidelberg, 1913), pp. 368–74.

[2] After the Arnim trial this incident received some publicity, especially in those newspapers that were opposed to Bismarck. Granville, the British Foreign Secretary, told Muenster, the German Ambassador, that Arnim's name had never appeared in any correspondence pertaining to the ambassadorial post in London at that time. All he, Granville, had done was to ask Bismarck to send him an ambassador in whom the Chancellor had the fullest confidence. (Muenster to Buelow, 3 Mar. 1876.)

[3] Bismarck to the Emperor, 14 Apr. 1873.

[4] The Emperor to Arnim, 24 May 1873.

that support from that quarter was, if not non-existent, certainly very weak. Bismarck had achieved his immediate aim. Beyond these partisan considerations, this incident gives a fair preview of the impending clash. The difficulties of balancing the claims and counter-claims, the motives and intentions of the main actors in the negotiations, have already been mentioned. The suspicion that Arnim used his official knowledge and influence for stock-market speculation was, and still is, very strong. On the other hand, Bismarck's actions in this case were not much less devious. The idea that the Chancellor manipulated the course of the negotiations to bring about Arnim's dismissal or resignation is quite plausible. It would certainly explain his extensive correspondence with Manteuffel and his early and articulate suspicion of Arnim. It would also explain the sudden substitution and subsequent equally sudden retraction of Toul for Belfort. It would, finally, provide a better and more logical reason for the transfer of the negotiations to Berlin.

XIII

THE FALL OF THIERS

THE ink on the Convention of March 1873 had hardly dried when a clash in the French National Assembly brought about Thiers's fall. Thus the latent conflict between Bismarck and Arnim on the most suitable form of government in France was brought to a climax. Their respective positions were well known. Bismarck had maintained throughout that the republican form of government would keep France weak and disunited internally and incapable of concluding alliances with any major European power. Arnim, on the other hand, had repeatedly expressed his belief that a republican France was a continuous source of danger to Germany because of its radical form of government as well as because of its revolutionary zeal. And although the Chancellor's point of view, which was at the same time the official policy of the German Government, was well known to Arnim, he steadfastly maintained his own opinion, believing it the only right and reasonable one, regardless of directives and official instructions.[1]

Since the beginning of the year (1873) a great number of Arnim's reports on the political situation in France had dealt with the weakness of Thiers's Government and the chances of a monarchical restoration.[2] When the situation in the National Assembly had reached a critical stage, however, Arnim became reluctant to make any predictions. He did not believe, or at least professed not to believe, that the parties of the Right were ready to overthrow Thiers.[3] It was quite conceivable that he appreciated neither the extent nor the seriousness of the crisis. And it seemed that Bismarck too did not, at that time, grasp the full implications of the parliamentary struggle that

[1] See H. L. Schweinitz, *Denkwuerdigkeiten*, 2 vols. (Berlin, 1927), i. 300–1, henceforth cited Schweinitz.

[2] Arnim to Bismarck, 17 Jan. 1873, no. 23, 8 Feb. 1873; no. 29, 23 Feb. 1873. Arnim to Foreign Ministry, no. 41, 1 May 1873; no. 43, 2 May 1873.

[3] Arnim to Foreign Ministry, no. 45, 19 May 1873.

was going on in Paris. For when Arnim reported that he had been approached by Goulard, a member of the Assembly, with a request that he influence the President to co-operate more closely with the conservative parties—a policy which might very well have saved Thiers's position—Bismarck noted on the margin, 'Should *we* help France to become stronger? Her strength will always be employed solely against us.'[1]

Arnim's part in Thiers's fall was a major problem, during the crisis and later at the trial. Bismarck accepted it as a well-established fact, and this view has been repeated innumerable times since. It would seem obvious that any influence Arnim might have used in bringing about the overthrow of Thiers would be impossible to determine with any degree of accuracy.[2] His influence could not have been decisive, though he apparently did nothing either to support the President or to prevent his fall. An indication of this can be found in two newspaper notices which appeared during and after the crisis in the French press. The *Univers* reprinted an item from the *Gaulois* of 22 May 1873, according to which, at a reception given by Count Apponyi, where the effects of Thiers's resignation on the liberation of French territory were being discussed, Arnim was supposed to have said, 'Really Gentlemen, you surprise me! The liberation has nothing to do with the maintenance or the overthrow of M. Thiers. For it is not with him but with the Assembly that we have negotiated. It is the latter which has given the guarantee and it is its authority which we hold much higher than that of M. Thiers.'[3] According to *Le Français* of 26 May Arnim, on an unspecified occasion, was supposed to have said that not only would Thiers's resignation 'not cause any tension in the diplomatic relationship between France and Prussia, but the Prussian Government would rather consider the taking over of a more conservative government in France as a guarantee of [its] greater solvency for Prussia and of security for Europe'.[4]

---

[1] Arnim to Foreign Ministry, no. 43, 2 May 1873.

[2] Rich and Fisher, i. 103–4.

[3] When the Foreign Ministry sent copies of these articles to Arnim with a request for an explanation, Arnim noted on the margin, 'How could I have said such nonsense.' See footnote 1, p. 119, below.

[4] A memorandum by Bucher of 15 June 1873 notes that Baron von Ungern-Sternberg had informed Bismarck that an Italian deputy had told him that many

When the crisis had passed and MacMahon had been installed President of the Republic, Bismarck sent Arnim copies of the two newspaper articles and asked him to report on these incidents.[1] Arnim replied that the pronouncements ascribed to him in the *Gaulois* and *Français* 'were, of course, entirely fabricated'.[2] A few days later, he complained to the Chancellor about articles that had appeared first in the *Koelnische Zeitung* and then in various other German newspapers, in which he had been accused of having shown too much sympathy to the new regime, contrary to the official position of the German Government. Allegations had also been made in this connection that he would be dismissed because of this attitude.[3] Bismarck ignored these complaints and, in his next communication, referred once more to the two items in the French newspapers and to Arnim's denial. This denial, the Chancellor observed acidly, was gratifying, though somewhat unexpected. For it would have meant that Arnim had made no remarks whatever that could have given rise to these reports. The remarks attributed to him were, however, so much in line with the reports he had sent since the previous autumn that he could only assume that Arnim had managed to evade any and all discussions on this subject. 'I can conclude therefore', Bismarck observed, 'that you expressed your opinion, which is contrary to my own, only to His Majesty.'[4]

Arnim's views on the new regime in France were contained in two lengthy reports; one to the Foreign Ministry, the other to the Emperor.[5] To the Ministry he told of the widespread support which the new Government found among the majority of the French people and the hope of many for a monarchical restoration, a possibility Arnim considered unlikely. He thought

Italians believed that Arnim had brought about a change of government in France; they based this on his pro-papal leanings and on the belief that he, or German policy, was counting on a rupture of German–Italian relations in the future.

[1] Bismarck to Arnim, 2 June 1873.

[2] Arnim to Bismarck, 10 June 1873. It should be noted that in neither case was a denial issued by the papers involved. Bismarck to the Emperor, (draft), (19) June 1873.

[3] Arnim to Bismarck, 13 June 1873; *Pro Nihilo*, pp. 29–31.

[4] Bismarck to Arnim, 18 June 1873.

[5] Arnim to Foreign Ministry, no. 49, 27 May 1873; Arnim to the Emperor, 8 June 1873; both are printed, with minor omissions, in *Pro Nihilo*, pp. 64–6, 70–3.

that a republic, or rather the then current form of government with neither emperor nor king, would have a better chance for a sustained and continuous existence. This assertion he supported with the argument that none of the royal parties could produce a universally acceptable candidate, while at the same time the Duc de Broglie seemed more and more to cherish the idea that he himself would be able to govern the country as president or regent.[1]

In his report to the Emperor, Arnim stressed in great detail the chivalrous, honest, and straightforward character of the new president. He discounted the imminence of a restoration, as he had to the Foreign Ministry, but for other reasons. The royalist parties were not so much interested in the restoration of a monarchy as in safeguarding their lives and property. For them pursuance of a conservative policy by the established government was more important than a king on the throne.

Therefore, if the neighbours of France have, as I believe, a fundamental interest that this country should not be made once again the disturber of the peace by radical or clerical crusaders and, if there exists, in this respect, a solidarity of conservative interests, there is no basis for the belief that the monarchical principle in Europe would receive considerable support, if a member of the old dynasty would come to the throne. For these same reasons there is no cause to prefer one or the other dynastic solution, or even to demonstrate a special sympathy for either. Any government within the next twenty years will most likely take advantage of complications so as to reclaim the 'robbery' perpetrated on France; no government will drive toward war, if it has no firm alliances. Only a radical or completely mad ultramontane government could disturb the peace even without alliances, because the one, as well as the other, counts on sympathizers in the camp of the enemy. The best one for us will always be the one which has to employ the greater part of its powers on the subduing of its internal enemies.[2]

The two reports make use of different arguments and stress different details. There can be no doubt that Arnim deliberately painted a favourable and detailed picture of MacMahon in order to impress the Emperor. Essentially, however, both reports present the same picture—the unlikelihood of either an

---

[1] Arnim to Foreign Ministry, 27 May 1873.
[2] Arnim to the Emperor, 8 June 1873.

imminent royalist restoration or the establishment of a conservative government. To accuse Arnim, in this connection, of
outright lies, sophistries, and the use of Bismarckian arguments
built on wrong premises seems highly exaggerated.[1]

Replying to these reports, Bismarck accused Arnim of con-
spiring against his policy in order to bring about Thiers's
downfall, and of influencing the Emperor to such an extent
that his, Bismarck's, advice had not prevailed.[2] Having reprimanded the Ambassador, the Chancellor now faced the
difficult task of recovering his position with the Emperor, of
persuading Wilhelm I of the soundness of his policy, and of
convincing the Emperor of the validity of his views.

The Emperor, as was to be expected, had expressed his
pleasure and satisfaction over the downfall of Thiers and the
ascendancy of MacMahon. In a long and detailed memorandum Bismarck now attempted to demonstrate the disadvantages
and the veritable dangers in this fateful change for German
policy.[3] It was a change, the Chancellor asserted, from a weak,
civilian, and anti-clerical France to a strong and military one,
friendly to the Jesuits. How this quick turnabout had suddenly
come to pass, the Chancellor did not elaborate, nor, for that
matter, did he explain why it had happened. Instead, he
painted a dark and threatening picture of Europe's political
landscape. The new French Government would, according to
Bismarck, sooner or later support the Carlist movement in
Spain and the vacillating policies of Victor Emanuel in Italy,
thus uniting the Latin part of Europe under the leadership of
papal Rome against Germany.[4] Austria might soon join this
coalition and Great Britain, too, would become part of it, if
for no other reason than its Asiatic interests. Germany, for all
practical purposes, would be isolated, because Russia, its only
ally, could not be depended upon. Nor would this be all. The

---

[1] Herzfeld, pp. 278–9.

[2] Bismarck to Arnim, 19 June 1873, *GP* i. 189–91; there was, apparently, no
reply by Arnim, but his views are printed in *Pro Nihilo*, pp. 73–6; they are also
expressed in his marginal notes on this directive; these were omitted in the *Grosse
Politik*.

[3] Bismarck to the Emperor, (19) June 1873; it seems doubtful, however, that
this memorandum, of which there is only a draft, was submitted to the Emperor;
see *GP* i. 191, fn. *.

[4] See, however, Bismarck's conversation with Odo Russell in Taffs, pp. 58–60,
and his report to the Emperor, 5 Dec. 1872, p. 99 above.

adverse effect of the governmental change in France would also be felt inside Germany, particularly in the South. This complete reversal of the balance of power, Bismarck concluded, was due to Arnim's activities and intrigues in Paris.

The Ambassador's view had prevailed over his own. Arnim's policy had been followed with the approval of the Emperor, against the advice of the Foreign Minister. Under these circumstances it would be better if the Emperor would choose another counsellor in foreign affairs whose views would be more in accordance with his own than those of the present one.[1]

The Chancellor's description of the political consequences following the change of governments in France was a mis-representation. So was the influence attributed to Arnim. The idea of the great Chancellor having to give way to the policies of the Ambassador in what he himself called the most important part of Europe was ridiculous. It would seem that Bismarck intended to use this memorandum to eliminate Arnim. That he apparently did not then submit it to the Emperor did not matter. The ideas and intentions were all there and would be used sooner or later.

[1] Bismarck to the Emperor, (19) June 1873.

XIV

THE PASTORAL LETTERS OF THE FRENCH BISHOPS AND ARNIM'S RECALL FROM PARIS

DURING the summer months, from July to September 1873, Arnim was on leave and away from Paris.[1] Before returning to his post he came to Berlin and on 1 September had an audience with the Emperor as well as a meeting with the Chancellor.

According to Arnim's account of the audience, he obtained complete satisfaction from the Emperor regarding his person, his behaviour, and his position. He asked the Emperor if his recall from Paris and his retirement from the service were desired. The Emperor rejected this idea with the remark that there were no reasons for such a step. The matter concerning the Convention of 15 March 1873 had also been cleared in Arnim's favour, and altogether there was nothing more involved than the Chancellor's rancour. This, according to the Emperor, was a main characteristic of the Chancellor which, unfortunately, had already been the undoing of many a faithful servant of the Crown: Golz, Thile, Savigny, Usedom, Werther, and others. 'Now it is your turn!' the Emperor concluded. Arnim replied that he considered himself the Emperor's, not the Chancellor's, servant and that he felt it his duty to tell Bismarck how baseless were all the assertions on which his ill feelings seemed to rest.[2]

The meeting with Bismarck was much less pleasant. Asked for the reasons for his enmity, the Chancellor replied,

you conspire with the Empress [against me] and you will not rest until you sit here at this table where I am sitting and [then] you too will see that this is nothing either.

I know you since your youth. You see in each superior[3] your natural enemy; this you said yourself, years ago. I am the enemy

---

[1] *Pro Nihilo*, p. 76.   [2] Ibid., pp. 77–8.

[3] Bismarck's marginalia: *Vordermann*, ibid., p. 78.

at the moment. You have procrastinated the conclusion of the Convention of 15 March to bring about the fall of Thiers[1] and I have to bear the responsibility for this political mistake. You have accused me before the Emperor, you have connections at Court which have prevented me, so far, from calling you back here earlier.[2]

Bismarck's speech then became incoherent according to Arnim, because of real or simulated rage. He confused the sequence of events and finally asserted, though in no way proved, that everything he had said about Arnim's behaviour had been taken from the official files. The meeting ended without a reconciliation.[3]

Toward the end of September Arnim returned to Paris. During his absence two events of more than ordinary significance had occurred. On 15 September 1873 the last German troops had left France, completing the evacuation.[4] And on 3 August the Bishop of Nancy had issued a pastoral letter in his diocese (which included parts of German territory recently acquired from France) calling for the reunification of Metz and Strassburg with France.[5] A month after this event, Bismarck directed Wesdehlen, the chargé d'affaires in Paris, to express his Government's displeasure over the incident and the hope that the French Government would take the necessary steps to prevent any similar incidents in the future.[6] When Wesdehlen reported his subsequent conversation with the Duc de Broglie, the new French Prime Minister, Balan replied that the Chancellor was not quite satisfied with the French attitude, especially because the Archbishop of Paris had, in the meantime, issued a similar pastoral letter.[7] After Arnim had returned to Paris he also had a conversation with the Prime Minister on this subject, but his report, too, failed to satisfy the Chancellor.[8]

From the reports and directives on hand—and they are

[1] Bismarck's marginalia: *Um zu speculieren, Pro Nihilo*, p. 78.

[2] Ibid., pp. 78-9; see also *GW* xv. 357.

[3] *Pro Nihilo*, p. 79. According to Odo Russel, however, Arnim had told him that his differences with Bismarck had been cleared up. Gontaut-Biron, p. 346.

[4] Manteuffel to Bismarck, 15 Sept. 1873, *GP* i. 192.

[5] Bismarck to Wesdehlen, 3 Sept. 1873, ibid., p. 211; see also E. Schmidt-Volkmar, pp. 156-8.

[6] *GP* i. 211.

[7] Wesdehlen to Bismarck, 12 Sept. 1873; Balan to Arnim, 20 Sept. 1873, ibid., pp. 211-13.

[8] Arnim to Bismarck, 29 Sept. 1873; Bismarck to Arnim, 10 Oct. 1873, ibid., pp. 213-16.

complete up to this point as printed in the *Grosse Politik*—it is quite clear that this was then a minor and fairly common incident in the relationship between France and Germany. The circumstances were neither unusual nor especially grave and the peace between the two countries was never endangered. It is all the more surprising, therefore, to have Bismarck describe this event to the Emperor as a major disturbance of the peace and serious enough to warrant a strongly worded *démarche* on the part of Germany.[1] The Chancellor took the opportunity to complain severely about the way Arnim had handled the matter and went so far as to imply that unless the Ambassador were called to task a grave situation might result. Submitting the pertinent documents to the Emperor, Bismarck pointedly asked for approval of his policy.

On 17 October Arnim had another conversation with de Broglie in which he took a very strong stand and repeatedly pressed the Prime Minister for definite action by the Government which would be satisfactory to Germany.[2] His urgings were in vain, none of Arnim's efforts impressed Bismarck, who could be neither pleased nor appeased. While Bismarck's marginal notes may have given an indication of moderate satisfaction, the Chancellor's reply to Arnim's report describing his conversation with de Broglie was sarcastic, complaining, unjust, and reprimanding.[3]

There can be little doubt that Bismarck intended to use this incident to make Arnim's position impossible. He was also using it to put pressure on the opposition at home and, at the same time, justify his domestic policy against the Catholic Church by exaggerating the episode abroad. That Bismarck did not expect the Arnim–de Broglie conversations to succeed is demonstrated by a short note from Bucher to Buelow[4] attached to the Chancellor's directives nos. 205 and 206 of 30 October to Paris.[5] Requesting the State Secretary to forward the enclosed directives, Bucher added,

After the directives have been sent off, Your Excellency should be good enough

---

[1] Bismarck to the Emperor, 11 Oct. 1873.
[2] Arnim to Bismarck, 17 Oct. 1873, *GP* i. 217–20.
[3] Bismarck to Arnim, 30 Oct. 1873, ibid., pp. 220–1.
[4] Bucher (to Buelow), 30 Oct. 1873.
[5] Bismarck to Arnim, no. 205, 30 Oct. 1873; no. 206, 30 Oct. 1873, *GP* i. 220–1.

(1) in the foreseeable event that the continued oral discussions should be unsuccessful, draft a note in German to de Broglie, which should recapitulate briefly the ideas of the directive of 10 October and of the one of today and which [should also] express the demand that the pastoral letter of the Bishop of Nancy should be publicly reprimanded.

(2) notify His Majesty of the intention of this note and stress, in this connection, that with regard to the other Powers these matters should be treated somewhat ostentatiously in order that the public opinion of Europe should notice them.[1]

Arnim saw de Broglie again on 8 November and discussed with him the affair of the Bishop of Nancy. The Prime Minister's attitude was most accommodating. He said he would have been willing to publish the reprimand sent by the Minister for Cultural Affairs to the Bishop of Nancy had Count Wesdehlen made this request in their original conversation. Now, three months after the event, this seemed most inopportune.[2] The report from Arnim recounting this meeting with the Prime Minister arrived in Berlin the following day, 9 November, at 8.30 a.m. The next day Buelow sent a directive to Arnim, reminding him of the Chancellor's directives of 4 and 7 November, and advising him once more to clear up the incident with the Prime Minister. 'The Chancellor is expecting your report on this matter immediately', Buelow closed his directive.[3] This directive was not based on a misunderstanding or oversight by the State Secretary, but was a deliberate attempt to exasperate the Ambassador. This is borne out by a communication from Bucher to Buelow, advising Buelow that the Chancellor had decided to have the pastoral letter of the Bishop of Nancy discussed in an article in the *Norddeutsche Allgemeine Zeitung*. 'I also want to note', Bucher wrote, 'that I have reasons to believe that the Prince [i.e. Bismarck] *does not want to see*[4] the report announced in the telegram from Paris[5] before this article has been launched.'[6]

---

[1] Bucher (to Buelow), 30 Oct. 1873.

[2] Arnim to Bismarck, tel. (no no.), 8 Nov. 1873; see also Arnim to Bismarck no. 131, 10 Nov. 1873, *GP* i. 221–3.

[3] Buelow to Arnim, no. 224, 10 Nov. 1873.

[4] Underlined in the original.

[5] Arnim's telegram of 8 Nov. and report of 10 Nov. 1873.

[6] Bucher to Buelow, 15 Nov. 1873; the article appeared in the *Norddeutsche Allgemeine Zeitung* of 18 Nov. 1873.

On 21 November 1873 Pope Pius IX issued his Encyclical *Etsi multa luctuosa*, protesting, among other things, against the *Kulturkampf* in Germany.[1] About the same time an assembly of bishops at Bourges expressed their gratification over the undaunted attitude of the German Roman Catholic clergy in their struggle against the State. Bishops from other parts of France, too, hastened to express publicly their support of the papal pronouncement and their condemnation of Bismarck's policy. Of these, the expressions of the bishops of Angers and Nimes were particularly offensive.[2]

Following these public expressions, the correspondence between the Foreign Ministry in Berlin and the German Embassy in Paris became increasingly acerbic. The Ministry, in the person of State Secretary Buelow, contended that the Ambassador had been negligent and procrastinating in his duties. Arnim, on the other hand, puzzled by the urgency and importance this affair had suddenly assumed in Berlin, did everything to satisfy the vague and changing demands of the home office.[3]

Before this controversy with France was settled Bismarck complained to the Emperor, criticizing Arnim's handling of the affair, and declaring himself unable to continue to work with the Ambassador. He accused Arnim of evading and ignoring instructions, of lacking firmness in his conversations with French officials, of an inability to grasp the seriousness of the problem involved, and of incompetence in finding applicable French legislation with which to counteract the excesses of the French bishops.[4] As to the last, it would seem that Bismarck intentionally overlooked Arnim's detailed and elaborate exposé on the legal aspects of the dispute written a few days earlier.[5] Since it could not be suppressed altogether, Buelow noted its existence in a postscript and explained to the Emperor that it

---

[1] Franz, pp. 235–6.   [2] Arnim to Bismarck, 30 Nov. 1873.

[3] Referring to this incident, Holstein testified during the Arnim trial that he had written a letter at that time to the Foreign Ministry saying 'that the French Government will do everything possible to fulfil the German demands as long as they are stated clearly and succinctly. What creates ill will [in Paris] is that the demands, instead of being expressed plainly, arrive piece by piece, and, no sooner has one been fulfilled, another is being put forward . . .' (*Darstellung*, p. 238). See also Buelow memorandum, 31 Dec. 1873, *GP* i. 225–7.

[4] Bismarck to the Emperor, 4 Jan. 1873; Gontaut-Biron, p. 681.

[5] Arnim to Foreign Ministry, 2 Jan. 1874.

had not altered the Chancellor's views but had only confirmed his original opinion.[1] Following his complaint, Bismarck asked the Emperor to approve Arnim's transfer from Paris.[2]

That Bismarck's accusations regarding Arnim's performance in connection with the pastoral letters of the French bishops were unjustified is clear from the record. While these accusations had little bearing on the substance of Franco-German relations, that they had been made at all made Arnim's position in Paris untenable. The questions remain why Bismarck chose this particular incident to tie the knot around Arnim's neck and why he selected this particular dispute with France to create an international crisis. The answers to these questions can probably be found in the developments governing the domestic policies of the Reich at this particular period. Two were outstanding: the increasingly embittered struggle against the Roman Catholic Church, and the less spectacular, but by no means minor, attempt by the Government to pass a new military law. Both developments had serious political implications at home as well as abroad.[3] To assure the passage of a new military law, foreign dangers had to be created. To overcome the resistance of the Roman Catholic Church, new threats had to be devised. Both predicaments could be solved by exaggerating and publicizing the pastoral letters of the French bishops. They were, no doubt, an interference in German internal affairs. Their appeal to German Catholics made those Germans traitors by association. At the same time, the French Government's apparent inability to curb the excesses of its own bishops opened possibilities for further and more serious entanglements which, in the end, could lead to a war scare.[4]

Bismarck's genius made it possible for him to exploit all these factors to the fullest. Except for the *Kulturkampf*, which proved a somewhat more complicated undertaking, he was successful all along the line. Arnim was recalled from Paris on 24 February, and the new army law became effective on 2 May.

[1] For Arnim's side of this episode, see *Pro Nihilo*, pp. 84–109.

[2] Undated and unsigned draft of a memorandum to the Emperor, probably written in January 1874. The following notation appears on the margin: 'This report has not been sent off; [its content] has been incorporated in the report to His Majesty of 3 February.' The report of 3 Feb. 1874 has not been found. For the text of the undated draft, see Appendix III of this study.

[3] Wahl, i. 107–15; Eyck, iii. 65–77.

[4] Gontaut-Biron, pp. 364 ff.; Wahl, i. 347 ff.

XV

THE 'DIPLOMATIC REVELATIONS'

THE same courier who brought Arnim official notification of his recall also brought a message that the Emperor intended to appoint him Ambassador to Constantinople.[1] The order confirming the appointment was issued on 19 March.[2] Arnim never reached his new post. Illness and death in his family—his daughter had died early in March—and the settling of his private affairs delayed his departure, and he spent all of March and most of April in the French capital.[3] Other events also interfered.

On 2 April 1874 the Vienna newspaper *Die Presse* printed two documents under the title 'Diplomatic Revelations' which Arnim had written during the Vatican Council. The first, of 8 January 1870, was a general report on the Council, addressed to Doellinger, in which Arnim expressed his regret that people in Germany were not fully aware of what was going on in Rome and that the Catholic Church was in danger of being dominated by 'five hundred Italians, of whom three hundred were dependants [*Kostgaenger*] of the Pope'. The second, of 17 June 1870, was a memorandum in which Arnim foresaw the dangerous consequences of papal proclamation of the dogma of the infallibility.[4]

These documents, especially the second, created a sensation. They seemed to show that Arnim foresaw the *Kulturkampf* when he wrote them in 1870. From this it was not difficult to conclude that the Government's policy toward the Roman Curia at the time of the Vatican Council was badly conceived, because, by not heeding the advice of its Ambassador, the Government had not foreseen the consequences. This attitude was widespread

[1] Bismarck to Arnim, nos. 68, 69, 24 Feb. 1874.
[2] Buelow to Arnim, 20 Mar. 1874.
[3] Arnim to Buelow, 18 Mar. 1874; Buelow to Arnim, 9 Apr. 1874; Arnim (to Buelow), 11 Apr. 1874; see also Schweinitz, i. 305.
[4] See pp. 35–6 above.

and was expressed by a number of newspapers, first in Austria, then in Germany.[1]

As soon as the *Presse* article came to the attention of the Foreign Ministry in Berlin, Bismarck had the documents reprinted in the *Norddeutsche Allgemeine Zeitung* of 8 April, with the comment that the documents had been published by the *Presse* of Vienna from an unknown source, that they were of considerable historical interest, and that they had originally been written by a very gifted man intimately familiar with the circumstances.[2] The Chancellor was, of course, fully aware of Arnim's authorship, but, for reasons of his own, took no official steps; he informed Arnim though, through an intermediary, that he did not consider the documents authentic.[3]

Arnim himself drew the attention of the Foreign Ministry to the article in the *Presse*. He implicitly acknowledged authorship of the memorandum, but denied having written the covering letter to Bishop Hefele, as printed in the newspaper, because he remembered, he wrote, that he 'had carried the memorandum personally to the Bishop's apartment'. Equally untrue, according to Arnim, was that Hefele, or any other bishop, had given him his word of honour that he would resign rather than submit to the dogma of infallibility, as had also been reported by the *Presse*.[4] 'I should not like to enter into direct correspondence with the *Presse*', Arnim wrote, 'but I would appreciate it very much if Hefele could be exonerated by a communiqué in an official paper, as far as breaking his word of honour and his receipt of this memorandum are concerned.'[4]

Although he apparently received no reply to this from Berlin, it would be wrong to conclude that the Foreign Ministry ignored the incident. Far from it. Bucher was busy compiling a list of directives to, and reports from, Arnim at the time of the Vatican Council which 'would be suitable for publication in total or in part'.[5] Two of these, Bismarck's directive of

---

[1] *Die Presse* (Vienna), 3 Apr. 1874, and its quotations from *Die Deutsche Zeitung, Das Neue Wiener Tageblatt, Das Vaterland.*

[2] Buelow (memorandum), 7 Apr. 1874.

[3] Bismarck to the Emperor, 28 Apr. 1874; there is no indication in the files that Arnim had been asked by the Foreign Ministry to explain the publication in the *Presse*.   [4] Arnim (to Buelow), 11 Apr. 1874.

[5] Bucher (memorandum), 9 Apr. (1874).

13 March 1870 and Arnim's report of 14 May 1869, were published in the *Norddeutsche Allgemeine Zeitung*. This was done 'to invalidate accusations in the ultramontane papers that *we* [the Prussian Government] had initiated the quarrel with Rome, to put on record our calm and waiting attitude toward Rome, and to prove that not only the official instructions but also the actual behaviour of Your Majesty's Ambassador had been of a *peaceful* nature'.[1]

Following these publications, the *Norddeutsche Allgemeine Zeitung* concluded that Arnim's memorandum, as published in the *Presse*, was at least partially spurious. This, in turn, was questioned by many newspapers, among them the *Deutsche Zeitung* of 19 April 1874. Final proof of the memorandum's authenticity was established by Arnim himself when he wrote a letter to Doellinger, which was printed in the *Augsburger Allgemeine Zeitung* on 25 April. In it Arnim expressed his regrets that from the recently published documents in the various newspapers Doellinger might have gathered the impression that he, Arnim, did not respect him as much as he actually did. In particular Arnim denied any important contradictions between his report of May 1869 and his memorandum of June 1870. (This the *Norddeutsche Allgemeine Zeitung* had attempted to prove, to discredit Arnim's views on the Council.) The question whether the dispatch of an ambassador to the Council would have changed events was futile, Arnim continued; still, he regretted that the ideas expressed in the Hohenlohe circular had not been followed more closely.[2] 'If one had succeeded in destroying the seeds of these rank weeds, which were nurtured by the Council, we would not find ourselves today in those incredible entanglements which call in question everything which seems to have been common property of Christendom for a long time.'[3]

Publication of this letter rekindled the flame of public controversy and the *Presse* used it to attack the German Chancellor in a front-page article. 'One cannot forget that the German Ambassador in Paris, as the then accredited diplomat in Rome,

---

[1] Bismarck to the Emperor, 28 Apr. 1874.
[2] See pp. 5 ff. above.
[2] Arnim to Doellinger, 21 Apr. 1874, in *Augsburger Allgemeine Zeitung* of 25 Apr. 1874.

had recognized the implications of the plans of the Jesuits and the importance of the dogma of infallibility from the beginning and much better than his chief, the Reich Chancellor.'[1] Reviewing events at the Council and recalling the opposition of twenty-six German and Austro-Hungarian bishops and their support from Hohenlohe, Daru, Beust, and the King of Bavaria, the paper went on,

there were so many excellent elements of opposition, the governments and bishops only needed to act in common and the infallibility would have disappeared like a ghost. At that time the North German Federal Chancellor maintained an impenetrable silence, disregarded the movement which, in his opinion, did not threaten North Germany, and dismissed the good counsel of Arnim. . . . The way things have developed since the year 1870 to this day makes it clear which one of the two diplomats was more perceptive in this question. . . .[1]

In Berlin, meanwhile, Bismarck considered the time ripe to inform the Emperor of the course of events. He noted the various documents that had been published, the public discussions that had ensued, and the counter-measures he had initiated.[2] While it would be simple, Bismarck told the Emperor, to prove publicly that Arnim's opinion during the Council was immature and that he never offered any advice of the sort he was now being credited with,[3] it would be incompatible with the dignity of the imperial service and with the respect German representatives enjoyed abroad for the Foreign Minister to enter into a public debate with one of his subordinates.[4] Arnim's action was inadmissible, unheard of, and punishable by all civilized standards. At least while the applicable laws and regulations were being studied for further action against him, to continue Arnim's employment in the foreign service seemed impossible.[5] In conclusion, the Chancellor asked the Emperor to order Arnim to appear in Berlin to vindicate himself.[6] Upon receipt of Bismarck's report, the Emperor indicated that most

---

[1] *Neue Freie Presse* (Vienna), 29 Apr. 1874.
[2] Bismarck to the Emperor, 28 Apr. 1874. When he read about Arnim's letter to Doellinger, the Emperor noted on the magin: 'This is pretty strong!'
[3] The Emperor's marginal comments: 'Did he not propose the Oratores?', ibid.
[4] 'Correct!', ibid.
[5] 'First we shall hear his side', ibid.
[6] 'He has already arrived 2/5', ibid.

of the published material had been unknown to him. 'After its examination, I cannot but severely reprimand Count Arnim's procedure; and I leave it to you to take steps as you see fit, after he has vindicated his action.'[1]

Meanwhile, Arnim had arrived in Berlin. In a letter to the Foreign Ministry he complained of 'the unheard-of public insults to which he was being exposed and which originated in the Foreign Ministry', making it impossible for him to appear there in person. He also protested against the interpretations of his letter to Doellinger.[2] Next, having been refused an audience, he wrote to the Emperor, denying that his letter to Doellinger had been intended to start a controversy with the Chancellor. 'I believe', Arnim wrote, 'that Prince Bismarck himself could have written this letter—as far as it deals with politics—without contradicting himself in any way.' Arnim also asserted that he had in no way provoked the newspaper campaign. 'I was, so to speak, dragged into the street and forced to defend myself.'[3] The Emperor asked the Foreign Ministry to have Arnim submit his views regarding the correspondence about the Council and other Church questions in writing and through official channels.[4]

Following the Emperor's directive, Buelow asked Arnim to justify his recent actions, particularly whether the publication in the *Presse* of 2 April had originated directly or indirectly with him; whether he had any knowledge of the person or persons involved who might have brought about this publication, and how they might have obtained the documents in question. Inasmuch as these documents were being used by the Opposition to attack the Government, it was Arnim's responsibility, Buelow wrote, to assist in the search. Information was also required about the authorship and publication of an article in the *Spenerschen Zeitung* of 15 April, and of a similar article in the *Schlesischen Zeitung* of 29 April. As to Arnim's letter to Doellinger which had been published in the *Augsburger Allgemeine Zeitung*, it was important to ascertain whether

[1] The Emperor's marginal comment on Bismarck's report of 28 Apr. 1874.
[2] Arnim to Foreign Ministry, 3 May 1874.
[3] Arnim to the Emperor, 4 May 1874.
[4] The Emperor's marginal notes on Arnim's letter. The Emperor informed Bismarck that he had received Arnim's letter but had not granted him an audience. The Emperor to Bismarck, 4 May 1874.

Arnim had indeed written it and caused its publication. Should he admit to authorship and publication of the letter (which Arnim had already done in an open letter to a Berlin newspaper), he would have to answer for the consequences of his disregard of the official policies of his Government. In conclusion, Buelow reminded Arnim that it had been his duty, as a government official, to get permission from the Ministry for the publication of any document and that any complaints on his part should have been made through official channels rather than attacking governmental policy through the press.[1]

Arnim replied to none of these questions. Instead he indignantly rejected once more the idea that he had, in his letter to Doellinger, expressed any opposition to government policies. He complained again of attacks on him in the official press and claimed that this was tantamount to being found guilty without a chance for a defence.

> The sense which Your Excellency reads into my letter is not there [Arnim wrote], and cannot be there for anyone who does not start from the erroneous premiss [and implicitly believes] that the author is fundamentally an opponent of the Government. I mentioned in my letter the undisputable fact that the unfortunate course of the Council had led to the present disturbance. It has not yet been proved by what expression I put the responsibility for this on the Government. Nobody has the right to interpret my letter to Herr von Doellinger in such a way that the reader would mentally have to add words in order to give it the interpretation it should have, according to the directive of 5 May.[2]

Arnim's interpretation of his letter to Doellinger was at best ambiguous. It probably was an attempt to build up a legal case and show some moral indignation. For the first and last impression of this letter on any reader was of its author's prescience and the Government's short-sightedness. The question whether Arnim did or did not want to create this impression was irrelevant. As to the 'Diplomatic Revelations' in the *Presse*, Arnim categorically denied any responsibility for it. He

---

[1] Buelow to Arnim, 5 May 1874.

[2] Arnim to Buelow, 7 May 1874. In acknowledging this letter, Buelow informed Arnim that the Foreign Ministry was not going to enter into a discussion on individual points. If a complete justification of his behaviour should be further delayed, disciplinary action against him would be considered by the Foreign Ministry. Buelow to Arnim, 10 May 1874.

enclosed a statement from the editor of this paper which did not divulge the name of the contributor but declared that Arnim was in no way implicated. As to the memorandum, which also appeared in the *Presse*, it was merely a short statement, Arnim averred, in which he had set down the possible consequences of the Council. The effects of its publication had not been at all as Buelow had described them.[1]

Arnim's denial of responsibility for the 'Diplomatic Revelations' was a typical evasion. For in *Pro Nihilo* he states 'that it is really incredible that one should have read into the text of Count Arnim's reply that he had denied every connection with the Viennese publication'.[2] He went on to say in this pamphlet that what he had really meant in his reply to Buelow was that he had not been responsible for its *publication*, but that he had never denied having given the memorandum to a third person,[3] especially because he had been within his rights to dispose of the memorandum as he saw fit.[4] Arnim claimed those rights on two counts. First, he asserted that the memorandum of June 1870 was not an official but a private document, which had never been part of the official files. Therefore, he could make any use of it he liked. Second, his reason for publication was purely defensive. Because he had been exposed to constant venomous attacks by partisans of the Chancellor, he was forced to present his side of the story so as to refute these attacks and clear his reputation as a diplomat.[5] Moreover, the memorandum disclosed nothing but his agreement with the aims of the Chancellor's policy as far as ecclesiastical matters were

---

[1] Arnim further denied having had anything to do with the articles in the *Spenerschen Zeitung* and the *Schlesischen Zeitung* but he did admit having written the letter to Doellinger and having authorized him to publish it if he so desired. He had done this, Arnim wrote, to make up for the injury which recent publications in the press had caused him. Arnim to Buelow, 14 May 1874.

[2] *Pro Nihilo*, p. 123.

[3] Ibid., p. 124, Bismarck's marginalia: 'with order.'

[4] Ibid., pp. 123–4. Arnim's hand in this affair was established by the Foreign Ministry through Bleichroeder, who was told by Landsberg that he, Landsberg, had, on Arnim's request, sent the documents to the *Presse* in Vienna. Landsberg also told Bleichroeder that he would be willing to tell all he knew about Arnim if he were called as a witness, except for this one episode, the 'Diplomatic Revelations', which he had promised not to divulge. Radowitz (to Buelow), 9 Nov. 1874.

For Landsberg's statement in court, see *Darstellung*, pp. 207–11, and pp. 173–4 below.

[5] *Pro Nihilo*, p. 115.

concerned. But this, according to Arnim, did not suit Bismarck. He did not want the public to know that Arnim had agreed with his policy and had, perhaps, foreseen some of the consequences which he, the Chancellor, had overlooked.[1] To prove his point, Bismarck had dug into the archives and had published official and confidential documents to show that the Ambassador's views, prior to the Vatican Council, had been different and contradictory to those he had held during the Council.[2]

Meanwhile, in spite of sympathetic assurances from friends and relatives,[3] the noose began to tighten slowly around Arnim's neck and opposition to him in the highest circles of the Court and in the Government became more pronounced.[4]

One of the Foreign Ministry's first efforts was to attempt to establish the origins of the manuscript of the 'Diplomatic Revelations'. To this end it sent an agent, von Schluga, to Vienna and advised the German Embassy there to put at his disposal up to 2,000 guilders to obtain the necessary information.[5] But Schluga was unsuccessful, and, although the Foreign Ministry suspected a German journalist in Paris, Landsberg, of having had a hand in this affair, nothing definite could then be established.[6]

Another effort by the Foreign Ministry produced better

[1] *Pro Nihilo*, pp. 137–8.

[2] Ibid., p. 116. Doellinger, in his reply to Arnim's letter, takes much the same position as Arnim: ibid., p. 125, fn. *.

[3] Arnim's brother-in-law, Hermann Arnim, wrote to him on 2 May 1874 that public opinion would soon have forgotten the deplorable events of his resignation had it not been for his recent publications.

[4] After his attempt to secure an audience with the Emperor had failed, Arnim tried to gain access to the Crown Prince. Eulenburg, the Lord Chamberlain, informed Buelow of Arnim's request and inquired about the Ambassador's current status. In his reply, the State Secretary described the situation and added that Arnim's status was, at the moment, difficult to define. His appointment as Ambassador to Constantinople was held in suspense, that to France had expired. The Emperor had refused an audience to Arnim without asking for the advice of the Foreign Ministry; had it been asked, the Ministry would have had to advise against it. Eulenburg (to Buelow), 7 May 1874; B(uelow) to Eulenburg, 8 May 1874.

[5] Schluga to Foreign Ministry, 14 May 1874; Foreign Ministry to Schluga, 17 May 1874; Foreign Ministry to Doenhoff, 17 May 1874 (Schluga had been a military agent of Waldersee when the latter was chargé d'affaires in Paris. Waldersee, i. 158).

[6] On 27 May 1874 the *Presse* printed a short notice under the title 'Pro Domo' in which it reported the attempts of Schluga, without, however, mentioning his name. (Doenhoff to Foreign Ministry, 3 June 1874.) On Landsberg see p. 135, fn. 4 above.

results. This concerned an investigation into the authorship of an article that had appeared in the *Écho de Parlement* of Brussels on 21 September 1872. It was to the effect that the German Ambassador in Paris, Count Arnim, had requested that he be recalled after the question of the French war indemnity had been definitely settled. Count Arnim had stated, so it was said, that his assignment to Paris exposed him to too many annoyances. Should the Ambassador's request be granted, the position would be left vacant indefinitely. Prince Bismarck would be inclined, so it seemed, to assign only a consul to Paris, who could take care of routine matters. This news item had found its way into other papers and had been discussed at length in the German and French press. Bismarck had instructed Thile at the time to treat all inquiries on the subject ironically,[1] and Arnim had reported from Paris that, according to a local paper, responsibility for this erroneous item was being attributed to a Herr von Kahlden in Berlin.[2] Buelow now asked Wesdehlen, the German chargé d'affaires in Paris, to interview Beckmann, a German journalist, whose part in this publication Bismarck had suspected as early as 1872, and to report anything else he might know in this connection. Beckmann readily admitted to Wesdehlen that he had placed the story in the Belgian newspaper, but only on orders from Arnim, then still his superior.[3]

These revelations hardly justified a major action against Arnim. Neither legal nor disciplinary steps could be taken on the basis of these meagre findings, and Bismarck suggested to the Emperor that Arnim simply be retired from the service. According to the Chancellor, Arnim's behaviour fully justified such action. It was also necessary because of the difficulties and uncertainties a continuous vacancy would cause in the administration of the foreign service. Arnim's retirement would, furthermore, attract the least outward attention and could take place at any time in pursuance of the applicable regulations, with no necessity to give a particular reason for it.[4]

While the Chancellor was preparing his report, the Emperor

[1] Holstein to Thile, 24, 25 Sept. 1872; Thile to Arnim, 26 Sept. 1872.
[2] Arnim to Foreign Ministry, 1 Oct. 1872, *Staatsarchiv*, xxviii. 142–3.
[3] Buelow to Wesdehlen, 6 May 1874; Wesdehlen to Foreign Ministry, 13 May 1874.
[4] Bismarck to the Emperor, 13, 14 May 1874.

was discussing the same subject with Otto von Buelow, the Foreign Ministry's representative in the Emperor's retinue, in Wiesbaden. The Emperor, so it seemed to Buelow, was quite willing to have Arnim retired, because the Chancellor could not be expected to continue to work with such a recalcitrant subordinate. In a letter to the Foreign Ministry, Buelow hinted that a request by the Chancellor for Arnim's recall would most likely be approved immediately.[1]

At the same time Arnim directed yet another petition to the Emperor, justifying his behaviour and protesting his innocence. This arrived together with the Chancellor's report. The issue, Arnim wrote, was to decide whether he had started the newspaper controversy. In this connection, it was important to determine with whom the 'Diplomatic Revelations' had originated. He, Arnim, had often declared that he had not sent to the *Presse* the documents published in that paper. Although its management had refused to give any information concerning the sender, it had stated that whoever it was had never been in touch with him. Therefore it seemed clear that he had had nothing to do with this matter. As to his letter to Doellinger, this had been construed as an act of opposition against the Government. This had not been his intention, Arnim assured the Emperor, nor had he expressed it in the letter to Doellinger. It was meant as an apology to Doellinger, who had been offended by another publication. This also proved that he had not brought about this controversy. From the contents of the 5 May directive it would seem, Arnim went on, that the Foreign Ministry intended to instigate disciplinary action against him. While he did not fear the outcome of such an action, there seemed no reason for it. On the other hand, there were serious considerations against such action. Should it be ordered, he would be unable to restrict his defence to those points which were the immediate cause of this controversy and he would have to mention all the unfounded accusations made against him at one time or another. The question was whether it was in the interests of the imperial

[1] Buelow II (to Buelow, State Secretary), 14 May 1874. ('Otto von Buelow, official in the German Foreign Ministry, 1874–79; Minister in Bern, 1882–92. Frequently the Foreign Ministry's representative in the Kaiser's retinue. He was referred to as Buelow II in official documents, to distinguish him from State Secretary Buelow.' Rich and Fisher, iii. 34, fn. 6.)

service and the royal house to disclose these matters to a disciplinary tribunal. It would be better, Arnim suggested, as had been the custom in such cases, to appoint an *ad hoc* committee of reputable and unbiased men, experienced in diplomatic affairs, to investigate his entire period of service. As soon as this commission had given its findings, which he had no doubt would prove his innocence, he would ask for the Emperor's permission to retire from the service.[1]

Having read the statements of the Chancellor and the Ambassador, the Emperor, with great reluctance, signed the order for Arnim's retirement.[2] His reluctance was caused by the consideration that Arnim might be able to clear himself so thoroughly that to retire him would then seem too harsh a measure. These thoughts were dispelled by Buelow, the Emperor's aide, who called his master's attention to the proved facts and pointed out that Arnim's temporary retirement could not be considered a punishment in the legal sense, but rather as a political measure.[3] But there were other, more tangible, arguments which carried greater weight with the Emperor than Buelow's equivocations.[4]

Bismarck, who must have sensed the Emperor's reluctance to take any firm action against Arnim, sent to Wiesbaden the Wesdehlen report and the Beckmann statement concerning the publication in the *Écho de Parlement* of September 1872. These proved that Arnim had knowingly made a false report and had abused his official position for unknown private purposes. It was enough to initiate disciplinary action against Arnim. But, the State Secretary wrote in a covering letter, it was not the Chancellor's intention to press these matters. All he wanted was that Arnim should be retired by royal command.[5] It was this disclosure of Arnim's part in the publication of the *Écho de Parlement* that quelled any scruples the Emperor had about Bismarck's original suggestion. That Buelow strongly supported the Chancellor's recommendations cannot be doubted.[6]

[1] Arnim to the Emperor, 14 May 1874.
[2] Buelow II to Foreign Ministry, 15 May 1874.
[3] Buelow II to State Secretary, 15 May 1874.
[4] In *Pro Nihilo*, p. 128, Arnim claims that Bismarck had threatened to resign.
[5] State Secretary to Buelow II, 15 May 1874.
[6] Buelow II to State Secretary, 16 May 1874; Buelow II to the Foreign Ministry, tel. no. 2, 16 May 1874. As further proof of Arnim's unsuitability, Bismarck had

The order for Arnim's retirement, together with his letter to
the Emperor, was sent from Wiesbaden to Berlin, and the
Emperor left it to Bismarck to inform Arnim of the royal
decision immediately, or to report his views on Arnim's letter
first.[1] Bismarck chose the first procedure. In his subsequent
comments on Arnim's letter he denied the Ambassador's contention that his case warranted a special commission of inquiry.
There were no precedents to justify such measures, Bismarck
thought. There were, furthermore, other objections to Arnim's
plan. From the point of view of official discipline it would, if
put into practice, make superior and subordinate equal before
such a commission. It would give purely disciplinary problems
the appearance of political questions and would elevate any
official's insubordination to the level and importance of a state
action. There was no basis for this in either law or tradition.
The complaints against Arnim, according to Bismarck, had to
do with his behaviour as an official toward his lawful superior
and could be dealt with adequately under existing regulations.
Only by following the steps prescribed by law for the Foreign
Ministry as well as for other government departments could
authority be upheld and responsibility be exercised. Otherwise,
orderly procedure in government service would be rendered
impossible.

The attitude which Count Arnim had assumed for the past two
years [Bismarck wrote to the Emperor] justified the assumption
that he was determined to make the official dissensions which he
had brought about between himself and his chief minister appear
outwardly in the light of a deep political cleavage, so as to enhance
his own political importance. In addition, there appeared to be
a clear intention to prolong the entire affair as much as possible.
This would probably succeed if a commission [as Arnim desired it]
were formed. It certainly would be to the detriment of Your
Majesty's service.[2]

As to Arnim's belief that a disciplinary action would be against
the interests of the foreign service and the royal house, Bismarck
contended that the contrary would be true. Neither would

the State Secretary send to the Emperor a derogatory report which was unsigned
and probably originated with Beckmann.
    [1] The Emperor (to Buelow II), 15 May 1874.
    [2] Bismarck to the Emperor, 17 May 1874.

a special commission be favourable to Arnim, because any impartial investigation would have to recommend either disciplinary or criminal proceedings in accordance with article 92, no. 3, of the penal code. For these reasons the Chancellor asked the Emperor not to grant Arnim's request for a special commission.

Regarding the information that Arnim had been asked to supply to the Foreign Ministry, Bismarck went on, the Ambassador had maintained that he himself had never sent the published letter and the memorandum to the *Presse* in Vienna. He had always evaded the question as to his prior knowledge or whether he had indirectly caused these documents to be published. Concerning his letter to Doellinger and his statement that it contained no opinion on official policy, this was contrary to the unanimous views of the political world. This letter alone would make Arnim's further employment impossible. In spite of all these factors, he did not wish to start disciplinary action against Arnim, Bismarck asserted, but was satisfied that the Ambassador had been removed, for the time being, from active service. This opinion took into account Arnim's former position as well as that of his family, and that official scrutiny of some of the Ambassador's official acts would probably involve him in criminal proceedings.[1]

It can be assumed, and there seems to be no evidence to the contrary, that Bismarck meant what he wrote to the Emperor and contemplated no further steps against Arnim. One reason for his lenient attitude may have been that the Chancellor wanted no public discussion of German foreign policy, which probably could not have been avoided at an inquiry, and that he did not want to create a rallying-point for the opposition, with Arnim playing the role of a martyr.

The decision to start disciplinary action against Arnim must have been taken shortly after Bismarck's report to the Emperor, because on 28 May the State Secretary referred to it in a letter to Arnim. He asked him to explain fully the item published in the *Écho de Parlement* and informed Arnim of the contents of the Wesdehlen and Beckmann reports.[2] Arnim put off replying and went to Karlsbad to take the waters.

[1] Ibid.
[2] No documents concerning such a decision have been found and it is not clear

When he finally answered Buelow's request, he tried to excuse and rationalize his part in the incident. He had sent a note to Beckmann, he wrote, while vacationing in Pomerania in the summer of 1872, and it was therefore incorrect to say that this note had originated from the Embassy in Paris. Besides, Count Wesdehlen had been in charge during his absence. It was not true that he had asked Beckmann to go to Brussels and to give the incident the exaggerated importance which, because of Beckmann's mistakes, it had finally assumed. The only thing he, Arnim, wanted to achieve with this news item was a certain effect in Parisian political circles. The note Beckmann had given to the newspaper was not exactly the same as the one he had received, Arnim went on, and the way in which Beckmann had handled the matter had left a bad impression all around. It had indeed been his intention to ask the Emperor's permission to retire as soon as the negotiations for the evacuation of French territory had been completed. But it was inaccurate to say that he had already done so at that time, as had been stated in the Belgian newspaper. This had been a mistake and he believed that Beckmann was responsible for it. The statement about the appointment of a consul in place of an ambassador had been intended, as everybody in Paris knew at the time, as a warning to the French, who were expressing their patriotism by assuming a hostile attitude toward the German Ambassador. Many Frenchmen had considered the appointment of ambassadors in Paris and Berlin a rash act and had believed that a chargé d'affaires would have been more appropriate for the duration of the occupation. The item in the *Écho de Parlement* had merely expressed these thoughts and observations. Conditions in France at that time were such, according to Arnim, that extraordinary steps had to be taken, and it had been necessary, from time to time, to pour cold water over French ambitions. This had also been the Chancellor's view, especially on this particular incident. Proof of this had been a note from Holstein, then acting as private secretary to Bismarck at Varzin, in which Holstein had informed him, Arnim, that the Foreign Ministry had requested permission to circulate the item from the *Écho de Parlement* in

when the decision was taken or who was responsible for it; Buelow to Arnim, 28 May, 20 June 1874.

Berlin newspapers. Permission had been granted by the Chancellor. When he had returned to Paris, Arnim went on, he had learned from Beckmann the details of this incident and, in order to lessen its effects, had asked him to put another notice in a Paris paper, saying that the sensational item in the Brussels paper had originated with a disgruntled German nobleman. As to his original report of 1 October 1872 about this matter, it was, so Arnim claimed now, purposely ambiguous, so that those officials in the Foreign Ministry who read it would be acquainted with the circumstances, but the clerks, who were not supposed to know the circumstances, were kept in the dark. In conclusion, Arnim stated that he had spoken to the Emperor about this incident, and the Emperor seemed at the time to have no objections.[1]

Arnim's tortuous explanations and feeble excuses had no effect. Bismarck observed that Arnim had knowingly reported an untrue statement in his report of October 1872, ascribing authorship of the article to von Kahlden, as well as in his recent letter in which he claimed that the Government had agreed with him about the publication in the Belgian paper.[2] It would be difficult to guess what the outcome of the controversy between Bismarck and Arnim might have been had the affair been limited to the developments up to this point. There can be little doubt that it would have been quite different from the eventual outcome.

[1] Arnim to Buelow, 20 June 1874.

[2] Buelow to Bismarck, 22 June 1874, in which he reported that there was nothing in the files to show that Arnim's authorship had been known in Berlin in Sept. 1872, or that the publication had been silently approved, as Arnim now implied. Eulenberg to Buelow, 25 June 1874.

XVI

THE MISSING DOCUMENTS

THE turning-point in the case against Arnim came when Holstein noted that several documents were missing from the archives of the German Embassy in Paris. Holstein made this discovery when he was asked by Hohenlohe, Arnim's successor in Paris, to assemble the Embassy files on ecclesiastical affairs.[1] Three reports and one directive were missing and this was at once reported to Berlin.[2] Five days later, still another directive from that series could not be found.[3]

Buelow, in Bismarck's absence, directed Hohenlohe to make a thorough search of the Embassy archives and to ascertain, with the help of the journal, which and how many documents were missing altogether.[4] The State Secretary at the same time informed Arnim of this incident, asked him to report at once on the whereabouts of these documents,[5] and informed Bismarck at Varzin of what had happened.[6] The Chancellor's reaction was instantaneous. Without asking for further details, he demanded that Arnim be threatened at once with legal proceedings if his first reply was unsatisfactory.[7]

Arnim took the position that the documents mentioned in Buelow's letter were notes and memos of private conversations which he had had with Thiers, which, in his opinion, did not belong to the Embassy archives. 'Since the Foreign Ministry seems to be of a different opinion in this matter, I shall return these documents to the Foreign Ministry before long, so it may do with them whatever it sees fit.'[8] In a subsequent communication Arnim stated that, inasmuch as the documents had been

[1] *Darstellung*, pp. 160–1.
[2] Hohenlohe to Foreign Ministry, 8 June 1874, ibid., p. 3.
[3] Hohenlohe to Foreign Ministry, tel. no. 27, 13 June 1874.
[4] Buelow to Hohenlohe, 13 June 1874.
[5] Buelow to Arnim, 15 June 1874, *Darstellung*, p. 4.
[6] Buelow to Bismarck, 15 June 1874.
[7] Eulenburg to Buelow, 16 June 1874.
[8] Arnim to Buelow, 19 June 1874, *Darstellung*, p. 4.

marked for his personal attention only, he had kept them separate and had told no one at the Embassy of their existence. On his departure from Paris, the question had arisen whether he should hand the documents to Prince Hohenlohe. He had not done so, Arnim explained, because he had been afraid of offending Hohenlohe's religious feelings with some of the terms he had used in these reports. He had never considered the documents his private property, but had intended to return them to the Foreign Ministry all along; only his illness had prevented him from doing so earlier.[1]

Meantime, the search in the Paris Embassy had been completed and Hohenlohe reported that there were altogether eighty-six documents missing—all from the period 1872 to 1874.[2] After returning some documents through his son and after further reflection, Arnim apparently decided to shift his defence tactics. In a letter to Buelow of 20 July[3] Arnim denied that the Foreign Ministry had any authority over him since his retirement; he was responsible only to the Emperor and therefore could not be asked to submit any official reports to the Ministry. He protested at Buelow's statement that the documents returned through his son had originally 'been taken' from the archives by him. These documents had never been part of the archives, Arnim wrote. He also denied the State Secretary's contention that he was primarily responsible for the missing documents. Examination of the archives in Paris had taken place two months after his recall and it would be difficult to prove that the documents had been missing before that date. There was also the possibility, Arnim averred, that the documents may have been lost during a time when a chargé d'affaires was in charge of the Embassy. Arnim then proceeded to account for the fifty-eight documents that Buelow had listed as missing. Of these, Arnim professed no knowledge of thirty-eight; seventeen he considered as belonging in his personal file and possession; three he had taken along with his personal papers by mistake—these he returned. Arnim justified his retention of the seventeen documents by saying that these

---

[1] Arnim to Buelow, 21 June 1874, ibid., pp. 5–7.
[2] Hohenlohe to Foreign Ministry, 26 June 1874, ibid., pp. 8–9. There was, at this point, some confusion about the exact number of missing documents. See Appendix IV in this study.
[3] *Darstellung*, pp. 10–14.

concerned his conflict with the Chancellor. They contained serious accusations against him and he needed these papers for his defence. Should the Foreign Ministry be of a different opinion, Arnim concluded, a judicial decision would have to be made.[1]

Obviously the Foreign Ministry could not let matters rest at this point. Aside from the legal aspect, questions of discipline and authority were involved which were especially important because the German imperial foreign service had been established only a few years and had as yet no tradition of its own. Precedents of this sort would certainly be detrimental to its future development; thus the Ministry was anxious to prove its point. It based its case for the return of the documents on two grounds. First, it denied Arnim's contention that he was no longer responsible to the Foreign Ministry and thus beyond its jurisdiction. Second, it contested his right to claim official documents as his private property.[2]

It would be difficult to challenge the logic of the Foreign Ministry's argument, though Buelow's threatening and blustering style was not conducive to an amicable settlement and was perhaps not meant to be. Arnim's reasoning, on the other hand, seemed clumsy and devious. Especially so if his recent controversy over the various newspaper publications is recalled. What then were Arnim's motives for this peculiar action which seemed to play straight into Bismarck's hand? It would seem that the reason Arnim had mentioned to Buelow that he needed these papers for his defence might have been the true one. But to defend what? Nobody was attacking him at the time and it can be assumed that Bismarck did not intend to publicize Arnim's dismissal any more than was absolutely necessary. Though the Chancellor had answered the 'Disclosures' of the *Presse* in the *Norddeutsche Allgemeine Zeitung*, nothing further had been published on this subject. It was precisely this that must have motivated Arnim. His vanity and exaggerated self-esteem would not let the matter rest and he could not let his opponent have the last word in this dispute. He had to answer him. He

[1] *Darstellung*, pp. 10–14.
[2] Buelow to Arnim, 5 Aug. 1874, ibid., pp. 14–18; see also Wilke's memorandum of 27 July 1874 on which Buelow's letter was based. Arnim replied on 11 Aug. 1874, maintaining his view without adding anything to the controversy, ibid., pp. 18–20.

had to show the public once more that it was he who possessed superior statesmanship and diplomatic skill and that he had been dismissed because of envy, intrigue, and opposition. To achieve this aim, he needed proof—proof similar to the memorandum that had been published in the *Presse*.[1] This could be found only among the official correspondence which he had carried on over the past three years. Mere copies of this correspondence would not have been suitable, because prospective editors and publishers had to be impressed with the authenticity of the papers in question. There was another consideration. Arnim, in his impulsiveness, had marked most of the critical directives of the Chancellor with marginal notes that were censorious as well as outspoken.[2] It would seem natural that he would have been hesitant to return documents which clearly revealed his innermost thoughts and his unflattering remarks about his superior's directives. (The idea, expressed at the trial later on, that these documents were Arnim's private papers, and that he could therefore make notations on them at will, may have occurred to him at the time he received these documents or only just at the time of the trial: fundamentally, it did not matter.) It can be assumed that these two considerations motivated him. It seems of little importance here to decide whether Arnim, on his departure from Paris, took the documents with him with a clear and well-formulated plan as to their future publication, or whether he took them as a precaution, undecided about his subsequent action and their future use, intending eventually to return them to the Foreign Ministry.

Arnim's plans during the summer and early autumn of 1874 seem to have been twofold—to play an active part on the domestic political scene by entering the Upper House of the Prussian Diet, and to publicize his views as widely as possible by acquiring ownership of a newspaper. His ambition to enter the Upper House was not new. Two years before, Arnim had made an attempt in that direction, but had failed because of

[1] The situation was, in some respects, similar to Bismarck's own dismissal later on. Of interest in this connection are Wilhelm II's remarks to Hohenlohe in November 1892: 'Compare what Bismarck is doing [the interviews and articles he published at that time were highly critical of the Emperor and the Government] with that for which poor Arnim had to suffer . . .' (Hohenlohe, ii. 495).

[2] See pp. 103–4 above; *Darstellung*, p. 395.

Bismarck's intervention with the Emperor.[1] In June 1874 he
wrote to several influential landowners in his district, soliciting
their vote in the forthcoming election. One, Count Krassow
of Pansewitz, replied that, though he recognized Arnim as 'an
experienced diplomat' and 'a perceptive statesman' who had
only recently demonstrated to the world that he had fully
recognized the overriding importance of ecclesiastical problems,
Arnim's opinions on other questions concerning internal policy
were unknown to him and to the other people in the neighbour-
hood.[2] Arnim explained that his views on internal policy were
not identical with those of any of the parties in the Upper
House. The most important problem of the day, in his opinion,
was how to terminate satisfactorily the struggle with the Roman
Catholic Church. He did not believe that the Government
could retreat from its policy in this struggle, nor that the Church,
even were its leadership to change, would give up its opposition.
In spite of these difficulties, Arnim thought that compromise
could be achieved. The root of the evil, as he saw it, was not
that Protestants were separated from their Catholic fellow
citizens by one or another dogma, but was the great dependency
of German Catholics on a foreign sovereign whose political
interest ran counter to those of their mother country. 'I feel
justified in doubting whether everything in the right direction
has been done by the Royal Government.'[3] Another problem
of internal policy was the reorganization of the Upper House,
Arnim continued.

Between universal suffrage on the one hand and the all-powerful
government on the other, there must, of necessity, exist a body,
which through its own independent authority can decisively
influence the policies of the government, without being accused of
partiality or selfishness.

There are, in our country, independent elements; but there are,
too, individuals whose advice should be listened to before political
decisions are taken. It is the task of a conservative policy to give to
those persons the right to participate in the public life of the nation,
if our political system should be [re]organized. The Upper House,
in its present composition, does not conform to those necessities.

[1] See p. 91 above, n. 5.
[2] Krassow to Arnim, 22 June 1874; on the political situation, G. Ritter,
pp. 369–74.
[3] Arnim to Krassow, 25 June 1874.

I am of the opinion that the influence of the independent elements of the country must not be made illusory by a wholesale creation of peers. At the same time it seems necessary to me that the seats in the Upper House should not become the privilege of one single category [of persons] only.[1]

The development of Arnim's other project—acquisition of a newspaper—was less clear. According to Landsberg, Arnim had mentioned the idea while he had been Ambassador in Paris and again after his recall. At the time he apparently considered the *Berliner Tageblatt* a suitable organ for his purpose.[2] In September 1874 the backers of the *Spenersche Zeitung*, which had been in financial difficulties for some time, were urgently seeking a buyer. Negotiations were going on intermittently with the *National Zeitung* and, through a middleman, with an anonymous party. On 23 September of that year a notice appeared in the *Berliner Boersen Courier* that Count Arnim was discussing terms with the *Spenersche Zeitung*. These discussions came to nothing when a member of the board of trustees of the *Spenersche Zeitung*, F. Schoenheimer, discovered that the anonymous party with whom he was negotiating was indeed Arnim.[3] This seems to have been the end of Arnim's newspaper project.

[1] Ibid. No answer to this letter has been found. There also seems to have been an attempt by Arnim to take an active part in the Old Catholic movement. Two letters from and to Doellinger, 23 Sept. and 3 Oct. 1874, indicate such an endeavour. See also Wemyss, ii. 303.

[2] *Darstellung*, pp. 208–9; (Landsberg) to Arnim, 21 July 1874. According to the *Berliner Tageblatt*, negotiations to obtain an influence on its editorial policies were conducted by Arnim as late as the middle of September 1874, and the sum of a quarter of a million thalers was mentioned in this connection. *Berliner Tageblatt*, 21 Nov. 1874.

[3] Schoenheimer to Heiberg, 23 Sept. 1874. An unsigned memorandum of 26 Sept. 1874 notes that Arnim's negotiations with a Dr. von Mugden about the sale of the *Spenersche Zeitung* can be considered a failure: Heiberg (to Phillipsborn), 19 Dec. 1874. Another indication of Arnim's interest along those lines is contained in a letter which informed Arnim that the *Preussische Reichs Correspondenz* could be acquired for 30,000 thalers and that articles published there would appear simultaneously in almost 100 newspapers: Zweigert to Arnim, 28 Sept. 1874.

XVII

THE INVESTIGATION

THE fight over the missing documents continued. Arnim's contention that as a temporarily retired civil servant of the Reich he was no longer under the jurisdiction of the Foreign Ministry, but responsible only to the Emperor,[1] prompted the Ministry to consult the Reich Chancellery.[2] The Chancellery agreed with the Foreign Ministry that an official on temporary retirement who denied the authority of his superior office would, according to article 119, be subject to disciplinary action and dismissal.[3]

In September Bismarck considered the time ripe to initiate legal action against Arnim and directed the Foreign Ministry to prepare a report to this effect, to be submitted to the Emperor for approval. Until then the Emperor had been opposed to such a step.[4] Following Bismarck's instructions, Wilke, the Ministry's legal adviser, reviewed the case and considered its legal aspects. Count Arnim had admitted having removed the official directives, as well as drafts of official reports, which were missing from the Paris Embassy archives. His statement that he had handed most of them over to his successor, Count Wesdehlen, had been refuted by the latter's official statement.[5] Arnim's contention that he regarded seventeen documents as his private property was unjustified, as he had been informed. It therefore followed, according to Wilke, that (1) Arnim had embezzled official documents, which was punishable under article 348 of the penal code, and (2) he had illegally taken possession of official documents, punishable under article 350 of the penal code. After the extensive correspondence Count Arnim had had with the Foreign Ministry, in which the legal implications

[1] Arnim to Buelow, 20 July 1874.
[2] Foreign Ministry to Reich Chancellery, 21 Aug. 1874.
[3] Reich Chancellery to Foreign Ministry, 31 Aug. 1874. Bismarck underlined the word dismissal and noted on the margin: 'This will not restore the archives.'
[4] Bucher to Buelow, 17 Sept. 1874.
[5] Statement by Wesdehlen, 24 Aug. 1874.

had been fully explained, it could not be doubted that he had acted with malice aforethought. The competence of a Prussian court to act in this matter was established by Arnim's residence in Prussia. And a search or a temporary arrest warrant issued by such a court might produce the documents or cause Count Arnim to hand them over. Criminal rather than civil proceedings were being recommended, because, Wilke argued, the preliminary conditions for a civil action—that is, pecuniary matters—were not present. Besides, criminal proceedings had priority over civil proceedings; the latter would, furthermore, in no way ensure the return of the documents.[1]

At a meeting in the Foreign Ministry on 20 September, at which Radowitz, for the political section, Buelow II, for the personnel section, Wilke as legal adviser, and Phillipsborn, in the absence of the State Secretary, participated, all aspects of the case were discussed once more. The consensus of the meeting was substantially the same as the conclusion Wilke had drawn in his report. Disciplinary action was not considered feasible, because Arnim's resulting dismissal would give him more freedom of action and would not lead to recovery of the missing documents. Civil proceedings could not be considered because official, not monetary, matters were involved. That left criminal proceedings the only possible action to be taken. This would also permit a search of Arnim's possessions and confiscation of the documents. To justify such a drastic step against a high state official to the Emperor, Phillipsborn suggested that the proposed action be approved by the Minister of Justice.[2]

Bismarck, informed of these deliberations, generally agreed with the recommendations of the Foreign Ministry officials. Because, judging from Arnim's previous behaviour, it was to be feared that he might use the documents for further publications which would endanger state secrets, Bismarck reminded the officials that speed and secrecy in recovering the documents were essential.[3] For this reason Bismarck considered it impractical

---

[1] Wilke memorandum, 20 Sept. 1874.

[2] Phillipsborn to Bismarck, 21 Sept. 1874.

[3] That Arnim's journalistic ventures were not limited to the *Presse* and the *Écho de Parlement* was proved later on during the pre-trial investigation when some of his private papers were seized. (See p. 155 below.) Among them was a draft of an article which had appeared in the *Koelnische Zeitung* of 29 May 1872, and was based on Arnim's official knowledge regarding Germany's policy toward France:

to consult the Minister of Justice. Instead, he directed Buelow II to get the Public Prosecutor's confidential opinion concerning the legal aspects of the case and his advice on the preliminary steps that should be taken. On the basis of the prosecutor's opinion and the Chancellor's further instructions, Buelow II was to report to the Emperor.[1]

Tessendorf, the Public Prosecutor, also considered criminal action the only feasible way of recovering the documents. He expressed himself willing to authorize a search of Arnim's house as soon as the Foreign Ministry gave official notification to start proceedings.[2] This much accomplished, Buelow II left for Baden-Baden on 28 September to report to the Emperor. After hearing the pertinent facts, the Emperor reluctantly agreed to the recommendations of the Chancellor and the Foreign Minister and expressed the opinion that 'personal considerations will have to be put aside and the responsibility for a possible scandal will have to be borne by Arnim and not by the Government'.[3]

Buelow II informed the Foreign Ministry of the Emperor's approval the very same day, and, when the news arrived in Berlin that evening, the official request to start criminal proceedings against Arnim was drawn up. The next morning, 3 October, Wilke presented this request to Tessendorf, who immediately obtained a decision from the Berlin City Court to start proceedings. The court issued a search warrant and authority for Arnim's arrest.[4]

Arnim, meantime, had left Berlin for his estate at Nassenheide.[5] There, the following day, his house was searched and he himself arrested. The missing documents were not found.[6]

Foreign Ministry to City Court, 4 Nov. 1874. See also Holstein's deposition of 1 Nov. 1874, Rich and Fisher, iii. 31–6.

[1] Bismarck to Buelow II, 26 Sept. 1874. In the meantime, all salary payments to Arnim were stopped. Buelow II to Foreign Ministry, tel. no. 25, 26 Sept. 1874.

[2] Phillipsborn to Bismarck, 29 Sept. 1874.

[3] Buelow II to Foreign Ministry, tel. no. 2, 2 Oct. 1874.

[4] Phillipsborn to Bismarck, 3 Oct. 1874. One reason for the great haste on the part of the Foreign Ministry was the fear that Arnim might leave Germany. According to Lindau, Arnim had asked him at the end of September to take an apartment for him in Paris for the middle of October. Radowitz memorandum, 2 Oct. 1874.

[5] Radowitz to Buelow II, 3 Oct. 1874.

[6] Pescatore to Foreign Ministry, 4 Oct. 1874; Phillipsborn to Bismarck, 4 Oct. 1874.

When asked their whereabouts, Arnim, remaining quite calm, explained that they were in a foreign country. Told that under the circumstances there was no alternative to his arrest, he declared himself willing to procure the documents immediately if the authorities would not arrest him and if their hiding-place and the name of their custodian were kept secret. These conditions were rejected by the examining magistrate and whatever papers were found were confiscated and Arnim placed under arrest.[1] In the company of his wife, his children, and a police inspector, Arnim travelled to Berlin to be imprisoned there on remand. He was given a cell to himself and was allowed to provide his own food. Following the failure at Nassenheide, searches of his mother's house and his son's house were made, without success.[2]

Arnim's arrest created a sensation in the capital and throughout Germany. 'First impression: painful. Form of the proceedings: shocking. Arrest unusual for this kind of offence. It comes as a surprise', Baron Muench, Counsellor of the Austrian Embassy in Berlin, wrote to Andrassy in Vienna, 'that the city court here [Berlin] has been chosen. Antagonism [between Bismarck and Arnim] still too fresh in everybody's mind not to interpret the trial as a personal affair . . .'.[3] That a man who had only recently been the personal representative of the German Emperor and the first Ambassador of the Reich in Paris should have been arrested and his house searched gave rise to endless speculation and much controversy. Arnim was of an old and well-known family with many influential members in high places of society and government. They, together with Bismarck's numerous adversaries, constituted a formidable and outspoken opposition, which used this incident, and later the

---

[1] In a report to the Emperor of 4 Oct. 1874, Buelow II described the event: '. . . this authority [the Berlin City Court], which is known to be completely independent and which looks upon these events [Arnim's transgressions] with impartiality and without prejudice, found Arnim's behaviour so very serious that it decided to start a search for the documents at Arnim's house immediately and to have him, if need be, arrested . . . the search for the papers was in vain and, finally, as the only legal means left at their disposal, they arrested Arnim today at 1.00 p.m. . . .'

[2] (Phillipsborn to) Buelow, 6 Oct. 1874.

[3] Muench to Andrassy, 8 Oct. 1874, as quoted by E. Wertheimer, 'Der Prozess Arnim', in *Preussische Jahrbuecher*, vol. 222, p. 274, henceforth cited, Wertheimer, *Arnim*.

trial, as a rallying-point to turn against the Chancellor and his policies. Their machinations, as much as the events, made this affair famous and known far beyond Germany's borders.

Officials in the Foreign Ministry were aware of these trends, and Phillipsborn promptly saw to it that this matter would be presented in the press in a way favourable to the Government, because, as he put it, 'what was involved here was a question of law and justice'. Should the press not accept this view, he was prepared to go further.[1]

Preparation for the trial continued. Close co-operation was established between the Foreign Ministry and the office of the Public Prosecutor; and from Varzin Bismarck kept a careful watch on proceedings. Having read copies of some of the missing documents, the Chancellor pointed out that it was of the utmost importance that the court should be convinced that Arnim's contention that the documents he withheld were his private papers was frivolous and false. The best thing, Bismarck thought, would be to present to the court the complete documents, regardless of any state secrets they might contain. By that time Bismarck thought it more important to have Arnim punished for his disobedience than to get the missing documents back to the Foreign Ministry.[2] Their recovery seemed to have receded into the background and punishment of Arnim had apparently become paramount. Bismarck had probably concluded that this was his opportunity to ruin Arnim completely.

The Chancellor also asked that the Public Prosecutor be made aware of other incriminating evidence; that Arnim had sent the documents abroad and that, as a result, there was grave suspicion that these too might be misused by Arnim; that the 'Diplomatic Revelations' had been published by Arnim in the Vienna *Presse*; that Arnim's untruthfulness had been established by Wesdehlen and Beckmann; and, finally, that Arnim's actions in connection with the evacuation of French territory had been counter to the Foreign Ministry's instructions.[3] In a following directive, Bucher explained to Phillipsborn that he did not think much of these points, but, since he had 'reduced the demands of the chief from a much more doubtful

---

[1] Phillipsborn to Bismarck, 5 Oct. 1874.
[2] Bucher (to Phillipsborn), 9 Oct. 1874.
[3] Bucher to Foreign Ministry, tel. no. 32, 9 Oct. 1874.

[position] to those expressed in telegram no. 32, he wished to cause no further opposition'. Bucher also doubted whether Tessendorf would be willing to use these arguments as the threat they were intended to be.[1]

A physical examination by the authorities showed that Arnim was suffering from severe diabetes and that a further stay in prison would endanger his life.[2] A request by his defence counsel that he be released from prison because of poor health was rejected by the court.[3] Instead Arnim was moved to the Charité hospital: two rooms were put at his disposal and he received medical treatment.[4] Rumours of Arnim's possible release reached Baden-Baden and agitated the Emperor considerably. Though he realized that it was illegal to interfere with the proceedings of the court, he thought that there should be a way of keeping 'as dangerous a man as Arnim in prison, regardless of his state of health'.[5] The State Secretary informed the Emperor that he had already called the attention of the Public Prosecutor to the dangers of Arnim's release and would repeat his warning.[6] His interest thoroughly aroused, the Emperor was anxious to be informed of all details of the preliminary proceedings. To comply with his master's wishes, Buelow II thought that, though anything that would appear as government interference should be avoided, it should be possible for the Foreign Ministry to obtain confidential information from the Public Prosecutor's office which could be presented to the Emperor.[7] The State Secretary complied and two days later reported on events which had occurred up to then. Arnim's private papers, which had been seized at Nassenheide, had been carefully examined and their contents had provided valuable material for the investigation. Arnim's correspondence with several journalists had been found, from which it was apparent that he had used the press for his own political purpose. In particular it had been established beyond any reasonable doubt that there existed a connection between Arnim and

[1] Bucher to Phillipsborn, 9 Oct. 1874.
[2] Phillipsborn to Bismarck, 10 Oct. 1874.
[3] Tessendorf to Wilke, 10 Oct. 1874.
[4] Buelow to Bismarck, 12 Oct. 1874.
[5] Buelow II to Foreign Ministry, 10 Oct. 1874.
[6] Buelow to the Emperor, 11 Oct. 1874.
[7] Buelow II to Buelow, 15 Oct. 1874.

the editor of the Vienna *Presse*. Thus his official explanation
that he had had nothing to do with the publication of the
'Diplomatic Revelations' was proved untrue.[1] Buelow also
noted that public opinion, which at first had favoured Arnim,
had recently turned against him. The public seemed to have
realized, Buelow believed, the necessity of the preservation of
order, discipline, and reliability in the foreign service by all
legal means against the transgressions of Count Arnim.

Buelow's observations of a turnabout in public opinion, as
expressed in various German newspapers, seems exaggerated.
Newspaper opinion in general followed an established pattern.
Those papers which supported the Government, and were in
one way or another subsidized by it, were, naturally enough,
against Arnim. Most of the others opposed the Government and
castigated its handling of this case.[2] It was noted, among other
things, that the president of the Berlin City Court had been
forced to issue a denial that the court had been exposed to
undue influence and pressure by the Government.[3] These
accusations had first been printed in the *Weser Zeitung* and had
been taken up by some Berlin papers. They singled out Tessendorf, the Public Prosecutor, and Pescatore, the examining
magistrate, and accused them of having consulted officials of
the Foreign Ministry three hours before Arnim's arrest warrant
had been issued. According to Tessendorf, this was an 'infamous
insinuation'. He and Pescatore had been at the Foreign
Ministry only after the court had decided on the arrest, he said,
which had been scheduled for the same day.[4] While Tessendorf's statement was true as far as it went, there had, in fact,
been a meeting of Foreign Ministry officials with the Public
Prosecutor on 28 September, during which the details of the
proceedings had been discussed.[5] Nor was that all. Bismarck's
interference by way of suggestions and recommendations has
been mentioned before; and so has the Emperor's.[6] In addition,
other officials of the Ministry, notably Wilke and Phillipsborn,

---

[1] Buelow to the Emperor, 16 Oct. 1874, and the Emperor's marginal note:
'A fact which, in a *letter* to me, he had explained to be untrue and about which
he wanted to tell me during an *audience*. W 18/10 74.'

[2] Wertheimer, *Arnim*, p. 275; *Frankfurter Zeitung*, 23 Oct. 1874.

[3] *Deutscher Reichs und Preussischer Staatsanzeiger*, 14 Oc 1.1874.

[4] Tessendorf (to Buelow), 13 Oct. 1874.

[5] See p. 152 above. [6] See p. 155 above.

had co-operated closely with Tessendorf. That the line of necessary official business had not always been strictly observed was quite clear. It was also plain from these incidents that the court was under considerable pressure from the Government to impose a harsh sentence upon Arnim. That it did not do so in the end was to its great credit and a testimony of its independence.

The public realized that this was not an ordinary trial and that more than legal matters were at stake. It was obvious that the Chancellor's prestige would suffer if Arnim were to be cleared by the court. But, with the power of the Government in Bismarck's hands, this was unlikely. 'Prince Bismarck will have to win the lawsuit against Count Arnim; he has to win it for the sake of his political prestige; because the acquittal of the Ambassador would incriminate him, even endanger his position. . . .'[1] While some of the political parties, such as the National Liberals, were reluctant to oppose Bismarck on that issue, society circles in Berlin were almost unanimous in their opposition to the Chancellor.[2] They could not forgive him for picking on a member of their own class, nor for the way he was treating him in public. 'Nobody [but Bismarck] knows so well how to use the *avilir puis détruir* and to ruin his victim in the eyes of public opinion through well-prepared poisoned correspondence, and to expose him to the deadly blow which awaits him . . .', Roggenbach wrote to Stosch on 30 August 1874.[3]

Arnim's diabetes had worsened during his incarceration, and, after a renewed petition by his defence counsel, the court agreed to release him on bail. This was fixed at the then enormous sum of 100,000 thaler and Arnim had to promise not to leave Germany before the investigation had been terminated.[4] He used his freedom to promote his cause, much to the displeasure of the Foreign Ministry and the court. In Grenville Murray, Paris correspondent of the *New York Herald*, he found a willing champion, and through him and his paper presented his side of the case. Many of the articles published

[1] *National Zeitung*, 10 Oct. 1874.
[2] Wertheimer, *Arnim*, p. 275.
[3] Quoted by J. Heyderhoff, *Im Ring der Gegner Bismarcks* (Leipzig, 1943), pp. 159–62. This, it should be noted, was not written in connection with the Arnim affair, but rather with reference to the Bismarck–Stosch entanglement.
[4] Buelow to the Emperor, 27 Oct. 1874.

in the *New York Herald* were taken over and reprinted in the German press. The *Herald* printed on 29 October a summary of the Arnim–Buelow correspondence of the previous July and August,[1] and, on the following day, the *Vossische Zeitung* printed the entire exchange verbatim. As a result, the court warned Arnim that he would be arrested once more if, as was stated in the official notification, he used his freedom 'to obscure the truth'.[2]

Disregarding these warnings, Arnim continued his activities. On 10 November his lawyer, Munckel, returned to the court eight of the missing documents; and though they contained highly classified material Munckel took no precautions whatever. He explained that his client had discovered these papers only recently because his belongings had been badly mixed up and packed during his absence from Paris. There was no hope of finding any more documents.[3] Following this incident, Arnim was called into court once more and, because of his questionable conduct, was again remanded into custody.[4] Because of his bad health, however, he was released shortly thereafter and put under house arrest. Tessendorf tried to cite Arnim for attempted treason because of the way Munckel had returned the documents, but, as he himself noted, this charge was not likely to be accepted by the court at that time.[5]

Preparations for the trial were almost completed and the indictment was ready to be published. All this, Tessendorf notes maliciously, 'will hardly be beneficial to his [Arnim's] state of health'.[5] One of the major questions was whether the trial should be conducted in public or secret session. The Foreign Ministry said it welcomed an open session in principle and deemed such a procedure desirable and useful.

It would not only not endanger public order and morality in Germany, but, on the contrary, by its open exposition and display of the entire course of events and of all pertinent points, it will greatly contribute toward nullifying a grave damage [which had been inflicted] on the sense of duty and discipline of the officials of the Foreign Ministry, and to invalidate the accusations and sus-

[1] See pp. 145–6 above.
[2] Buelow to the Crown Prince, 5 Nov. 1874.
[3] Buelow to the Emperor, 10, 11 Nov. 1874.
[4] Buelow to the Emperor, 12 Nov. 1874.
[5] Tessendorf (to Wilke), 14 Nov. 1874.

picions to which they had been systematically exposed. It is therefore decidedly in accordance with the wishes of the Foreign Ministry and in the general interest of the state that the procedure in this affair, now as well as in the future, be given full publicity.[1]

But there were other factors to be taken into account. The trial would deal to a great extent with the contents of diplomatic directives and reports concerning the relationship of Germany with foreign powers. Clearly it would not be in the interest of the State should the contents of certain documents be made known to the public. These documents, the Foreign Ministry thought, should be omitted from the indictment and the trial. It would be up to the accused whether he wanted to respect these restrictions concerning the security of the Reich. Should he choose not to do so, the responsibility for such action would be his, and public opinion would realize all the better the implications and dangers to which Arnim, by keeping the documents, had exposed the security of the country.[2]

This seemingly equitable proposition had one great advantage for the Foreign Ministry. By withholding documents which allegedly jeopardized the country's security, the Foreign Ministry also withheld those which illustrated the conflict between Bismarck and Arnim and reflected their respective views on German policy toward France. Some of these documents contained Bismarck's reprimands and these the Foreign Ministry wanted to introduce in court. It instructed Tessendorf that part of these documents should be read in open session.[3] The Public Prosecutor expressed his doubts about this procedure and solicited, informally, the opinion of the court. He was told, and so informed the Foreign Ministry, that the court would refuse any document that was incomplete.[4] In spite of this decision the Foreign Ministry persisted in its attempt to have it both ways, and Wilke suggested to Tessendorf that he should mention in his covering letter to the indictment that, on recommendations from the Foreign Ministry, passages from

[1] Foreign Ministry to the Public Prosecutor, 4 Nov. 1874; another reason to hold a public trial might have been the threat of the *Daily Post* of Liverpool to publish all documents pertaining to the trial if it were conducted in secret session. *Frankfurter Zeitung*, 28 Oct. 1874.

[2] Foreign Ministry to the Public Prosecutor, 4 Nov. 1874.

[3] Foreign Ministry to the Public Prosecutor, 6 Nov. 1874.

[4] Wilke (memorandum), 7 Nov. 1874.

certain documents should be omitted for political reasons. Should the court reject this argument, Tessendorf could suggest that those documents that were incomplete should, though part of the indictment, not be considered as such.[1] Tessendorf did as he had been told, but the court refused to permit such sophistries and stated that it would consider only complete documents as part of the indictment.[2] Since the Chancellor insisted on a public trial, those documents which the Foreign Ministry had intended to submit in extract only had to be withdrawn.[3]

The presentation of suitable government witnesses and experts also proved somewhat more difficult than was generally expected. One of the more recalcitrant witnesses was Field-Marshal Manteuffel. The Public Prosecutor was particularly interested in having him appear in court to testify against Arnim. But Manteuffel declined and was supported by the Emperor. Bismarck and the officials in the Foreign Ministry were much irritated by Manteuffel's uncooperative attitude. At a meeting with Wilmowski, the chief of the Emperor's civil cabinet, Bismarck grudgingly conceded that he attached no great importance to Manteuffel's appearance, especially because the Field-Marshal's deep-seated reluctance would make an unfavourable impression on the court and would nullify all advantages of his testimony.[4] As far as the testimony of experts was concerned, Bismarck expressed the desire that Thile, the former State Secretary, should not be called, nor should Bleichroeder, the banker, appear as a witness, if that were at all possible.[5] The objection to Bleichroeder was later retracted and Tessendorf was advised that either Bleichroeder

[1] Wilke to Tessendorf, 8 Nov. 1874.
[2] Tessendorf (to Wilke), 9 Nov. 1874.
[3] Buelow to Tessendorf, 9 Nov. 1874; Bismarck's insistence on a public trial was, at least partly, the result of public opinion as expressed by various newspapers. In a directive to Hohenlohe, after the trial, Buelow asserted, however, that admission or exclusion of the public was solely a matter for the court to decide, inasmuch as the Government lacked any means to exert its influence. B(uelow) to Hohenlohe, 21 Dec. 1874.
[4] Wilke memorandum, 1 Dec. 1874. Tessendorf also decided to forego Manteuffel's testimony, unless the defence or the court insisted upon it. Manteuffel's persistent refusal to testify was creating a most unfavourable impression and might prejudice the Government's case, Buelow believed. Buelow to Wilmowski, 4 Dec. 1874.
[5] Wilke to Tessendorf, 6 Dec. 1874.

or his principal secretary, Dr. Pauly, could appear in court.[1]
But Tessendorf declined this offer. He considered Dr. Pauly's
testimony unnecessary and his naming as a witness positively
dangerous, because of his earlier discussions with Landsberg.[2]
Another difficulty arose when the court tried to obtain the
testimony of the editors of the Vienna *Presse*. The Austrian
courts, which had been approached in this matter, refused their
co-operation on the grounds that according to Austrian law
witnesses could be forced to give testimony only in important
criminal cases, and the case in question was not considered such
by the Austrian judiciary.[3] Annoyance over this refusal was
particularly strong in the Foreign Ministry in Berlin, because
public opinion in Austria, and especially in Vienna, had consistently favoured Arnim. This was most openly expressed by
the newspapers, which almost without exception had attacked
the German Government over this case. The case of the *Neue
Freie Presse* was of special significance because this paper was
close to the Austrian Government and could not have maintained its anti-German policy without the Government's
sanction.[4]

As the day of the trial approached, newspaper reports about
the case became more frequent in Germany and their comments
more scathing. The lines for or against Arnim became more
sharply defined. In their attempt to discover the real motives
for the struggle between the Chancellor and the former
Ambassador—for very few papers believed it to be a case
involving legal matters only—many indulged in quite fantastic
speculations. The most common theory concerning the origins
of the conflict ascribed it to personal animosity and rivalry
between the two men. Some papers went further and gave more
specific details. The *Berliner Tageblatt*, for example, believed
that there was an international ultramontane conspiracy

---

[1] Wilke to Tessendorf, 12 Dec. 1874.

[2] Wilke (to Buelow), 12 Dec. 1874. Landsberg had apparently been enter-
tained by Bleichroeder and had been put up by him while in Berlin to testify.
Bleichroeder (to Bismarck), 13 Dec. 1874.

[3] Wilke memorandum, 15 Nov. 1874.

[4] Buelow to Schweinitz, 29 Oct. 1874. Schweinitz was asked to call the attention
of the Austrian Prime Minister to this deplorable situation and to express his
regrets that the Austrian Government had not found any means to interfere with
these aberrations of the press: Buelow to Schweinitz, 14 Nov. 1874; Schweinitz,
i. 307–8.

between Berlin, Paris, and Vienna, of which Arnim was the only visible link.[1] The *Neue Freie Presse* of Vienna wrote that Arnim's opposition to the Chancellor's policy toward France was shared by influential conservative circles in Germany. It was their support, the *Presse* asserted, which had made it possible for Arnim to hold out against Bismarck for so long. This also explained the severity and ruthlessness of the Chancellor and his supporters and their attempt to ruin Arnim.[2]

While the *Presse* did not name the influential circles that allegedly stood behind Arnim, another Viennese paper, the *Tagespresse*, came right out with it and called Augusta, the German Empress, Arnim's protector.[3]

[1] *Berliner Tageblatt*, 18 Nov. 1874.
[2] *Neue Freie Presse*, 12 Dec. 1874.
[3] *Tagespresse*, 15 Nov. 1874.

XVIII

THE TRIAL

THE trial before the City Court of Berlin began on 9
December 1874 amidst great excitement fostered by
clandestine rumours and wild speculations by some of
the newspapers, which predicted sensational disclosures. Arnim,
confident and undaunted, had requested twelve seats for his
friends, 'claiming that, as host, he had the right to invite more
people'.[1] The indictment, far from creating a sensation, simply
accused Arnim of having knowingly suppressed official documents which had been in his custody and of having illegally
appropriated documents which he had received in an official
capacity.[2]

Arnim was represented by three lawyers: Munckel, Dockhorn, and Holtzendorf. Munckel opened the defence by
questioning the competence of the court—holding that his
client's domicile was his estate, Nassenheide, situated in the
judicial district of Stettin—and by complaining about Arnim's
treatment during the preliminary investigation.[3] The court
rejected both contentions. Next, and this became one of the
main issues of the trial, Dockhorn challenged the prosecution's
statement that the papers in question were official documents.
His challenge was not altogether unsuccessful. Koenig, from
the Foreign Ministry, called as an expert on this subject, had
to admit upon cross-examination that the nature of a document was determined by its content. Thus, correspondence
dealing with granting leaves and transfers could be considered
private papers. In this connection Arnim pointed out that the
directives bearing on these matters had not been considered
private documents by the Foreign Ministry. The defence was
further able to prove that merely because directives and reports
carried journal numbers was without significance as far as their
deposition and safe keeping in the archives was concerned. And

---

[1] *Deutsche Nachrichten*, 5 Dec. 1874, as quoted by Taffs, p. 45.
[2] *Darstellung*, p. 43.   [3] Ibid., pp. 51 ff.

it was established through the testimony of another expert that a number of documents received from and sent to the Foreign Ministry were transmitted without such registration numbers, although their contents were highly political. In connection with the safe keeping of documents, the defence could also call the attention of the court to the fact that the facilities and working-conditions in the building of the Paris Embassy were very restricted and the archival system exceedingly poor.[1] It was at this point in the trial that an incident occurred which gave birth to a long-standing myth: the spying of Friedrich von Holstein, Second Secretary at the German Embassy in Paris.[2]

Following the testimony of several officers and employees of the Paris Embassy about the daily routine there, Dockhorn revealed that Holstein had confessed to Arnim that the Foreign Ministry had employed him in Paris to spy on Arnim and to report continuously on his activities and his behaviour. Since it had been established in the course of previous testimony that it was Holstein who had first discovered the missing documents and that he too had had access to the secret archives, Dockhorn strongly insinuated that it had been Holstein himself who, on orders from his superiors, had taken the missing documents.[3] This statement by the defence was made on Friday, 11 December, apparently in the hope that the testimony of witnesses would be terminated by the court on Saturday and that there would be no time for Holstein to appear before the tribunal.[4] This proved a mistake. The trial lasted for another week, and Holstein, hastily summoned to Berlin by the Foreign Ministry, appeared in court on Monday, 14 December. Before he appeared on the witness stand, Dockhorn retracted part of his previous statement and denied that he had said or implied that Holstein had taken any documents.[5] This in itself would invalidate the suspicion cast upon Holstein. There was, in addition, the undisputable fact that Arnim himself had retained certain documents and returned others. For these reasons alone, Holstein could not have done what Dockhorn implied. Nor is this the point that popular imagination fastened upon. It was rather Holstein's 'spying' on Arnim that excited the popular

---

[1] *Darstellung*, pp. 78–130.
[2] Rich, *Holstein*, i. 74 ff.
[3] *Darstellung*, p. 164.
[4] Buelow to Hohenlohe, 20 Dec. 1874.
[5] *Darstellung*, pp. 230–1.

fantasy and provided the foundation for the subsequent legend about the 'Grey Spectre'.[1]

Immediately after Dockhorn had made his oblique accusation, the Foreign Ministry issued a denial. In a letter to Tessendorf, Buelow rejected the statement by Arnim's defence counsel, at the same time insisting on the right of the Foreign Ministry to issue orders to its agents to supervise and report on their superiors should such a need arise.[2] On the witness stand, Holstein categorically denied ever having received orders from the Chancellor or from anybody else to report on Arnim. He admitted having corresponded with friends in the Foreign Ministry and that he had mentioned this to Arnim when the Ambassador had questioned him in December 1872.[3]

This statement left several questions unanswered. While it may have been true that Holstein had not received any explicit orders and had not 'reported' on Arnim in the strictest and most formal meaning of these terms, he could have, and probably did, write in his private letters comments none too favourable to the Ambassador. That these letters found their way to Bismarck can be easily assumed. But what of it? Holstein's correspondence, whatever it contained, did not contribute to nor would it explain anything concerning the conflict between the Chancellor and the Ambassador. Even if Holstein's derogatory letters about Arnim were taken as fact, they would not change the picture. Bismarck needed no secret reports on Arnim to be aware of his activities. Arnim's own reports were quite sufficient.

There is one aspect about this Arnim–Bismarck–Holstein triangle worth speculating about which is generally overlooked. While it can be assumed that Holstein did not spy and report on Arnim, the possibility that he actively intrigued against him cannot be disregarded. As a witness in court, Holstein testified that in April 1872, when Bismarck talked about retiring, he, Holstein, believing that Arnim would be the successor best suited to the Chancellorship, had possibly written to Arnim

[1] N. Rich, 'Holstein and the Arnim Affair', *Journal of Modern History*, vol. 28, no. 1 (Mar. 1956), pp. 35–7.

[2] Buelow to Tessendorf, 11 Dec. 1874, Rich and Fisher, iii. 36–7. According to Odo Russell, Lindau had been sent to Paris by Bismarck to watch Arnim: Newton, ii. 46.

[3] *Darstellung*, p. 232; Rich and Fisher, i. 95, iii. 34 ff; Rich, *Holstein*, i. 82–3.

along these lines.[1] According to Frankenstein, the Austrian Ambassador in Berlin, such a letter did indeed exist and was, together with Arnim's reply—in which Arnim had apparently had the imprudence to agree and accept Holstein's proposition —in the files of the court.[2] Holstein's statement of his belief in Arnim's suitability for the Chancellorship was all the more surprising because he must have known at the time that Bismarck and Arnim were not on the best of terms and that their opinions on German policy toward France were quite different. Holstein himself did not share Arnim's views on German policy, according to a statement he made at a conference in the Foreign Ministry about his relationship with Arnim at Paris.[3] Thus it was possible that Holstein contributed materially to poisoning the atmosphere between Bismarck and Arnim and aggravating the conflict. Though Holstein's intrigue would be more difficult to prove than his 'spying', it would be more plausible and would better accord with the known facts.[4]

It was only natural that the Foreign Ministry should have backed Holstein's statement in court. But it did more. A full-fledged campaign was set in motion to rehabilitate his honour and erase the bad impression created by Dockhorn's insinuation. Not only the newspapers in Germany, but the Embassies in Paris and London, were asked to see that public opinion there should be informed.[5] The most important and, for Berlin society, decisive factor in favour of Holstein was his special audience with the Emperor.[6]

With Holstein's testimony, examination of witnesses was completed and the Public Prosecutor began his summation.

---

[1] *Darstellung*, pp. 232–3.   [2] Wertheimer, *Arnim*, p. 287.
[3] Rich and Fisher, iii. 31 ff.
[4] In spite of the wealth of documents on Arnim and the trial, there are a few important gaps. The protocols of the court's secret sessions are not available and neither are Arnim's private papers. A passage in a letter from Tessendorf to Wilke of 12 Dec. 1874 refers to a secret session in which Arnim had produced 'a letter from Herr von Holstein to him, in April 1872, which *heavily compromises* v.H.' Rich and Fisher, iii. 37–8. For a different and more sympathetic interpretation of Holstein's part, see Rich, *Holstein*, i. 74 ff.
[5] Buelow to Hohenlohe and Muenster, 16 Dec. 1874.
[6] Buelow to Hohenlohe, 20 Dec. 1874, Rich and Fisher, iii. 38–9. That so much fuss was made on behalf of a mere secretary of legation would, under ordinary circumstances, seem odd. It should be kept in mind, however, that it was not only Holstein who was being slandered but through him the Foreign Ministry and the Chancellor.

Tessendorf's role during the trial had not been outstanding—
defence counsel had gained many telling points against him,
his cross-examination had been weak, and his presentations
perfunctory—but his summation was clear and concise. He
stressed Arnim's contradictory answers to why he had kept the
documents, his probable motives for keeping them at all, and
his hand in the reports of the Brussels *Echo de Parlement* and the
Viennese *Presse*. In conclusion, he asked the court to sentence
Arnim to two years and six months' imprisonment.[1]

For the defence, all three lawyers made their presentations
in turn. The most significant and, without doubt, the best
statement in Arnim's defence was made by Professor Holtzendorf, the famous jurist of Munich.[2] Basing his arguments on
purely technical and legal grounds, he denied that the Reich
had any property claims on the papers in dispute.[3] Next, he
tried to prove that these papers were not records within the
strict meaning of the law, and, finally, he asserted that there
could be no question of Arnim having suppressed or mis-
appropriated these papers. The only accusation that could be
made—and that was a disciplinary matter—was that Arnim
had failed to deliver the papers at the right time and that he
had shown negligence while they were in his custody.[4]

The verdict, pronounced by the court on Saturday, 19
December 1874, found Arnim innocent of misappropriation of
documents and of misbehaviour while in office. He was found
guilty of an offence against the public order—because he had
not returned, in time, the papers pertaining to Church policy.
For that offence he was sentenced to three months in prison.[5]

Supporting the verdict, the presiding judge accepted part of
the argument of the defence that the contents of the documents
determined their official status and he also accepted Arnim's
good faith and his claim that he could have regarded some such
documents as his private property. He rejected Arnim's contention that after his retirement he was no longer subject to
the disciplinary powers of the Foreign Ministry, but held,
on the contrary, that the former Ambassador should have

---

[1] *Darstellung*, pp. 245–82.
[2] F. von Holtzendorff, *Fuer den Grafen von Arnim. Vertheidigungsrede gehalten am
14. December 1874* (Berlin, 1875).
[3] *Darstellung*, pp. 298 ff.   [4] Ibid., pp. 302 ff.
[5] Ibid., pp. 389–408.

returned the documents when asked to do so by his one-time superiors. This offence was a disciplinary one, however, and the court could not deal with it. As to the documents that were still missing and those that Arnim had returned through his counsel just before the trial, the judge declared that there was no proof that Arnim had deliberately retained them. Likewise, the court held that Arnim's untrustworthiness had not been established in connection with the various publications in the *Echo de Parlement*, the *Presse*, and the *Spenersche Zeitung*, as the prosecution had tried to show. It was then a matter of thirteen documents, concerning Church policy, which Arnim had knowingly taken from the Paris Embassy archives. He had brought these documents to Berlin but, instead of delivering them to the Foreign Ministry, had kept them and, although requested to hand them over, had refused. On that basis, Arnim was judged guilty.[1]

Considering the case as it was presented in court, the verdict seems fair and well founded. If there was bias at all, it was in favour of Arnim, especially regarding his trustworthiness in connection with the newspaper publication. Noteworthy too was the independence demonstrated by the court in the face of considerable pressure by the Government.

The officials of the Foreign Ministry were greatly disappointed in the leniency of the verdict. While they professed to be indifferent about the length of the prison sentence, they were concerned about the substantiation the court gave in support of its verdict.

The Chancellor would not attach any great weight to the fact that only one-tenth of the penalty which the Public Prosecutor had asked for had been granted. There were, however, the material principles of the verdict which, in the opinion of the Chancellor, will have to be redressed, by an appeal, in the interest of judicial dignity and the welfare of the state. For, if such principles should become valid law in Germany, no civil-service practice, much less a diplomatic one, could be maintained in the future. The judicial views expressed in the Arnim verdict would make proper government impossible. Should they be carried out, no correspondence between official departments could expect legal protection, if it should not, at the same time, represent rights of property. Its sup-

[1] *Darstellung*, pp. 389–408.

pression by the official to which it had been entrusted would not be an offence, because such correspondence could not be regarded as records in the sense of the penal code.[1]

Aside from these legal considerations, the State Secretary was incensed by the incompetence of the court, particularly its presiding officer, whom he characterized 'a very unimportant, weak-minded, miserable man'.[2] A jurist from the provinces, according to Buelow, he was no doubt overpowered by the importance of the case and the prestige of the accused and the defence counsels. If, despite of this handicap, Arnim had been sentenced to three months, one could easily be justified in assuming that he would have deserved three years.[2]

Public opinion after the trial was generally favourable to the Chancellor. Publication of his directives contributed much to this change. Compared to Arnim's reports, they were admired for their lucidity of style and their content and as an indication of the clarity and directness of the Chancellor's policy.[3] Only a few German and foreign newspapers continued to support Arnim. Of the latter, the *New York Herald*, which had been Arnim's main champion throughout the proceedings, wrote on its editorial page, under the headline 'Bismarck defeated by von Arnim':

Prince Bismarck in this bitter struggle has the shadow of victory in the shape of a meaningless legal decree, but von Arnim has the substance in the vindication of both his private and public character. He has triumphed over his opponent and may even exult in his past sufferings, when he considers that they have contributed to the interests of his party. Thus, the great trial which Bismarck provoked has inured to the benefit of his enemies.[4]

Of the pro-Bismarckian papers, the *Norddeutsche Allgemeine Zeitung* agitated against the sentence and, in support of its opinion, used the very same arguments that Buelow had employed in his letter to the Emperor.[5]

Reactions from abroad, as reported by various German diplomatic representatives, were also favourable to the Government.

[1] Buelow to the Emperor, 26 Dec. 1874.
[2] Buelow to Hohenlohe, 20 Dec. 1874.
[3] Taffs, pp. 45–6; *Fremdenblatt* (Vienna), 11 Dec. 1874.
[4] *New York Herald*, 20 Dec. 1874.
[5] *Norddeutsche Allgemeine Zeitung*, 23 Dec. 1874.

In France, the trial and the publication of documents disclosing the recent political events made an extraordinary impression. The frankness of the German Government won great respect among those who had followed the trial. The French Foreign Minister, though regretting the stir these publications had created, was glad to have learned from them that the German Government had, on the whole, only peaceful intentions toward France.[1]

In Italy, Count Arnim's arrest created a most unfavourable impression, though public opinion in Rome had not been as critical as in Vienna. The trial brought about expressions of admiration for German legal institutions and their practices. The political leadership of German affairs was being praised beyond bounds, 'and publication of the most intimate dispatches was considered good fortune for the enlightenment of the entire political world'.[2]

Opinions in Russia, as reflected by the St. Petersburg and Moscow newspapers, were divided, but the majority was on the side of the German Chancellor.[3] Others had condemned Arnim's arrest and had expressed the opinion that Bismarck could have forced Arnim to return the documents without employing such drastic action.[4]

British periodicals in general applauded the court's verdict but regretted the undue hardship to which the former Ambassador had been exposed.[5]

Repercussions within the Foreign Ministry, following the trial, were unspectacular. There was a minor shake-up in the Paris Embassy personnel, owing to some not quite satisfactory performance at the trial, and Beckmann had to leave Paris in a hurry because some of his activities during the trial had caused resentment among his French colleagues.[6] A minor but interesting consequence of the trial, as far as the foreign service was concerned, was a circular directive issued by the State Secretary to all heads of missions. He cautioned them to be

[1] Hohenlohe to Bismarck, 17 Dec. 1874.
[2] Keudell to Buelow, 21 Dec. 1874.
[3] Survey of press reports from Russia, 21–9 Dec. 1874.
[4] Langenau to Andrassy, 10 Oct. 1874, as quoted by E. Wertheimer, *Arnim*, p. 280.
[5] *Saturday Review, Spectator, Economist*: ibid., pp. 280–1.
[6] Hohenlohe to Bismarck, 17 Dec. 1874.

more circumspect in their reporting in the future, and warned them, especially, not to use derogatory expressions about measures of the Government to which they were accredited, or to attack personalities. At least they should do so no more than was absolutely necessary and needed for the understanding of their reports. The recent events in connection with the Arnim trial were particularly pointed out as a warning.[1]

Another more far-reaching result of the trial was the inclusion of a special paragraph in the new penal code which later became known as the 'Arnim Paragraph'. Legal opinion, especially in government circles, considered the then existing law inadequate. It was pointed out that the Public Prosecutor had had no means to include in his presentation Arnim's official conduct in Paris, which had been contrary to the Chancellor's instructions, nor could he mention his use of official documents for publication purposes. The court, on the other hand, had to disregard the arguments of the prosecution, which had been based on paragraphs 348 and 350 of the penal code, and had based its verdict on paragraph 133. This, in turn, was being challenged by many people as a distortion of the facts of the case. The new law, taking into consideration the facts and circumstances of the Arnim trial, was drafted in 1875 and submitted to the Reichstag on 23 November of that year. It was debated on 3 December, and, after being amended, was passed and adopted on 10 February 1876.[2]

---

[1] Buelow to Missions, 14 Jan. 1875.
[2] For text of the law, see Appendix V of this study.

XIX

PREPARATIONS FOR A NEW TRIAL

As soon as the trial was concluded, both sides made preparations to appeal against the verdict. The Foreign Ministry and the Public Prosecutor agreed to submit to the Appellate Court once more those points on which the lower court had not been convinced of Arnim's guilt. Tessendorf intended to call the Chancellor or Bleichroeder as a witness to establish Arnim's authorship of the 'Diplomatic Revelations' printed in the *Presse*.[1] But at this the Foreign Ministry demurred. Bismarck did not want to appear as a witness. He did not cherish the idea 'of being exposed to the invectives of the defence to which he had no means of replying'.[2] This was in contrast to Bismarck's views about the duty of the highest government officials to take the witness stand if the welfare of the State demanded it, as he had done in the case of Manteuffel.[3] Concerning Bleichroeder's testimony, the Foreign Ministry thought that this would be even more awkward for the prosecution than the Chancellor's.[4] No further explanation for this attitude was given, but it can be assumed that Bleichroeder's connection with Landsberg might have had something to do with it.[5] Bismarck may also have been afraid that the banker's testimony would not be restricted to Arnim's connection with the *Presse*, but might extend to Bleichroeder's activities in connection with various loans during the German occupation of France.[6] Tessendorf also decided that Beckmann should be called as a witness, though his personality did not inspire trust. The main reason for calling Beckmann was Holstein's statement that Arnim had told Beckmann that he would be neither transferred nor dismissed because he had documents in his possession whose publication the Chancellor feared.[7] When

[1] Tessendorf (to Wilke), 19 Jan. 1875.
[2] Wilke (memorandum), 24 Jan. 1875.
[3] See p. 160 above.
[4] Wilke (memorandum), 24 Jan. 1875.
[5] See p. 161, n. 2 above.
[6] See p. 84 above.
[7] Tessendorf (to Wilke), 19 Jan. 1875.

Arnim's defence counsel learned of the prosecution's intention to call Beckmann, he asked the court that Buelow II be called to testify about Beckmann's unreliability and bad character. For Beckmann, so it seemed, had been an agent and journalist for the King of Hanover and, after the King's expulsion, worked in the same capacity for Bismarck and was being paid by him with moneys from the *Welfenfond*.[1] The court denied the request of both the prosecution and defence and Beckmann did not appear as a witness. When the Emperor learned the court's decision he was nettled. He had been told earlier that Beckmann, who knew about Arnim's responsibility for the publication in the *Presse*, would tell everything he knew after Arnim had been convicted by the lower court. At the first trial, the Emperor noted, Beckmann had only hinted at Arnim's guilt in this matter, and the judge, as if reluctant to explore Arnim's responsibility in this instant, had not pursued the question. It was important that Beckmann be heard so as to establish Arnim's guilt quite clearly.[2]

In his new indictment, the Prosecutor charged Arnim with having wilfully taken documents on Church policy from the Paris Embassy. Arnim's excuse that he did not want to offend the religious feelings of his successor was absurd, Tessendorf thought, because Hohenlohe's views on the *Kulturkampf* and on German Church policy were, as Arnim well knew, identical with those of the Chancellor. Besides, Hohenlohe did not arrive in Paris immediately after Arnim's departure, and the Embassy was, for a considerable time, in the charge of Wesdehlen, who had been familiar with the contents of the documents. Tessendorf also tried to prove that Arnim had intended to keep those documents as his private property and had had no intention of returning them, as the lower court had assumed. He also rejected the city court's finding that the papers in question were private and not official records as stated in the original indictment. In support of his views, Tessendorf advanced no new arguments, but merely enlarged on his old ones. Concerning Arnim's part in the various newspaper publications, the prosecution submitted no new evidence. It criticized the failure of the lower court to force Landsberg to testify about his

[1] Dockhorn's reply (Apr. 1875).
[2] The Emperor's marginal comments to Buelow's report of 20 May 1875.

knowledge of Arnim's authorship of the 'Diplomatic Revelations'.[1]

The defence again raised the question of the court's competence and argued, rather weakly, that Arnim had had no intention of keeping the documents pertaining to Church policy and that he had been prevented from returning them by other, more pressing, business after his arrival from Paris in April 1874.[2]

Arnim, whose health had been none too good before and during the first trial, left Germany—although he was forbidden to do so while his case was being appealed—and travelled to Italy to recuperate. On his way to Nice he stopped over in Munich to consult with Holtzendorff, his former defence counsel. There, at the house of Morier, the British Minister, he also met Doellinger. Morier was shocked at Arnim's appearance, especially when he recalled their last meeting in 1872, when Arnim had been on his way to Rome to present his letter of recall to the Pope. He also remembered their conversation then and was much impressed with Arnim's views, which, Morier thought, 'had a far truer outlook into the future and far sounder diagnosis than [those of] the man who, with such wanton cruelty, has so pitilessly crushed him'.[3]

The trial before the court of appeals was set for 15 June. Arnim was not present.[4] For the defence there were Munckel and Dockhorn. Chief prosecutor was von Luck. The prosecution asked that Arnim be sentenced to one year's imprisonment.[5] The trial lasted only a few days, and on 24 June 1875 the court announced its verdict. Arnim was sentenced to nine months'

---

[1] Tessendorf to Foreign Ministry, 3 Feb. 1875.

[2] Munckel's justification for an appeal, 20 Feb. 1875. The prosecution as well as the defence submitted briefs in answer to each other's arguments. The one of the prosecution contained nothing new; that of the defence cited the former acting State Secretary Balan as the recipient of Arnim's letter regarding the incident of the *Echo de Parlement*. The advantage being that Balan had died and could not testify. The defence also admitted now that Arnim might not exactly have told the truth about his responsibility regarding the 'Diplomatic Revelations' in the *Presse*.

[3] Wemyss, ii. 303.

[4] Arnim sent a letter to the court from Ouchy in Switzerland on 10 June 1875, in which he excused his absence because of ill health and recapitulated some points in his defence. The letter was printed in the *Neue Freie Presse* (Vienna), 20 Oct. 1875.

[5] W(ilke) to Buelow II (17 June 1875).

imprisonment. Contrary to the city court, the court of appeals recognized that the documents on Church policy were public records, and thus paragraph 348 of the penal code applied, which demanded a severer sentence for the accused.[1] Arnim's lawyers appealed but were turned down by the High Court (*Obertribunal*).[2] By this action the verdict was confirmed.[3] But the sentence was never carried out, for Arnim did not return. He had left Germany for ever.

[1] W(ilke) to the Emperor and Crown Prince, 25 June 1875.

[2] Chief Public Prosecutor to Bismarck, 20 Oct. 1875.

[3] Notifying the Emperor of the verdict, Buelow pointed out that, by recognizing diplomatic papers to be documents and records in the legal sense and that their illegal removal was punishable, the safeguarding of the Foreign Ministry's correspondence had been assured. It was also a great satisfaction to know, Buelow stated, that the considerations which had led the Foreign Ministry to initiate proceedings against Arnim had been upheld and recognized by the court. The Emperor indicated through his marginal comments his complete agreement with these views. (Buelow to the Emperor, 28 Oct. 1875.)

XX

PRO NIHILO AND AFTER

IN the autumn of 1875 Arnim took up temporary residence in Vevey, Switzerland. From there he sent a petition to the Emperor, asking clemency and satisfaction. Recapitulating the recent events, he pointed out that he had been convicted of an offence against the public order because he had withheld secret documents. These documents, Arnim asserted, had been read only in secret session and that was against the existing laws. They were, furthermore, in no case of such importance that they could not have been made public; especially because the Chancellor himself had had those printed which dealt with the election of the Pope in May 1872. Arnim denied that he had intended to keep the documents for later use. Had that been his intention, he would not have returned thirteen documents when he had been asked to return five by the Foreign Ministry. He reminded the Emperor of his achievements in the past: 'many affairs which have brought honour to the Chancellor have been accomplished by myself or through my proposals', Arnim wrote. 'Many of the phrases by which the nation has become accustomed to express its most noble desires have been first expressed by myself.' He mentioned Bismarck's caprices which, as the Emperor had once said himself, were the cause of the Chancellor's hatred of him. 'Against this passion I have once sought protection from Your Majesty. And I have to continue to seek it, until I shall find it. . . .'[1]

His petition, which did not so much ask for clemency as demand satisfaction, was badly phrased and ill conceived. Instead of presenting his case humbly, in as few words as possible, and appealing to the magnanimity of the Emperor, Arnim argued and scolded, accused and attacked, bragged and complained. Nor was this the worst of Arnim's follies. At the time his petition arrived in Berlin, there appeared in bookstalls and shops throughout Germany the pamphlet *Pro Nihilo*. *The*

[1] Arnim to the Emperor, 27 Oct. 1875.

Prelude to the Arnim Trial.[1] No author was indicated on the title-page but everyone immediately assumed that it must have been Arnim. The pamphlet was a bitter diatribe against the Chancellor, the Emperor, and the courts. It was a glorification of Arnim. Any chance his petition might have had of changing the Emperor's mind immediately and irrevocably vanished.

There were many indications that Arnim had not been wasting his time in Switzerland. As early as 20 September 1875 the Foreign Ministry had received news of Arnim's activities from Professor Tschischwitz, a Swiss citizen of German origin and a great admirer of Bismarck and the Empire.[2] Further investigation indicated that Arnim and his brother-in-law, Hermann, were preparing a pamphlet and that it was being printed by a publishing firm in Zurich.[3] Though an agent of the German Embassy attempted immediately to prevent its publication, he failed.[4] The only way to prevent shipment of the pamphlet to Germany and its distribution there was to obtain a court injunction and for that Arnim's authorship had to be established.[5] Tschischwitz threw himself enthusiastically into the task but was too late to prevent the shipment. He learned that 4,000 copies had been printed, 3,500 of which had been sent to Leipzig for distribution from there.[6] They arrived in small lots and the Prussian Legation in Dresden tried at once to have them confiscated by the authorities.[7] One copy was sent to Berlin, where it arrived at the same time as Arnim's petition to the Emperor.

Buelow, meanwhile, had asked Count Eulenburg, Minister of the Interior, to issue a ban on the distribution of *Pro Nihilo* because 'it contained the severest accusations and insults against the Chancellor; repeatedly attacked, in offensive fashion, the impartiality of the High Court, and also made

---

[1] Buelow to Bucher, 8 Nov. 1875.
[2] Tschischwitz to Simon, 20 Sept. 1875; Pindter (to Foreign Ministry), 20 Sept. 1875.   [3] Roeder to Buelow, 2 Oct. 1875.
[4] Roeder to Buelow, 12 Oct. 1875.
[5] Buelow to Roeder, 14 Oct. 1875.
[6] Tschischwitz (to Pindter), 16, 19 Oct. 1875.
[7] Solms to Buelow, 7, 9 Nov. 1875. Attempts to have Saxon authorities confiscate the pamphlets before distribution ran into difficulties because the local police were unable to find offences in the pamphlet against the German Emperor. In the end it was confiscated because of offences against the Chancellor, of which there were many. Buelow to Solms, 12 Nov. 1875.

statements in which, most likely, offences against the Emperor could be detected'.[1] Buelow's request was speedily granted and Eulenburg issued an order to all chiefs of police and administrative heads of districts to confiscate the pamphlet.[2] In spite of these measures, *Pro Nihilo* enjoyed a brisk sale and wide distribution.[3] Its popularity, mainly in anti-Bismarckian circles, was based primarily on the attacks it made on the Chancellor. Its claim to be an impartial account of the preliminaries to the trial, from 1872 onward, can be disregarded. It was an apologia for and by Arnim which, by its exaggerations, incorrect statements, and excessive admiration for the greatness and capabilities of Arnim, defeated its own purpose.[4] Aside from all this, it does, within limits, present the Arnim–Bismarck conflict from Arnim's point of view and cannot be ignored. After reading it, Bismarck expressed his disappointment. It was a web of lies, full of contradictions, of meagre content, and altogether below expectations.[5] Public reaction was strictly along partisan lines. Officials in the Foreign Ministry thought that it contained enough material, aside from offences against the Emperor, the Chancellor, and the High Court, to prosecute Arnim for high treason.[6]

---

[1] Buelow to Eulenburg, 8 Nov. 1875. Arnim's description of an audience he had had with the Emperor on 1 Sept. 1873 (*Pro Nihilo*, pp. 77–8) was essentially untrue; this was sufficient to provide a legal basis for a charge of *lèse-majesté*. (Buelow to Wilmowski, 10 Nov. 1875.) In his reply Wilmowski informed Buelow that the Emperor had found in Arnim's account both truth and fiction and that many of his (the Emperor's) replies had been given a tendentious twist. He clearly remembered that he had not characterized the attitude of the Chancellor as 'intriguing'. For the rest, the Emperor forbade that this incident be made the subject of a legal investigation against Arnim. He would like the matter straightened out at a suitable occasion, however, and the incorrectness of Arnim's version put on record. (Wilmowski to Buelow, 11 Nov. 1875.)

[2] Eulenburg to Buelow, 9 Nov. 1875.

[3] Later on an English and French edition appeared but not, as had been announced by the publishers, a second part.

[4] In an editorial of 19 Feb. 1876, *The Times* characterized *Pro Nihilo* as follows: 'The literary merits of the pamphlet are quite inconsiderable. The laudation of Arnim is fulsome and the abuse of Bismarck ridiculous. The rhetoric is extravagant and the satire blunt and ponderous.'

[5] Bismarck also suggested that somebody should reply to Arnim and expose his lies and contradictions (Bucher (to Buelow) 11 Nov. 1875). This was done by A. A. von Harlessen, in a pamphlet *Pro Multo, Entgegnung der Brochure Pro Nihilo* (Leipzig, 1876). The copy of *Pro Nihilo* which bears Bismarck's marginal comments has been filmed as part of the *Holstein Nachlass* on serial 5377.

[6] Though it was stated in the Introduction (p. vi) that no documents were

Following the appearance of *Pro Nihilo*, Arnim's petition to the Emperor remained unanswered. The pamphlet was handed over to the Public Prosecutor to establish evidence of Arnim's authorship.[1] Proceedings against the former Ambassador were begun once more and again Tessendorf was put in charge. From the papers of the Paris Embassy he discovered discrepancies and false entries regarding postage and cable expenses made while Arnim had been Ambassador; Tessendorf thought by starting criminal proceedings against Arnim for these transgressions he might force Arnim to come to Germany. Because in this case the extradition treaty with Switzerland would apply and Arnim would be handed over by the Swiss authorities to a German court.[2] But Bismarck opposed this scheme. He worried about public opinion and was afraid lest the impression be created that the Foreign Ministry was proceeding against Arnim because of his pamphlet. This would be especially bad if the court were to clear Arnim, which, after all, was possible. Instead, Bismarck believed, disciplinary action should be started, and, if in the course of these proceedings Arnim should be discovered guilty of criminal offences, the case could then be turned over to a criminal court. In this way time would be lost, but the case would reach the court without unpleasant connotations.[3]

The Chancellor's suggestion was followed and disciplinary action against Arnim was started, based on the following points:

(1) The verdict of the court of appeals of 24 June 1875.
(2) That Arnim not only supervised improperly the registration and the journals in the Paris Embassy archives, but made these functions impossible by his own behaviour.
(3) His seizure of the so-called 'conflict files'.

published that had not been published already, *Pro Nihilo* did contain the full text of eight unpublished documents and also revealed the contents of ten others, which had been kept secret up to that time. According to Holstein, the State Secretary 'pressed the Chancellor to bring charges of treason [against Arnim]. But to other people [Buelow], father and son, laid the blame on the Chancellor . . .' (Rich and Fisher, ii. 188).

[1] Buelow to the Minister of Justice and the Public Prosecutor, 10 Nov. 1875; Buelow (memorandum), 10 Nov. 1875.

[2] Buelow to Bucher, 11 Nov. 1875.

[3] Bucher (to Buelow), 14 Nov. 1875.

(4) The negligence displayed in returning the documents by his counsel, Munckel.[1]

To carry out the preliminary investigations, Buelow appointed three officials from the Foreign Ministry.[2] While comments about *Pro Nihilo* in Germany were mainly restricted to the conflict between Arnim and Bismarck and its implications for domestic affairs, French interests in the pamphlets concentrated on its disclosures about Franco-German relations. The *Moniteur universel,* which was close to the French Government, had pointed out in an article of 11 November that the pamphlet's publication of diplomatic indiscretions made normal diplomatic relations between France and Germany impossible and endangered the necessary confidence between the two governments.[3] From the German point of view, the disclosures of German policies during the occupation and evacuation of French territory, the German attitude toward French personalities and parties, German views on the episcopal letters of the French bishops, and similar items, were most unfortunate and complicated current German policy toward France.[4] All these considerations influenced the Superior Court (*Kammergericht*) to start formal proceedings against Arnim on 23 November 1875.[5] The preliminary charges included insults to the Emperor, the Chancellor, and the Foreign Ministry, as well as unspecified treasonable activities. To buttress this last charge, officials in the Foreign Ministry drew the chief prosecutor's attention to Arnim's activities in the negotiations of the convention with France of March 1873 for the evacuation of French territory and payment of the war indemnity.[6] In this connection, Wilke compared Arnim's activities during this period as described in the pamphlet with those reconstructed

---

[1] By Bismarck's order this was extended to include Arnim's behaviour before the fall of Thiers, which had been counter to the instructions he had received; Arnim's insubordination regarding the pastoral letters of the French bishops (next to this is a notation 'insufficient evidence'); misuse of the press for his own purposes and to publicize his own political views, which were opposed to those of the Government, especially the spreading of the false news that Bismarck wanted war; the deceptive reporting about Herr von Kahlden regarding the publication in the *Echo de Parlement*; various discrepancies in the financial affairs of the Paris Embassy concerning private use of stamps, telegram fees, and stationery. (Wilke memorandum, 24 Dec. 1875.)   [2] Buelow directive, 18 Nov. 1875.
[3] Buelow to Tessendorf, 16 Nov. 1875.
[4] Ibid.; Wilke to Luety, 10 Jan. 1876.
[5] Luck to Foreign Ministry, 23 Nov. 1875.   [6] See pp. 109 ff. above.

from the official documents. From this it would appear, Wilke concluded, that 'Count Arnim had conducted the affairs of state with France . . ., probably fully aware that this would be to the detriment of the German Reich,[1] in order to advance his private interests'. In his covering letter to the chief prosecutor, Buelow expressed the opinion that Arnim had indulged in stock-market speculations and had delayed negotiations for this purpose. His opinion was supported, Buelow wrote, by a letter from Count Henckel-Donnersmarck to Arnim, found among Arnim's private papers.[2]

To justify the charge of treason, Arnim's authorship of *Pro Nihilo* had to be established and proved beyond reasonable doubt. This was more difficult than it had first appeared. Though everybody who had read the pamphlet assumed that it must have been written by Arnim, and though it was an open secret in Switzerland that Arnim had been working on the pamphlet for some time, nobody wanted to get involved in court proceedings and testify about these rumours under oath.[3] More successful than the investigations of Roeder, the German Minister in Bern, were those of Professor Tschischwitz, who had originally announced the pamphlet's appearance. He discovered the firm in Zurich which had published the pamphlet and persuaded an apprentice of this establishment, Matthiae, to go to Berlin and testify to his knowledge of Arnim's activities in connection with the printing of *Pro Nihilo*.[4] From Matthiae's testimony it was established that Arnim had indeed been the author of *Pro Nihilo* and that he had been assisted in his endeavour by Counts Hompesch, Bollheim, Bassenheim, and Hermann Arnim.[5]

---

[1] Wilke memorandum, 30 Nov. 1875.

[2] Buelow to Luck, 4 Dec. 1875; Buelow to the Emperor, 15 Dec. 1875. As there was no date on Henckel's letter, Buelow had assumed that it must have been from the year 1873 and that Arnim's stock-market speculations had thus been established conclusively in connection with the Convention of March 1873. This was, however, not the case. Henckel, in the course of the investigation, was called as a witness and on that occasion testified under oath that he had written this letter in 1872 and that the correct date was 30 Aug. 1872. (Luck to Foreign Ministry, 15 May 1876.) See also p. 84 above.

[3] Roeder to Buelow, 12 Oct., 15 Dec. 1875.

[4] Tschischwitz (to Pindter), 27 Dec. 1875; 10, 19, 24 Jan. 1876. Matthiae was asked to come to Berlin and 450 marks from the *Welfenfond* reimbursed him for his travel expenses. (Wilke to Luety, 13 Jan. 1876; Wilke to Pindter, 26 Jan. 1876.)

[5] Unsigned and undated memorandum.

At this stage of the proceedings the family tried to come to the rescue of its wayward member. At a gathering of the clan a resolution was passed and a petition submitted to the Emperor, asking him to pardon Count Harry and to withdraw disciplinary action against him. The petition also mentioned the illustrious services the Arnims had rendered to the Crown in the past and the Count's faithful and creditable behaviour during thirty years' service.[1]

The Emperor sent the petition to Bismarck and Leonhardt, the Minister of Justice, for consideration and comment.[2] The advice of the two ministers was unfavourable. They cited the offences committed by Arnim and the sentences imposed by the courts. They pointed out that the former Ambassador had not himself asked the Emperor's pardon but had demanded satisfaction. Instead of admitting his guilt and trying to atone for it, he had brazenly challenged the authority of his superiors, of the courts, and even of the Emperor, and had not yet ceased to do so. He was, at the moment, being investigated by the Superior Court on suspicion of having committed treason and the full measure of his guilt had not as yet been established. As to the past services of the Arnim family, they had differed in no way from those of any other noble house and its members had been amply rewarded. Count Harry's own services had also been honoured far more than was usual by assigning him to the choicest posts in the foreign service and by bestowing upon him an earldom. All these favours should have produced in him greater respect and fidelity in the service of his king and country. Instead, he had put himself beyond and above the laws. Arnim himself could stop the disciplinary action by submitting his resignation. As long as he was unwilling to do this, termination of these proceedings could not be advocated. For all these reasons, Bismarck and Leonhardt asked the Emperor not to grant the petition.[3] The Emperor agreed with his ministers and the head of the Arnim family was informed accordingly.[4]

---

[1] Arnim family to the Emperor (25 Jan. 1876); while the majority of the family approved this step, two, the Emperor's aide-de-camp, and a former court chamberlain, indicated their dissent. (Arnim-Kroechlendorff to the Emperor, 29 Jan. 1876.)

[2] Wilmowski to Bismarck and Leonhardt, 25 Jan. 1876.

[3] Bismarck and Leonhardt to the Emperor, 10 Feb. 1876.

[4] Bismarck and Leonhardt to Arnim-Boitzenburg, 19 Feb. 1876. A petition by

Arnim, meanwhile, had left Switzerland and gone to Italy. His health continued to deteriorate. A medical examination in June 1876 showed that his illness had progressed since a similar examination two years earlier. The physician, who upon a request from the Superior Court had examined Arnim, stated in his official report that Arnim's arrest and imprisonment would endanger his life.[1] In spite of these findings, the Public Prosecutor and the Foreign Ministry maintained that Arnim's illness was not as bad as he had made it out to be and that his imprisonment would not endanger his life.[2]

When the Superior Court assembled on 5 October 1876, Arnim was not present.[3] His defence counsel attempted to justify his absence, but the court refused to hear him. After deliberating in secret session, it announced the verdict. Arnim was sentenced to five years in prison because of treason, *lèse-majesté*, and offences against the Chancellor and the Foreign Ministry.[4]

Still, Arnim did not give up. In October 1876 there appeared yet another pamphlet of his in reply to a letter by the Chancellor published in the *Reichsanzeiger*.[5] And in the following year he directed yet another petition to the Emperor, asking his pardon and his permission to return to Germany to restore his health.[6] In December 1879 he wanted his case reopened and, through his lawyer, Dorn, sent a request to the Reich Court asking for a safe-conduct pass for his personal appearance. The request was refused.[7] He died in Nice on 19 May 1881.

Arnim's wife for a safe conduct for her husband to visit his dying son in Berlin was likewise rejected. The Emperor (to Bismarck), 6 Feb. 1876; Leonhardt to Bismarck, 7 Feb. 1876.

[1] Liman (memorandum), 28 June 1876.

[2] Tessendorf (to the Superior Court), 1 July 1876.

[3] The session of the trial had originally been set for 11 May 1876. Upon Arnim's request it was postponed. Buelow explained to the Emperor, who was quite angry about the delay, that this was done to give Thiers, who had been called as a witness, a chance to appear. It was also done to avoid giving the impression that the court wanted to restrict Arnim in his defence, especially because the indictment had not reached him in time. (Buelow to the Emperor, 11, 12 May 1876.)

[4] Luck to Foreign Ministry, 5 Oct. 1876. A disciplinary court had found Arnim guilty and dismissed him from the service (Wilke to Buelow, 27 Apr. 1876).

[5] *Brief des Grafen Harry von Arnim an den Fuersten von Bismarck* (Zuerich, 1876).

[6] Arnim to the Emperor, 7 June 1877; this too was rejected. Minister of Justice to Arnim, 26 July 1877.

[7] Ministry of Justice to Foreign Minister, 15 Jan. 1880. Wertheimer, *Arnim*, p. 290, says that this request was granted but gives no source.

XXI

CONCLUSION

THE conflict between Bismarck and Arnim was essentially a struggle for the Emperor's confidence. To Bismarck this confidence was vital if he were to remain the undisputed head of the Government. Arnim, who considered himself a principal adviser and personal representative of the Emperor, used this time-honoured concept of his position to present his views and thus influence his imperial master against the policies of the Chancellor. In this he was supported by his connections at Court and by his clever presentations, which were astutely attuned to the Emperor's ears and played on his prejudices.

Bismarck, as Chancellor and Foreign Minister, could not and did not condone Arnim's manœuvres. Had he not challenged Arnim, the orderly conduct of government as he saw it would have been impossible. A system that had been good enough and had at times worked well for Prussia no longer worked for Germany. Then, too, there was the Chancellor's personality. Well versed in the art of intrigue, determined to hold on to his power with all the means at his disposal, ever watchful for rivals and over-suspicious of conspiracies, with his firm grip on affairs of state, his great influence on the Emperor —and the Emperor's attachment to him—all this made Arnim's schemes utterly hopeless. This fight, in retrospect seeming so completely absurd, was not thought so while it raged. That Arnim undertook it at all was due partly to his own exaggerated self-esteem and partly to his misjudgement of the Emperor. For the Emperor was vacillating and irresolute. In many instances his basic sympathies were with Arnim— when he advocated active support for the minority bishops at the Council and when he expressed his dislike for a republican government in France—and he apparently agreed with the Ambassador when he discussed foreign and domestic policy during his frequent audiences. Once Arnim had left, however, the overpowering personality of Bismarck changed the Emperor's views in favour of the Chancellor. That Arnim was unaware of these changes and placed too much reliance on his own influence with the Emperor proved his undoing.

There is no doubt that Arnim at one time seriously considered himself a contender for the Chancellorship and a rival of Bismarck. He was supported by some opposition groups in Germany which, in the end, proved too weak to support their candidate effectively. It is certain that Bismarck knew of the ambitions and machinations of his subordinate. He successfully blocked Arnim's attempt to be nominated to the Upper House, kept him under his own jurisdiction, and waited for the appropriate moment to get rid of him. Arnim, through his own offensive behaviour, made Bismarck's task relatively easy. Once the fight was in the open, the Chancellor used all the means at his disposal to crush Arnim. The latter played into his hands by appropriating official documents for his own use. Arnim's hope that these, when published, would demonstrate his superiority over Bismarck was a grave error in judgement.

As a diplomat Arnim was neither as brilliant as his friends have claimed, nor as incompetent as his enemies have asserted. His judgement of people and events was, in some instances, as good as and sometimes better than Bismarck's, but was marred by the extravagant style of his reporting, by his inappropriate comments, and his impolitic recommendations. His views were not so much changeable as the quality of his reports was uneven.

The Bismarck–Arnim episode was the last serious assault on the personal position of the Chancellor as head of the Government. From Bismarck's point of view it had to be repulsed at all costs. After that he remained undisputed master until the death of the old Emperor.

APPENDIX I

(See Chapter VII, p. 64, n. 1)

THIS is the last part of Arnim's report no. 97 to Bismarck of 2 September 1871, which has been omitted in the *Grosse Politik*, i. 77–8.

Schließlich erlaube ich mir noch zu erwaehnen, dass Herr Declerq hier anwesend ist und an den hiesigen Verhandlungen zwar keinen ostensiblen aber durch seinen Einfluß jedenfalls einen wirksamen Anteil nimmt. Er ist mir insofern unerwuenscht, als ich glaube durch direkte Verhandlungen mit Herrn Pouyer-Quertier die Sache rascher zu foerdern. Unter diesen Gesichtspunkten, kann ich daher nicht umhin, mein Bedauern darueber auszusprechen, daß die Verhandlungen in Frankfurt durch die unsererseits getroffenen Maßregeln im Widerspruch mit Eurer Durchlaucht erster (Bismarck's Randglosse: 'auch letzter') Auffassung sistirt worden sind, weil in Folge dieser Wendung der Dinge jeder Anlaß fehlt, den Wunsch auszusprechen, daß Herr Declerq sich nach Frankfurt zurueckbegeben moege. Arnim

APPENDIX II

(See Chapter X, p. 90, n. 2)

Arnim's report to Bismarck of 3 October 1872 has been printed in the *Grosse Politik*, i. 150–3. Three sections of this report were left out. The first section, the beginning of the report, on page 150, the second on page 151, and the third on page 152. All three omissions are marked by pp. in the *Grosse Politik*.

Die Konversation, welche der Praesident der Republik vor einiger Zeit mit einem Journalisten, Namens Arnoult gehabt hat, ist bereits durch die Zeitungen bekannt und von der Presse kommentiet worden.

An der Authentizitaet der Darstellung ist nicht zu zweifeln. — Herr Thiers hat mir haeufig in demselben Sinne gesprochen, wenn er auch die vortrefflichen Beziehungen zu allen anderen Laendern weniger accentuierte.

Herr Thiers hat mit dem Papst Pius nicht nur die Infaillibilitaet, sondern auch die Redseligkeit gemeinsam. Die Summe aller Konversationen des Praesidenten resumirt sich in den Saetzen:

Le pays est sage — tout le monde veut la paix — je mène le pays ou je veux — les passions se taisent — l'armée est incomparable — l'Europe nous admire, et attend avec impatience que nous reprenions notre position en Europe.

Ueber die Zustaende der Armee geben die Berichte des Herrn von Buelow Auskunft. — Sie wird wohl ungefaehr in demselben Zustande sein, wie beim Ausbruch des Krieges.

Was die sagesse du pays betrifft, so hat die Rundreise des Herrn Gambetta dazu einen uebeln Kommentar geliefert. Haeufig hat mir der Praesident die Versicherung gegeben, daß die Rolle Gambettas zu Ende sei. — Das Gegentheil ist wahr, und es fragt sich schon heute, ob Thiers, welcher einen Pakt mit dem Agitator geschlossen zu haben glaubte, ihm noch gewachsen ist. — In seinem Optimismus ging der Praesident zwar wie ich hoere, bei den ersten Nachrichten ueber die Erfolge des Herrn Gambetta so weit, sie nicht unangemessen zu finden, weil er glaubte, daß die Furcht vor der rothen Republik ihm die konservative Majoritaet in die Arme treiben wuerde. — An einer solche[n] Wendung ist aber doch sehr zu zweifeln. — Es waere wohl denkbar, daß die konservativen Parteien in Schrecken vor dem Abgrund, an welchen Thiers das Land nach ihrer Ansicht gefuehrt hat, seiner Diktatur muede wuerden. Nur die Unmoeglichkeit der Einigung zwischen den Fraktionen der Majoritaet kann sie veranlassen sich noch einmal der Fuehrung des Praesidenten anzuvertrauen.

Unter anderen sind es Mittheilungen des Herrn Kleczko [*sic*], welche darauf hingewirkt haben, die Berliner Feste als ein Fiasco — namentlich

Oesterreichs — erscheinen zu lassen. Nach Herrn Kleczko [sic] werden dem Grafen Andrassy Vorwuerfe gemacht, daß er den Kaiser nutzlos in Preußische Uniform gesteckt habe. In einem gewissen Grade ist mir gegenueber auch der Graf Apponyi beschuldigt worden, daß er durch ganze Haltung Illusionen bei den Franzosen erwecke. — Ja, die Persoenlichkeit, welche mir diese Mittheilungen machte, und welche zu dem Grafen Andrassy in etwaigen Beziehungen steht, hat sich sogar bemueßigt gefunden den oesterreichisch-ungarischen Minister auf die verfehlte Haltung des Botschafters in einem vertraulichen Schreiben aufmerksam zu machen. — Dieselbe Persoenlichkeit fuegte hinzu, dass der Graf Andrassy in Bezug auf die Allianz mit Deutschland ganz aufrichtig und der einzige Aufrichtige in Oesterreich sei. Er versicherte aber auch in Widerspruch mit den hier verbreiteten Nachrichten, dass der Kaiser selbst von Berlin sehr zufrieden zurueckgekommen waere. Was den Grafen Apponyi betrifft, so ist derselbe ein korrekter, sehr zuverlaessiger und ehrenwerter Diplomat. — Er wird wissentlich keine Linie halten, welche nicht den Intentionen seiner Regierung entspricht, und von allen oesterreichischen Diplomaten ist er mir der Erwuenscheste. Aber da er seine Jugend in Paris verlebt und mit den Franzosen intime Beziehungen hat, waehrend ihn norddeutsche Personen und Namen so unbekannt sind, wie etwa chinesische, so ist es nur natuerlich, daß er allmaelig mit den franzoesischen Kuemmernissen [?] sympathisiet, und ein wenig die Intimitaet der Franzosen mit wohlwollenden Eingehen auf ihre Auffassungen bezahlt. — Das ist nicht ganz gleichgueltig, aber soweit ich die oesterreichischen Diplomaten kenne, gibt es unter denselben niemand, der nicht schlimmer waere. Wie dem auch sei — der Praesident der Franzoesischen Republik glaubt nicht an die Oesterreichisch-Deutsche Intimitaet. Ebensowenig an die Russisch-Deutsche. — Ich kann nicht sagen, daß mir authentische Angaben ueber Insinuationen des Fuersten Orloff zugekommen waeren. — Aber der allgemeine Eindruck, welchen das franzoesische Publikum aus den Aeußerungen des offiziellen und nicht offiziellen Rußlands zu schoepfen sich berechtigt glaubt steht nicht im Einklang mit den Intentionen des Kaisers Alexanders. — Von hier aus wird jedes Mittel benutzt, um den Russen die Solidaritaet der Interessen zum Bewußtsein zu bringen. — Als Beleg dafuer will ich beispielsweise anfuehren, daß das franzoesische Kriegsministerium, auf den Wunsch des Russischen Militaer-Attachés, einige Zeichnungen von franzoesischen Krankenwagen zu haben, der Russischen Regierung sofort 4 vollstaendig ausgeruestete Ambulancewagen zum Geschenk machte.

Ich will in dieser Beziehung nur erwaehnen, daß Gambettas jetzige Rundreise hauptsaechlich im Hinblick auf Italien — vielleicht unter Billigung des Praesidenten — gemacht worden ist, und daß die Komplimente, welche er Italien gemacht hat, nicht ohne Nachhall jenseits der Alpen geblieben sind. — Auch in Oesterreich hat man in den Kreisen, welche uns am freundlichsten sind, mit einiger Befriedigung von dem gewußt, was Gambetta bei seiner Reise thun und sagen wuerde, und ich habe konstatiert, daß seine Unternehmung sowohl in der Oesterreichischen wie in der Italienischen Presse eine offenbar vorher bestellte Billigung gefunden hat.

APPENDIX III

(See Chapter XIV, p. 128, n. 2)

Berlin den   ten Januar 1874
An des Kaisers und Koenigs Majestaet

Ew. K. und K. Majestaet habe ich unterm 4ten d. Mts. ueber den Verlauf der diesseitigen Beschwerden gegen das Auftreten der franzoesischen Bischoefe sowie ueber das Verhalten des Botschafters Grafen Arnim allerunterthaenigst Bericht erstattet und spaeter Gelegenheit gefunden, Allerhoechstdenselben ueber die in diesem Anlasse eingegangenen Schriftstuecke ehrfurchtsvoll Vortrag zu halten. Bei der großen Wichtigkeit dieser Angelegenheit gestatte ich mir auf dieselbe noch einmal, namentlich im Hinblick auf ihre politische Bedeutung zurückzukommen.

Ew. Maj. haben seit der glorreichen Beendigung des franzoesischen Krieges als das Ziel der Deutschen Politik, wie als Allerhoechstdero Wunsch und Absicht festgehalten, auf Grund der durch schwere Opfer und große Erfolge errungenen Machtstellung Deutschlands den allgemeinen Frieden zu sichern und auch mit der franzoesischen Nation, soweit solches moeglich, ein gutes und friedliches Verhaeltniß festzustellen. Jenes Ziel erscheint durch die Aufrechterhaltung und Kraeftigung der freundschaftlichen Beziehungen zu den Beherrschern von Rußland und Oesterreich, so wie durch unsere durchaus befriedigende Stellung zu Großbritannien und Italien, soweit menschliche Voraussicht reicht, verbuergt, waehrend gleichzeitig Deutschland jetzt maechtig genug ist, um den inneren Hader der franzoesischen Parteien und das diesen allen mehr oder minder gemeinsame Bestreben, die Nation zu einem Revanche-Krieg vorzubereiten, mit Ruhe und in der Erwartung zu beobachten, daß dort die Leidenschaften und Illusionen allmaelig einer besseren Wuerdigung der vollendeten Thatsachen Platz machen werden. Laeßt es sich freilich nicht verkennen, daß die franzoesische Nation im Allgemeinen ihr Verhaeltniß zu Deutschland mehr wie einen voruebergehenden und drueckenden Waffenstillstand als wie einen dauernden Frieden aufzufassen geneigt sei, so spricht andererseits die bisherige Erfahrung und die gesammte politische Lage dafuer, daß ein leidlich gutes Verhaeltniß zu Frankreich und die allmaelige Abwendung der Gefahr von Friedensstoerungen moeglich und wahrscheinlich ist. Es kann nicht unsere Aufgabe sein, die

Wirkungen zu berechnen und abzumessen, welche aus den inneren
franzoesischen Zustaenden und dem moeglichen Wechsel in der
Verfassung und Regierung Frankreichs zu Deutschland hervorgehen
koennen. Letzteres kann die Entscheidung darueber um so ruhiger
der Franzoesischen Selbstbestimmung ueberlassen, als kaum eine
der allenfalls moeglichen Regierungsformen fuer uns die Hoffnung
ausschließt, gute oder doch friedliche Beziehungen mit den
Machthabern zu unterhalten. Nur in einem Fall wuerde an die
Stelle dieses Vertrauens sofort das Gegentheil an uns herantreten.
Naemlich alsdann, wenn die bald nach Beendigung des Krieges
auftretenden Bestrebungen der clericalen Partei in Frankreich zur
Alleinherrschaft oder doch zu ueberwiegendem Einfluß zu gelangen
Erfolg haben sollten. Daß diese Partei, deren Machinationen die
frivole Kriegserklaerung im Jahre 1870 großentheils verschulden,
seitdem der erste Eindruck der Niederlagen in Frankreich ueber-
wunden war, unter Inspiration des Vatikans darauf hinarbeitet,
durch einen Europaeischen Krieg zum Umsturz des Deutschen
Reichs und zur Suprematie in Europa zu gelangen, ist ebenso
unzweifelhaft, als dass sie Frankreich als das hiezu auserwaehlte
Ruestzeug betrachtet. Man hat im Vatikan sehr wohl erkannt, daß
dem unablaessig verfolgten Plan der paepstlichen oder jesuitischen
Alleinherrschaft kein groesseres Hinderniß entgegenstehe, als die
ruhige und friedliche Entwicklung und Befestigung eines einheit-
lichen Deutschen Reiches. Eben deshalb finden wir die clericale
Partei ueberall, wo es sich von offner oder versteckter Feindschaft
gegen Deutschland handelt, und erblicken dieselbe namentlich in
Frankreich nicht immer mit Geschick, aber mit rastlosem Eifer
bemueht, die Leidenschaften aller Volksklassen und aller politischen Combinationen jenen Zwecken dienstbar zu machen. Ich
darf in dieser Beziehung nur an die waehrend der sogenannten
Fusion vom Clerus in Scene gesetzten Pilgerfahrten, bei denen die
Wiedereroberung des Elsaß und die Wiederherstellung des Papstes
von der Geistlichkeit als Parole ausgegeben waren, an die Hirten-
briefe der franzoesischen Bischoefe und an die Sprache der clericalen
Presse erinnern, welche an Haß gegen Deutschland all anderen
Partei-Organe weit hinter sich laeßt. Ebenso haben die Vertreter
dieser Richtung in der Nationalversammlung zu aller Zeit die
Herstellung der weltlichen Herrschaft des Papstes verlangt und
keinen Zweifel darueber gelassen, daß, wenn sie zur Herrschaft in
Frankreich gelangten, als Mittel fuer diesen Zweck einen Krieg
nicht scheuen wuerden.

Es wuerde aber schon ein ueberwiegender Einfluß der clericalen
Partei in Paris mit der inneren Sicherheit Deutschlands und mit
den Zielen unvereinbar sein, welche Ew. Maj. mit und seit der

Gruendung des Deutschen Reiches erreichen wollten. Die Ultramontanen fuehlen sich so wenig wie die internationalen Socialisten
an die Pflichten und die Ehre der eigenen Nation gebunden, und die
Solidaritaet derselben in allen Laendern ist notorisch.

Die eigentlichen Fuehrer der ultramontanen Agitation, welche
vor dem franzoesischen Kriege auf Deutschlands Uneinigkeit
gerechnet hatten, suchen jetzt dessen politische Einheit und den
Ausbau seiner Einigkeit durch confessionellen Hader zu lockern.
Der Zusammenhang der Deutschen und Polnischen Ultramontanen
mit den Katholiken anderer Laender und den subversiven Bestrebungen des Vaticans ist unzweifelhaft; jede Schwierigkeit im
Deutschen Reich, jede Verstimmung eines unklaren reichsfeind-
lichen Particularismus, jeder Wahlsieg der Ultramontanen wird als
ein Erfolg des Vaticans und Frankreichs gefoerdert und gefeiert.
Was bei einer den Frieden ernstlich wuenschenden Regierung in
Frankreich nicht gelingt, wuerde, sobald dort der ultramontane
Einfluß maechtig bleibt, eine Gefahr herbeifuehren, der Deutsch-
land aller Wahrscheinlichkeit nach nur durch Energie und raschen
Entschluß werde begegnen koennen.

Um so mehr erscheint es als die naechste Aufgabe fuer Ew. Maj.
Politik, nicht bloß die ultramontanen Feinde Deutschlands,
ueberall wo diesselben aus dem Dunkel hervortreten, offen und
rueckhaltlos zu bekaempfen, sondern ihnen auch, ehe noch die
Gefahr zur Wirklichkeit wird, entgegenzutreten. Die gegenwaertige
franzoesische Regierung, unter clericalem Einfluß entstanden und
so lange die Thronbesteigung des Grafen von Chambord in der
politischen Rechnung Platz fand, diesem Einfluß mehr und mehr
anheimfallend, hat sich seit dem klaeglichen Ende jenes Plans
allmaelig von demselben geloest und schwankt jetzt zwischen den
alten Neigungen und der praktischen Erkenntniß, daß ein gutes
Verhaeltniß mit Deutschland und die verstaendige Politik der
Resignation fuer Frankreich die vortheilhafteste sei. Es wird unsere
Aufgabe sein, gerade weil wir ernstlich und aufrichtig ein friedliches Verhaeltniß mit Frankreich wuenschen, diese letztere Richtung zu staerken, die Spaltung zwischen den Klerikalen und den
besonnenen Conservativen zu benutzen und zu erweitern und
diesen letzteren keinen Zweifel darueber zu lassen, daß Ew.
Majestaet den Frieden wollen, zu einem guten und haltbaren
Verhaeltniß gern bereit sind, aber nur unter der Voraussetzung,
daß die Machthaber in Frankreich sich von den clericalen Ein-
fluessen unzweideutig emancipieren.

Daß die jetzigen Franzoesischen Minister wenigstens der Minister
des Auswaertigen solchen Erwaegungen zugaenglich sind, hat die
Erfahrung der letzten Wochen bewiesen, wo das Ew. Majestaet

bekannte Rundschreiben an die Bischoefe sofort erfolgte, nachdem die Monate lang vom Grafen Arnim unterlassenen oder unvollstaendig ausgefuehrten Reclamationen ernstlicher und offener gestellt waren. Ebenso habe ich in diesen Tagen aus einer eingehenden Unterredung mit dem franzoesischen Botschafter die Ueberzeugung gewonnen, daß eine friedliche aber bestimmte Sprache in Paris ihre Wirkung nicht ganz verfehlt.

Es bedarf nicht der naeheren Darlegung, daß und weshalb die auf Deutschlands Verhaeltniß zu Frankreich bezuegliche politische Action die wichtigste und schwierigste Aufgabe fuer die Leitung von Ew. Politik z. Z. ist und noch lange bleiben wird. Daß in der Verhandlung ueber die Bischoefe der Botschafter Gf. Arnim nicht bloß die ihm ertheilten Instructionen unvollstaendig und ungenuegend befolgt, sondern deren politische Bedeutung nicht verstanden hat, habe ich in dem Eingangs erwaehnten allerunterth. Bericht sowie in muendlichem Vortrag auszufuehren mir gestattet. Durch die dabei gemachte bedauerliche Erfahrung zeigt sich nur zu deutlich, wie unentbehrlich fuer Erfuellung der in Paris zu loesenden Aufgaben ein zur Ausfuehrung geschickter, ruhiger und voelliges Vertrauen erweckender Staatsmann ist, und daß sich als solcher der Graf Arnim nicht mehr bewaehrt hat. Derselbe hat sich vielmehr, unerachtet seiner hervorragenden Begabung ohne politisches Urtheil und unerachtet seiner großen Gewandtheit ohne das rechte Geschick fuer Einhaltung der richtigen Linie gezeigt. Ich lasse dahingestellt sein, ab und wieweit etwa anderweitige persoenliche Interessen und der Mangel lebendiger patriotischer Empfindung auf seine dortige Haltung influirten und lege darauf nicht mehr Werth als auf sonstige Privatnachrichten, darf aber doch nicht unbemerkt lassen, daß nach solchen Notizen Gf. Arnim gerade in dieser Zeit Ew. Politik in Paris durch Andeutungen verdaechtigt haben soll, als suche und wolle dieselbe la guerre à tout prix und sei er das verkannte Opfer seiner gemaeßigten und friedliebenden Haltung, waehrend gerade umgekehrt, Ew. pp. den Frieden mit dem jetzigen Frankreich dauernd erhalten und befestigen wollen und Unklarheit oder Unentschlossenheit gegenueber den jetzigen franzoesischen Machthabern beide Laender der Gefahr ernster Verwicklungen zufuehren wuerde.

Es wird allerdings anzuerkennen sein, daß die von Ew. pp. Vertreter in Paris zu erfuellenden Aufgaben durch die ganze Situation in ungewoehnlichem Masse erschwert werden. Indessen sind, was den Grafen Arnim angeht unparteiische Beobachter der Meinung, daß seine Persoenlichkeit und sein Auftreten nicht ohne Schuld an den Reibungen und Empfindlichkeiten sei, die dort immer wieder hervortreten. Daß Gf. Arnim, unerachtet seiner

angeblichen Maeßigung und bei allem Esprit der Franzosen keine
Sympathien einfloeßte, ist bekannt und kann nicht ueberraschen,
da derselbe ueberhaupt selten die Sympathien der mit ihm in
amtlicher Beruehrung stehenden Personen gewinnt. Sein Ver-
haeltnis zu dem gesammten Personal der Botschaft (vielleicht mit
einer Ausnahme) ist in unerwuenschter Weise schlecht und als er
vor einigen Jahren fuer den Posten des Staatssekretaers im Ausw.
Amte in Betracht stand, trat bei dessen Angehoerigen der Wunsch
sehr allgemein und sehr lebhaft hervor, nicht unter einem so
eigensinnigen und so hochfahrenden Mann gestellt zu werden.

Ist nun, wie ich unterth. hervorgehoben habe, Paris noch fuer
lange Zeit die wichtigste diplomatische Stelle, welche mehr als jede
andere eines durchaus zuverlaessigen Inhabers bedarf, so bin ich
auch verpflichtet zu wiederholen, daß der jetzige Botschafter die
Ziele von Eurer Majestaet Politik nicht foerdert, sondern erschwert
und gefaehrdet. Ich gestatte mir daher, bei Eurer Maj. ehrfurchtsvoll
darauf anzutragen, Allerhoechst zu genehmigen, daß der Graf
Arnim nunmehr von seinen Posten abberufen werde.

Indem ich nicht in Abrede stellen kann, daß eine solche, immer
unerwuenschte Entschließung großes Aufsehen machen und zu
unbegruendeten und selbst schaedlichen Conjekturen Anlaß bieten
wird, darf ich unterthaenigst zur Erwaegung stellen, ob sich nicht
hieraus sowie durch die langjaehrigen und bedeutenden Dienste des
Grafen Arnim das Anerbieten eines anderen Postens an denselben
empfehlen moechte. Zwar wuerde derselbe schwerlich einen anderen
Posten annehmen als etwa Rom, und dort walten ziemlich genau
dieselben Bedenken ob, wie gegen seine Beibehaltung in Paris: die
angedeuteten Erwaegungen moechten aber doch dafuer sprechen,
daß Eure Maj. mich Allerhoechst zu ermaechtigen geruhten, dem
Grafen Arnim den durch das Entlassungsgesuch des Grafen Per-
poncher zur Erledigung kommenden Gesandtschaftsposten im
Haag anzutragen. Da Graf Arnim verhaeltnißmaeßig sehr frueh
u. unter außerordentlichen Umstaenden zum Botschafter in Paris
ernannt wurde, so waere weder fuer ihn, noch ist an und fuer sich
die Uebertragung eines Posten zweiten Ranges eine Zuruecksetzung,
und es wuerde jedenfalls ein solches Anerbieten beweisen, daß
Eure Maj. die Dienste und Talente des Grafen auf einer anderen
Stelle ersprießlich verwenden zu koennen wuenschen.

APPENDIX IV

(See Chapter XVI, p. 145, n. 2)

A List of Missing Documents

OF the eighty documents which were reported missing originally, Arnim returned fourteen on 23 June, dealing with the future election of the Pope. On 20 July he returned three, dealing with the pastoral letters of the Bishop of Nancy and the attitude of the French and German press. In the meantime, eight documents were found at the Paris Embassy. Of the fifty-five documents still missing, Arnim wrote that twenty-two might be in Paris and that his search for them among his own papers was unsuccessful. These included the following:

1. Directive No. 16 of 24 Jan. 72, concerning the relationship of Prince Bismarck to Prince Orloff.

2. Directive No. 17 of 24 Jan. 72, concerning a conversation of Grand Duchess Marie with General Fleury.

3. Directive No. 18 of 24 Jan. 72, concerning the attitude of Prince Orloff to Germany.

4. Directive No. 34 of 10 Feb. 72, concerning a conversation of Prince Orloff with Thiers.

5. Directive No. 35 of 12 Feb. 72, concerning the attitude of the *Kreuzzeitung* to the Government.

6. Directive No. 91 of 1872 [*sic*], concerning the nomination of Cardinal Hohenlohe as Ambassador [to Rome].

7. Directive No. 96 of 12 May 72, concerning a handwritten letter of His Majesty to Count Arnim.

8. Directive No. 99 of 12 May 72, concerning the parties in France.

9. Directive No. 210 of 21 Oct. 72, concerning the Austrian and Italian newspapers on Gambetta.

10. Directive No. 273 of 20 Dec. 72, concerning funds for press and intelligence purposes.

11. Directive No. 15 of 2 Feb. 73, concerning the position of Germans in Paris and the duties of the imperial representative there.

12. Directive No. 295 of 30 Dec. 73, concerning instructions about the affair Rothschild.

13. Report No. 10 of 22 Jan. 72, concerning the solution of the crisis at Versailles.

14. Report No. 97 of 21 Aug. 72, concerning loan of three milliards.

15. Report No. 99 of 29 Aug. 72, concerning the loan of three milliards.

16. Report No. 155 of 1 Dec. 72, concerning the budget of 1873.

17. Report No. 158 of 2 Dec. 72, concerning the German journalists in Paris.

18. Report No. 13 of 21 Jan. 73, concerning the social situation in Paris.

19. Report No. 21 of 7 Feb. 73, concerning the attitude of Germany toward France.

20. Report No. 24 of 15 Feb. 73, concerning the events in Spain.

21. Report No. 105 of 22 Sept. 73, concerning the pastoral letter of the Bishop of Nancy.

22. Report No. 30 of 11 Apr. 74, concerning the attitude of Germany toward France.

Of the rest—thirteen directives and reports—Arnim maintained either that they had originated with Wesdehlen or that he had given them to him. Wesdehlen, when asked about this, expressed his doubt about the accuracy of this statement and declared that he had returned these documents to Arnim later on. This group contained the following:

1. Directive No. 186 of 18 Sept. 72, concerning the reporting of Count Wesdehlen.

2. Directive No. 26 of 18 Jan. 74, concerning the instructions regarding the attitude of France to Italy.

3. Directive No. 39 of 23 Jan. 74, concerning the attitude of France toward Italy.

4. Report No. 61 of 22 Apr. 72, concerning Gambetta's appearance in the provinces.

5. Report No. 70 of 6 May 72, concerning the political situation in France.

6. Report No. 3 of 7 Jan. 74, concerning the frigate *Orénoque*.

7. Report No. 7 of 13 Jan. 74, concerning Tunisian affairs.

8. Report No. 8 of 13 Jan. 74, concerning the situation in France.

9. Report No. 9 of 13 Jan. 74, concerning the frigate *Orénoque*.

10. Report No. 10 of 13 Jan. 74, concerning the ministerial crisis.

11. Report No. 11 of 13 Jan. 74, concerning the financial affairs of the King of Italy.

12. Report No. 12 of 13 Jan. 74, concerning the 'Septennat'.

13. Report No. 13, the contents of which could not be established.

Seventeen directives were claimed by Arnim as his private property, which he refused to hand over. These were:

1. Directive No. 224 of 8 Nov. 72, concerning the remarks of Count Arnim to Count St. Vallier.

2. Directive No. 239 of 23 Nov. 72, concerning remarks of the Reich Chancellor on Count Arnim's reporting.

3. Directive No. 271 of 20 Dec. 72, concerning instructions to Count Arnim regarding his reporting.

4. Directive No. 281 of 23 Dec. 72, concerning the reporting of Count Arnim regarding the remarks of M. Thiers in the XXX commission.

5. Directive No. 90 of 2 June 73, concerning the article in the *Gaulois* regarding remarks of Count Arnim at the fall of Thiers.

6. Directive No. 102 of 18 June 73, concerning the articles of the *Gaulois* and the *Français* on M. Thiers.

7. Directive No. 104 of 1873 [*sic*], concerning alleged remarks of Count Arnim.

8. Directive No. 103 of 1873 [*sic*], concerning the change of government in France and its influence on Germany.

9. Directive No. 2 of 3 Jan. 74, concerning the pastoral letters of the bishops.

10. Directive No. 6 of 7 Jan. 74, concerning the appointment of French ministers in the lesser German states.

11. Directive No. 14 of 11 Jan. 74, concerning the procedures against the Bishop of Nancy.

12. Directive No. 33 of 21 Apr. 74, concerning the appointment of French ministers at German courts.

13. Directive No. 68 of 24 Feb. 74, concerning the recall of Count Arnim from Paris, respectively leave and transfer to Constantinople.

14. Directive No. 69 of 24 Apr. 74, concerning the same subject.

15. Directive No. 74 of 4 Mar. 74, concerning information about a personal report to the Emperor about his reporting.

16. Directive No. 93 of 20 Mar. 74, concerning the appointment of Count Arnim to be Ambassador to Constantinople.

17. Directive No. 130 of 9 Apr. 74, concerning the delayed presentation of letters of recall to MacMahon.

There were, finally, three documents missing which Arnim, in his reports to the Foreign Ministry, had not mentioned at all. It was assumed that he considered these also as his private property. These three documents were:

1. Directive No. 291 of 23 Dec. 72, concerning the representation of France in the lesser German states.
2. Directive No. 5 of 1874 [sic], concerning the appointment of French ministers in the lesser German states.
3. Report No. 120 of 17 Oct. 73, concerning the position of Germany toward France.

(Memorandum, 20 Sept. 74.)

APPENDIX V

(See Chapter XVIII, p. 171, n. 2)

The Arnim Paragraph

EIN Beamter im Dienst des Auswaertigen Amts des Deutschen Reiches, welcher die Amtsverschwiegenheit dadurch verletzt, daß er ihm amtliche anvertraute oder zugaengliche Schriftstuecke oder eine ihm von seinem Vorgesetzten erteilte Anweisung oder deren Inhalt, anderen widerrechtlich mitteilt, wird, sofern nicht nach anderen Bestimmungen eine schwerere Strafe verwirkt ist, mit Gefaengnis oder mit Geldstrafe bis zu 5000 Mark bestraft.

Gleiche Strafe trifft einen mit einer auswaertigen Mission betrauten oder bei einer solchen beschaeftigten Beamten, welcher den ihm durch seinen Vorgesetzten amtlich erteilten Anweisungen vorsaetzlich zuwider handelt, oder welcher in Absicht seinen Vorgesetzten in dessen amtlichen Handlungen irre zu leiten, demselben erdichtete oder entstellte Tatsachen berichtet.

Diese Vorschriften finden Anwendung ohne Unterschied, ob das Vergehen im Inlande oder im Auslande begangen worden ist.

(W. Contag, *Die Amtsdelikte im auswaertigen Dienst*, n.d., n.p.)

A NOTE ON SOURCES

THIS study is based primarily on documents in the Foreign Ministry Archives of the German Federal Republic in Bonn; microfilms of these documents are in the Public Record Office in London. (See *A Catalogue of Files and Microfilms of the German Foreign Ministry Archives, 1867–1920*, Oxford, 1959, pp. 14, 15, 311–12, 316–21, 372–3.)

Unless otherwise indicated, documents referred to in the footnotes are from the German Foreign Ministry Archives. Efforts to locate the personal papers of Harry von Arnim were unsuccessful.

The material listed on the following pages is a compilation of primary and secondary sources used in the preparation of this study. It is not a comprehensive bibliography.

PRIMARY SOURCES

Documents from the Archives of the German Foreign Ministry:

Italien 40, 'Acta betreffend die durch die Ausfuehrung der Convention vom 15. September 1864 notwendig gewordene Regelung der Roemischen Frage', vols. 6–8, 1867–70.

Italien 41, 'Acta betreffend Schriftwechsel mit der koeniglichen Gesandtschaft zu Rom, sowie mit anderen kgl. Missionen und fremden Kabinetten ueber die inneren Zustaende und Verhaeltnisse des Kirchenstaates', 1 vol., 1867–8.

Italien 42, 'Acta betr. Schriftwechsel mit der kgl. Gesandtschaft zu Florence, etc.', 1 vol., 1867.

Italien 43, 'Acta betr. Schriftwechsel mit der kgl. Gesandtschaft zu Florence, etc.', 1 vol., 1868.

Italien 46, 'Acta betr. das durch den Papst zum 8. Dec. 1869 nach Rom berufene oecumenische Konzil', vols. 1–6, 1868–70.

Italien 47, 'Acta betr. Schriftwechsel mit der kgl. Gesandtschaft zu Rom, etc.', 1 vol., 1869–70.

Italien 48, 'Acta betr. Schriftwechsel mit der kgl. Gesandtschaft zu Florenz, etc.', 1 vol., 1869.

Italien 50, 'Acta betr. die politischen Beziehungen Preußens zu Italien', 1 vol., 1869–71.

Italien 51, 'Acta betr. Schriftwechsel mit der kgl. Gesandtschaft zu Florenz, etc.', 2 vols., 1870.

Italien 53, 'Acta betr. Schriftwechsel mit der kgl. Gesandtschaft zu Rom, etc.', 1 vol., 1871.

Frankreich 70, 'Akten betreffend Krieg mit Frankreich, 1870–71', vols. 1–141, 1870–1.

Frankreich 70g, 'Geheime Akten', vols. 1–4, 1870–86.

Frankreich 71, 'Schriftwechsel mit der Botschaft zu Paris', vols. 1–3, 1871.

Frankreich 72, 'Acta betr. die Friedensverhandlungen mit Frankreich', vols. 1–18, 1870–1.

Frankreich 73, 'Acta betr. Umtriebe der Bonapartistischen Partei in Frankreich', vols. 1–2, 1871–9.

Frankreich 74, 'Acta betr. die Bildung anti-deutscher Vereine und die Verfolgung der Deutschen in Frankreich', 1 vol., 1871.

Frankreich 75, 'Schriftwechsel mit der Botschaft zu Paris', vols. 1–3, 1872.

Frankreich 75 u. 78 adh., 'Acta betr. das Verhalten des Botschafters Graf Arnim', 1 vol., 1872–3.

Frankreich 76, 'Acta betr. die Verhandlungen ueber die Handelsvertraege Frankreichs mit Oesterreich, Belgien, England, Italien, Rußland', 2 vols., 1872–4.

Frankreich 78, 'Schriftwechsel mit der Botschaft zu Paris', vols. 1–4, 1873.

Frankreich 79, 'Schriftwechsel mit der Botschaft zu Paris', vols. 1–2, 1874.

Frankreich 82, 'Acta betr. die Agitation des franzoesischen Clerus', vols. 1–2, 1873–4.

Europa Generalia 52, 'Acta betr. das gegen den k. Botschafter Grafen von Arnim eingeleitete Verfahren', vols. 1–9, 1874–7.

Europa Generalia 58, 'Acta betr. das Verfahren gegen den ehemaligen k. Botschafter Harry v. Arnim aus Anlaß der Herausgabe der Druckschrift Pro Nihilo', vols. 1–8, 1875–7.

Europa Generalia 59, 'Acta betr. die Disciplinaruntersuchung gegen den ehemaligen k. Botschafter Harry v. Arnim', 1 vol., 1875.

Europa Generalia 63, 'Acta betr. ganz vertrauliche Correspondenz Sr. Durchlaucht Fuerst von Bismarck', vol. 2, 1866–73.

The Holstein Nachlaß

Documents from the Archives of the French Ministry of Foreign Affairs:

Correspondance politique, Allemagne, vols. 6, 7, 9, 13, 15, 1872–4.

Mémoires et documents, Allemagne, vol. 161, 1871.

PRINTED PRIMARY SOURCES

Acta et Decreta Sacrorum Conciliorum Recentiorum, vol. vii, Freiburg, 1890.

Die auswaertige Politik Preußens, 1858–71, 10 vols., Munich, 1932–45.

BISMARCK, OTTO VON, *Die gesammelten Werke,* 15 vols., Berlin, 1923–35.

Darstellung der in der Untersuchungssache wider den Wirklichen Geheimen Rath

Grafen von Arnim vor dem koeniglichen Stadtgericht zu Berlin im Dezember 1874 stattgehabten oeffentlichen Verhandlung, Berlin, 1875.

DOELLINGER, IGNAZ von, *Briefwechsel 1820–1890*, 2 vols., Munich, 1965.

France, Ministère des Affaires Étrangères, *Documents diplomatiques français, 1871–1914*, 31 vols., Paris, 1929–59.

—— *Occupation et libération du territoire, 1871–73*, 2 vols., Paris, 1903.

FRIEDBERG, E., *Aktenstuecke die altkatholische Bewegung betreffend*, Tübingen, 1876.

—— *Sammlung der Aktenstuecke zum ersten vatikanischen Concil*, Tübingen, 1872.

GOLDSCHMIDT, H., *Bismarck und die Friedensunterhaendler 1871*, Berlin, 1929.

LEPSIUS, J., MENDELSSOHN-BARTHOLDY, A., and THIMME, F. (eds.), *Die Große Politik der Europaeischen Kabinette 1871–1914*, 40 vols., Berlin, 1924–7.

ONCKEN, H., *Die Rheinpolitik Kaiser Napoleons III. von 1863–1870 und der Ursprung des Krieges von 1870–71*, 3 vols., Stuttgart, 1926.

RICH, N., and FISHER, M. H. (eds.), *The Holstein papers*, 4 vols., Cambridge, 1955–63.

Das Staatsarchiv, 86 vols., Leipzig, 1861–1919.

Die Vorgeschichte des Kulturkampfes, Quellenveroeffentlichung aus dem deutschen Zentralarchiv, Berlin, 1956.

MEMOIRS

BEUST, F. F. VON, *Aus drei Vierteljahrhunderten*, 2 vols., Stuttgart, 1887.

BUSCH, M., *Tagebuchblaetter*, 3 vols., Leipzig, 1902.

EULENBURG-HERTEFELD, P. ZU, *Aus 50 Jahren*, Berlin, 1923.

GONTAUT-BIRON, *Meine Botschafterzeit am Berliner Hofe 1872–77*, Berlin, 1909.

HOHENLOHE-SCHILLINGSFUERTS, C. ZU, *Denkwuerdigkeiten*, 2 vols., Stuttgart, 1906–7.

LERCHENFELD-KOEFERING, H. VON, *Erinnerungen und Denkwuerdigkeiten 1843–1925*, Berlin, 1935.

MEISNER, A. O., *Denkwuerdigkeiten des General-Feldmarschalls Alfred Grafen von Waldersee*, 2 vols., Stuttgart, 1922.

MOHL, O. VON, *Fuenfzig Jahre Reichsdienst*, Leipzig, 1921.

NEWTON, LORD, *Lord Lyons*, 2 vols., London, 1913.

REMUSAT, C. DE, *Mémoires de ma vie*, 2 vols., Paris, 1958–9.

SCHWEINITZ, H. L. VON, *Denkwuerdigkeiten*, 2 vols., Berlin, 1927.

STOSCH, U. VON, *Denkwuerdigkeiten des Generals und Admirals Albrecht von Stosch*, Stuttgart, 1904.

THIERS, A., *Memoirs 1870–73*, London, 1915.

WEMYSS, R., *Memoirs and letters of Sir Robert Morier*, 2 vols., London, 1911.

GENERAL ACCOUNTS

AUBERT, R., *Le Pontificat de Pie IX*, Paris, 1963.

BASTGEN, H., *Die Roemische Frage*, 3 vols., Freiburg, 1917–19.

BLAKISTON, N., *The Roman Question. Extracts from the despatches of Odo Russell from Rome 1858–70*, London, 1962.

BONNIN, G., *The Hohenzollern candidature*, London, 1957.

BUCHHEIM, K., *Ultramontanismus und Demokratie*, Munich, 1963.

BURLER, D. C., *The Vatican Council*, 2 vols., London, 1930.

CASE, L. M., *Public opinion on war and diplomacy during the Second Empire*, Philadelphia, 1954.

COLLINS, I., *The Government and the newspaper press in France 1814–1881*, Oxford, 1959.

EGGERS, K., *Rom gegen Reich. Ein Kapitel deutscher Geschichte um Bismarck*, Berlin, 1941.

ENGEL-JANOSI, F., *Oesterreich und der Vatikan 1846–1918*, 2 vols., Graz, 1958.

FERNESSOLE, P., *Pie IX*, 2 vols., Paris, 1960–3.

FISCHER-FRAUENDIENST, I., *Bismarcks Pressepolitik*, Münster, 1963.

FLETCHER, W. A., *The mission of Vincent Benedetti to Berlin 1864–70*, The Hague, 1965.

FRANZ, G., *Kulturkampf*, Munich, 1954.

FRANZ-WILLING, G., *Die bayerische Vatikangesandtschaft 1803–1934*, Munich, 1965.

FRIEDRICH, J., *Geschichte des Vatikanischen Konzils*, 3 vols., Bonn, 1877–87.

—— *Tagebuch, Waehrend des Vaticanischen Concils*, Nördlingen, 1873.

GEUSS, H., *Bismarck and Napoleon III*, The Hague, 1959.

GIESBERG, R. I., *The Treaty of Frankfort*, Philadelphia, 1966.

GIMPL, M. C. A., *The correspondent and the founding of the French Third Republic*, Washington, D.C., 1959.

GRAHAM, R. A., *The rise of the double diplomatic corps in Rome*, The Hague, 1952.

GRANDERATH, T., *Geschichte des Vatikanischen Konzils*, 3 vols., Freiburg, 1903.

GREGOROVIUS, F., *The Roman journals 1852–74*, London, 1907.

HALPERIN, S. W., *Italy and the Vatican at war*, Chicago, 1939.

—— *Diplomat under stress. Visconti-Venosta and the crisis of July 1870*, Chicago, 1963.

HANUS, F., *Die preußische Vatikangesandtschaft 1747–1920*, Munich, 1954.

HERZFELD, H., *Deutschland und das geschlagene Frankreich*, Berlin, 1924.

HEYDERHOFF, J., *Im Ring der Gegner Bismarcks*, Leipzig, 1943.

HOLBORN, H., *Aufzeichnungen und Erinnerungen aus dem Leben des Botschafters Joseph Maria von Radowitz*, 2 vols., Berlin, 1925.

HORNE, A., *The fall of Paris. The siege and the Commune 1870–1871*, New York, 1965.

JEMOLO, A. C., *Church and State in Italy 1850–1950*, Oxford, 1960.

JOHNSON, D. W. J., *Guizot: aspects of French history 1787–1874*, London, 1963.

KARDORFF, S. VON, *Bismarck im Kampf um sein Werk*, Berlin, 1943.

KISSLING, J. B., *Geschichte des Kulturkampfes in Deutschland*, 3 vols., Freiburg, 1911–16.

MEDLICOTT, W. N., *Bismarck, Gladstone and the Concert of Europe*, London, 1956.

—— *The Congress of Berlin and after*, London, 1938.

MIKO, N., *Das Ende des Kirchenstaates*, 2 vols., Vienna, 1962–4.

MILLMAN, R., *British foreign policy and the coming of the Franco-Prussian War*, Oxford, 1965.

MORSEY, R., *Die oberste Reichsverwaltung unter Bismarck 1867–90*, Münster, 1957.

MULLEN, T. E., *The Role of Henri de Blowitz in International Affairs 1871–1903*, University Microfilms 59-6950.

NIELSEN, F. K., *The history of the Papacy in the XIXth century*, 2 vols., New York, 1906.

OLLIVIER, E., *L'Église et l'état au concile du Vatican*, 2 vols., Paris, 1879.

OSGOOD, S. M., *French royalism under the Third and Fourth Republic*, The Hague, 1960.

PFLANZE, O., *Bismarck and the development of Germany*, Princeton, 1963.

RICH, N., *Friedrich von Holstein*, 2 vols., Cambridge, 1965.

RITTER, G., *Die preußischen Konservativen und Bismarcks deutsche Politik 1858–76*, Heidelberg, 1913.

ROGGE, H., *Friedrich von Holstein*, Berlin, 1932.

—— *Holstein und Hohenlohe*, Stuttgart, 1957.

SANDFUCHS, W., *Die Außenminister der Paepste*, Munich, 1962.

SCHLOEZER, K., *Roemische Briefe 1864–69*, Berlin, 1926.

SCHMIDT, E., *Bismarcks Kampf mit dem politischen Katholizismus*, Hamburg, 1942.

SCHMIDT-VOLKMAR, E., *Der Kulturkampf in Deutschland 1871–90*, Göttingen, 1962.

STEEFEL, L. D., *Bismarck, the Hohenzollern candidacy, and the origins of the Franco-German War of 1870*, Cambridge, Mass., 1962.

TAFFS, W., *Ambassador to Bismarck. Lord Odo Russell*, London, 1938.

TAYLOR, A. J. P., *The struggle for supremacy in Europe 1848–1918*, Oxford, 1954.

TROTHA, F. VON, *Fritz von Holstein als Mensch und Politiker*, Berlin, 1931.

WAHL, A., *Deutsche Geschichte*, 4 vols., Stuttgart, 1926–36.

WALLACE, L. P., *The Papacy and European diplomacy 1869–78*, Chapel Hill, 1948.

WERTHEIMER, E., *Graf Julius Andrassy*, 3 vols., Stuttgart, 1910–13.

WINDELBAND, W., *Bismarck und die europaeischen Großmaechte 1879–85*, Essen, 1940.

ZELDIN, T., *Émile Ollivier and the Liberal Empire of Napoleon III*, Oxford, 1963.

PAMPHLETS

Brief des Grafen Harry von Arnim an den Fuersten Bismarck, Zürich, 1876.

HARLESSEN, A. A., *Pro Multo. Entgegnung der Broschuere Pro Nihilo*, Leipzig, 1876.

HOLTZENDORFF, F. VON, *Fuer den Grafen von Arnim. Vertheidigungsrede gehalten am 14. Dezember 1874*, Berlin, 1875.

LUCK, L. F. W. VON, *Anklage des Oberstaatsanwalts beim koeniglichen Kammergericht zu Berlin wider den einstweiligen in Ruhestand versetzten kaiserlichen deutschen Botschafter Harry von Arnim* [Berlin, 1876].

Pro Nihilo. *Vorgeschichte des Arnim'schen Prozesses*, Zürich, 1876.

ARTICLES

ACTON, LORD, 'The Vatican Council', *The North British Review*, liii (Oct. 1870).

ALBERTINI, R. VON, 'Regierung und Parlament in der Dritten Republik', *Historische Zeitschrift*, vol. 188, no. 1 (1959).

CONZEMIUS, V., 'Die Verfasser der "Roemischen Briefe vom Konzil" des Quirinus', *Freiburger Geschichtsblaetter*, vol. 52 (1963–4).

CRAIG, G. A., 'Bismarck and his ambassadors', (U.S.) *Foreign Service Journal* (June 1956).

DEUERLEIN, E., 'Bismarck und die Reichsvertretung beim Heiligen Stuhl', *Stimmen der Zeit* (June 1959).

ENGEL-JANOSI, E., 'Die Beziehungen zwischen Oesterreich-Ungarn und dem Vatikan von der Einnahme Roms bis zum Tode Pius IX.', *Mitteilungen des Österreichischen Staatsarchivs* (1957).

—— 'Zwei Aspekte der Beziehungen zwischen Oesterreich-Ungarn und dem Vatikan im Jahre 1870', in H. Hantsch, A. Novotny, *Festschrift für H. Benedikt*, Vienna, 1957.

——'Die oesterreichische Berichterstattung ueber das Vatikanische Konzil 1869–70', *Mitteilungen des Instituts für Österreichische Geschichtsforschung* (1954).

—— 'The Roman question in the diplomatic negotiations of 1869–70', *Review of Politics* (1941).

—— 'Liberaler Katholizismus und die Minoritaet im Vatikanischen Konzil', *Mitteilungen des Österreichischen Staatsarchivs*, vol. viii (1955).

HALPERIN, S. W., 'Bismarck and the Italian envoy in Berlin on the eve of the Franco-Prussian War', *Journal of Modern History* (Mar. 1961).

—— 'Visconti-Venosta and the diplomatic crisis of July 1870', *Journal of Modern History* (Dec. 1959).

HARTSHORNE, R., 'The Franco-German boundary of 1871', *World Politics*, 1949.

HARTUNG, F., 'Bismarck und Graf Harry Arnim', *Historische Zeitschrift* (Jan. 1951).

HOLBORN, H., 'Bismarcks Realpolitik', *Journal of the History of Ideas* (Jan./Mar. 1960).

MARRARO, H. R., 'American opinion on the occupation of Rome in 1870', *South Atlantic Quarterly* (Apr. 1955).

MIKO, N., 'Der Untergang des Kirchenstaates und Österreich-Ungarn im Jahre 1870', *Römische historische Mitteilungen* (1956/7), Heft 1, pp. 130–76.

—— 'Zur Frage der Publikation des Dogmas von der Unfehlbarkeit des Papstes durch den deutschen Episkopat im Sommer 1870', *Römische Quartalschrift* (1963).

MIRBT, K., 'Die Geschichtschreibung des Vatikanischen Konzils', *Historische Zeitschrift* (1908).

RANDALL, A., 'A British agent at the Vatican. The mission of Odo Russell', *The Dublin Review* (1959).

RICH, N., 'Holstein and the Arnim Affair', *Journal of Modern History*, (Mar. 1956).

WEINZIERL-FISCHER, E., 'Bismarcks Haltung zum Vatikanum und der Beginn des Kulturkampfes nach den österreichischen diplomatischen Berichten aus Berlin 1869–71', *Mitteilungen des Österreichischen Staatsarchivs* (1957).

WERTHEIMER, E., 'Der Prozeß Arnim', *Preußische Jahrbücher* (Oct./Dec. 1930).

INDEX

Abeken, Heinrich, 13, 14, 20, 35, 41 n., 66 n., 81.

Acton, Lord John Emerich Edward Dalberg, 24, 27 n.; influence on Arnim, 24 n.

Aegidi, Ludwig Karl, 97, 98, 99.

Alexander II, Tsar of Russia, 72, 90, 188.

Alsace-Lorraine, 54; custom duties, 56, 63, 64, 65 n., 66; debts, 49, 53, 54.

American bishops, 20.

Ampthill, Odo Russell, Lord, 10 n., 14, 29, 32 n., 38 n., 42 n., 79, 121 n., 124 n., 165 n.

Andrassy, Julius von, 73, 153, 188.

Anti-Council, proposed by Arnim, 22.

Antonelli, Cardinal Giacomo, 5, 10 n., 12, 14, 29, 30, 32, 42; and the French Note, 29.

Arnim, Harry Carl Curt Eduart von, accused of illegal financial and stock market operations, 83–4, 112, 116, 124, 181; advised to submit his complaints through official channels, 115; allegedly subordinates official duties to personal interests, 115; appointed ambassador to Constantinople, 129, 196; appointed ambassador to France, 77; arrested, 84, 152, 153; asks the Emperor's pardon and permission to return to Germany, 183; audience with the Emperor, 67, 92, 94, 123, 178 n.; audience with Pius IX, 13, 17, 39–40, 80; on the Bavarian Note, 6; beginning of conflict with Bismarck, 93 n.; birth, education, marriage, and early diplomatic career, 1; characterization of his personality, 23–4, 63 n.; characterization of his position at the Council, 15; charged with treason, 180, 181; claims Bismarck threatened to resign, 139; comparison of his reports, 104–5; complains to the Emperor, 113–14; connection with the editor of the *Presse* established, 155–6; on the consequences of the Council, 35–6; considered for State Secretary in the Foreign Ministry, 193; considers French *démarche* in Rome a defeat for French diplomacy, 34; conversations with Thiers, 78–9, 83; on the Council, 6–8, 12, 14–15, 25, 37–8; counsels against the occupation of Rome, 39; defence in Court, 167; denies Foreign Ministry's jurisdiction over him, 145; denies responsibility for 'Diplomatic Revelations' in the *Presse*, 134; desires appointment in Upper House, 91; dies in Nice, 183; disciplinary action not considered feasible, 151; the Écho de Parlement affair, 142–3; the Emperor's not the Chancellor's servant, 123; end of his assignment in Rome, 46; fails in reconciliation with Bismarck, 123–4; found guilty by a disciplinary Court and dismissed from the service, 183 n.; on the French Government, 67–9, 70–1, 73, 117, 119–21; on the French Note, 26, 29, 30, 34; on governmental intervention at the Council, 21, 25; influence at Court, 61; intends to resign, 89 n., 91; on internal Prussian policy, 148–9; intrigue against Balan, 49; leaves Germany, 174; his marginal notes on Bismarck's directives, 103–4, 147; memorandum in support of the French Note, 30–2; on negotiations in Brussels, 50–4; negotiations with Thiers, 63, 66–7, 107–12; on opposition at the Council, 20, 21; on papal election, 85–6; on papal infallibility, 18–19; on peace negotiations in Brussels, 50–4; plan for accommodation between Italy and the Vatican, 3; on political situation in France, 90, 94–5, 104–6; on his position in Paris, 75; prefers monarchical restoration in France, 93, 94; presents his letter of recall to the Pope, 78, 79, 80; proceedings by Superior Court, 180; proposes an Anti-Council, 22; proposes that

PRINTED IN GREAT BRITAIN
AT THE UNIVERSITY PRESS, OXFORD
BY VIVIAN RIDLER
PRINTER TO THE UNIVERSITY

DATE DUE

5/22/70			